Domestications

FLASHPOINTS

The FlashPoints series is devoted to books that consider literature beyond strictly national and disciplinary frameworks, and that are distinguished both by their historical grounding and by their theoretical and conceptual strength. Our books engage theory without losing touch with history and work historically without falling into uncritical positivism. FlashPoints aims for a broad audience within the humanities and the social sciences concerned with moments of cultural emergence and transformation. In a Benjaminian mode, FlashPoints is interested in how literature contributes to forming new constellations of culture and history and in how such formations function critically and politically in the present. Series titles are available online at http://escholarship.org/uc/flashpoints.

A complete list of titles begins on p. 242.

Domestications

American Empire, Literary Culture, and the Postcolonial Lens

Hosam Aboul-Ela

NORTHWESTERN UNIVERSITY PRESS | EVANSTON, ILLINOIS

Northwestern University Press
www.nupress.northwestern.edu

Printed in the United States of America

10 9 8 7 6 5 4 3 2 1

Library of Congress Cataloging-in-Publication Data

Names: Aboul-Ela, Hosam M., author.
Title: Domestications : American empire, literary culture, and the postcolonial lens / Hosam Aboul-Ela.
Other titles: FlashPoints (Evanston, Ill.)
Description: Evanston, Illinois : Northwestern University Press, 2018. | Series: FlashPoints | Includes bibliographical references and index.
Identifiers: LCCN 2018004072 | ISBN 9780810137493 (pbk. : alk. paper) | ISBN 9780810137509 (cloth : alk. paper) | ISBN 9780810137516 (ebook)
Subjects: LCSH: Literature, Modern—20th century—History and criticism. | Literature, Modern—21st century—History and criticism. | Imperialism in literature. | Postcolonialism in literature. | World politics in literature. | Imperialism—History—20th century. | Imperialism—History—21st century.
Classification: LCC PN56.I465 A26 2018 | DDC 809.933581—dc23
LC record available at https://lccn.loc.gov/2018004072

To Shankar

Contents

Acknowledgments ix

Introduction: Living with U.S. Imperialism 3

Chapter 1 (*Novel*). The Specter of Normativity: Paul Bowles and the American "Third World" Novel 19

Chapter 2 (*Idea*). Other Moroccos: Representation, Historicism, and the North African Lens 47

Chapter 3 (*Perspective*). Domestication and Eastern Asia: America Imagines the World 81

Chapter 4 (*Gender*). Normative Feminism: On Saving Women in the Postdevelopment World 113

Chapter 5 (*Space*). In Spite of the Land: Partitions, Terror Wars, and the New Idealism 151

Conclusion: The End of "Foreign" 191

Notes 197

Works Cited 223

Index 235

Acknowledgments

I owe a significant debt to a great many interlocutors, friends, and fellow travelers who kept my research moving on this project as it spiraled across the globe.

My first debt is to those who took the time to read drafts of parts of the manuscript along the way. They include Tarek El-Ariss, Margot Backus, Karen Fang, Ahmad Joudah, j. Kastely, Duy Lap Nguyen, Ussama Makdisi, Laila Parsons, Samah Selim, S. Shankar, Cedric Tolliver, Julie Tolliver, and Rebeca Velasquez.

The opportunity to present these ideas at a series of forums and diverse university settings has been a privilege that I feel has greatly enriched my research. These exchanges would not have been possible without the generous collegiality and hospitality of Nandini Bhattacharya, Nouri Gana, Ferial Ghazoul, William Granara, Said Graiouid, Jens Hansen, Michelle Hartman, Neville Hoad, Fadwa Kamal, Eralda Lameborshi, Francesca Orsini, Sangeeta Ray, Joseph Slaughter, Annette Trefzer, Max Weiss, and Jennifer Wenzel.

The group of colleagues and friends whose ideas have contributed materially to this project is far too extensive to be listed here, so many times have I found myself at a dead end, only to find myself saved by a thought shared, a reading recommended, or an idea debated. I am thankful to all those who have contributed to this book in such ways, and add that the following members of that expansive group simply cannot be left unnamed: Hosna Abdel-Samie, Latif Adnan, Mohamed

Badawi, Tani Barlow, Ann Christensen, Abdel Hamid Akkar, Ayman Eldesouky, Ahmad Hassan, Salah Hassan, Kimberly Kay Hoang, Christopher Hudson, Grace Koh, Kwon Bodurae, John T. Matthews, David Mazella, Paik Nak-chung, Doreen Piano, Abdallah Saaf, Elora Shehabuddin, Deborah Smith, Jonathan Smolin, Gayatri Chakravorty Spivak, Nirvana Tanoukhi, and Lynn Voskuil. My beloved, intrepid, and exemplary mentor Barbara Harlow did as much as any other single individual to instill in me the academic and intellectual tools necessary to survive the writing of this book. I am deeply saddened that she will not see the finished product.

The Martha Gana Houstoun Research Fund at the University of Houston provided generous financial support that made this research possible. A section of chapter 3 appeared previously in *Global South* 11, no. 2. I thank the editors for permission to reproduce the text, as I thank the curators of the University of Delaware Library's Paul Bowles collection for access to travel notes.

Domestications

INTRODUCTION

Living with U.S. Imperialism

As with any project of intellectual inquiry, mine can be traced back to more than one starting point. For me, an important beginning was a weekend afternoon in the summer of 1995. I was a year into a three-year residence in Cairo, Egypt, and I had made one of my regular rituals walking to a nearby hotel bookshop on my day off and buying a copy of *The Manchester Guardian Weekly* for a dose of news from outside the region.

Martin Woollacott's opinion piece, "Europe Losing Faith in American Leadership," which appeared in that week's issue, examined the aftermath of a successful military mission carried out by marines to save a U.S. pilot, Scott O'Grady, who had been shot down behind enemy lines in Bosnia. During that time, avid consumers of news were reading constantly about the brutal wars that broke up the former Yugoslavia. This column stuck in my memory because it chose the occasion of the O'Grady incident to read U.S. culture from an outsider's perspective. This was at a time when several years' worth of public debate inside the United States had been devoted to the question of what the new global role of the United States should be after the collapse of the Soviet Union and the end of the Cold War. For Woollacott, a strange and pernicious paradox inhered in the scenes of exuberant celebration provoked within the United States by the news of O'Grady's rescue. "Nothing could better illustrate the neurotic inwardness of America today," he began, "than the extraordinary over-reaction of the American president, of the

American media, and perhaps of the American people to the rescue of Captain Scott O'Grady."[1] Most of the world had experienced the Balkan wars as a tragedy, with their civilian massacres, massive displacements, ethnic cleansings, and destabilizing threat to the rest of Europe. Within that context, some more measured response, Woollacott rightfully argued, seemed called for: an acknowledgment of relief alongside an expression of concern for the ongoing dangers to innocents living in the region, for example. Indeed, under the circumstances, the sight of flag-waving mobs chanting "USA" struck European onlookers as at best clueless and provincial, and at worst brutish and venal. President Clinton himself, he notes, offered a particularly glib and inappropriate response in his "hankering to blur the boundaries between reality and fiction [by] already look[ing] forward to what 'I'm sure one day will be a very great movie' of the O'Grady rescue."[2] Such responses led the writer to contrast the moment of the Bosnian conflict with earlier periods in U.S./European relations. On the one hand, "the American idea has been for a long time a vital element in European life," but on the other, "Europeans, bombarded with the OJ Simpson trial, killings after chat shows, the Waco siege, or the Oklahoma bombing, are beginning to see America not as a powerful society with serious problems but as a deranged and dangerous place."[3]

Woollacott was hardly the first European journalist to criticize the global role of the United States. Still, this column appeared at an important historical moment in the working out of the contemporary place of the United States in the world. Also, I have thought of it not only for its contents or its connection to a temporal moment. Rather, I have explicitly cited the occasion, the circumstances, and the location within which I found myself reading it, outside of both the United States and Europe. I had lived all but a few years of my life up to that point inside the United States. In retrospect, that moment seemed to me to represent an initial insight into the idiosyncrasy of viewing the world from inside the homes, institutions, and general media and cultural environment of the United States. If intellectuals living outside the United States probably do not command a detailed knowledge of its inner workings, and thus may at times be led astray in their analysis (and indeed, the causal arguments proffered by Woollacott for the new American weirdness are highly problematic), the saturation in domestic American life that engulfs citizens, educators, and opinion makers in the United States is at least equally skewed. If there is no objective lens through which to view the great question of America's historical role in the world, that does not justify U.S. public culture's relentlessly heightened emphasis on some of the most subjectively celebratory lenses.

This study, then, explores the large question of the U.S. role in the world through contemporary culture and its immediate antecedents, and it does so with particular emphasis on the geohistorical and geopolitical circumstances of reading. Where we sit when we view America as a global power contributes much to what we see. Therefore, studying the United States and its global role leads to multiple global histories and global texts, including ones that are very difficult to access from inside the frame of high academic culture within the United States. In this sense, the American point of view can be said to have a domesticating effect against which this study has been fashioned to push back.

The definition, interpretation, and study of the global took on particular urgency as a topic of critical discussion in the years after the collapse of the Soviet Union, not only in the United States but also throughout Europe and the Global South. More recently, this discussion has become the central question in comparative literary studies as the field attempts to move away from its historical foundation in studies that universalize Europe. The by now familiar initializing texts in this discussion are Franco Moretti's "Conjectures on World Literature" (2000), Pascale Casanova's *La république mondiale des lettres / The World Republic of Letters* (1999/2004), and David Damrosch's *What Is World Literature?* (2003).[4] These authors together issued a call for literary critics to undertake disciplinary practices that incorporate a sense of the global so as to transcend the historical resilience of nationalist categories in literary studies. The responses to this call have been voluminous, and after more than a decade, many important critical voices have stepped forward to suggest expansions, corrections, and reformulations of the question of the global in literary studies.[5]

The world literature debate has advanced literary study by exposing the limits of thinking of literature in terms of the nation. Indeed, it has made questions of global culture, including literary cultures beyond the North Atlantic, feel urgent for most practicing critics, especially critics in comparative literature. The work of Emily Apter, S. Shankar, Gayatri Spivak, Shaden Tageldin, and others has appropriately emphasized translation, and thus made visible what was previously erased: the heavy dependence of every literary culture on translations, translators, and the institutions that produce and disseminate translated work. Thus, the centering of questions of translation also represents an advance forged by this discussion. Another important contribution of world literature criticism is the introduction of the work of the sociologist Immanuel Wallerstein, important because of its persistent emphasis on the inequalities on a world scale that are produced by global capitalism and its particular emphasis on the results visited upon the Global South, which he calls the "periphery" and "semi-periphery." In his initiating provocation, Moretti cites Wallerstein as a modeler of mechanisms to rethink literary studies globally. Since then, the question of a "world-system" and the place of peripheries and semi-peripheries has regularly been taken up by comparatists interested in thinking literature globally, with the question of Wallerstein's potential for a more global lens in both literary study and other disciplines elaborated with particular acumen in the essays collected on the topic by David Palumbo-Liu, Bruce Robbins, and Nirvana Tanoukhi.

The importance of this type of work is the way it makes unequal development an inescapable component of analyses of the world. World-systems theory sheds light on the processes of global capitalism by drawing on earlier work by Latin American intellectuals sometimes grouped together as *dependentistas*, or dependency theorists.[6] In following the dependency theorists, Wallerstein regularly emphasizes the relational quality of the global, thus subverting the tendency implicit in area studies and nationalist approaches toward regional exceptionalisms. Although a few literary critics in the United States have misunderstood references to the "periphery" and "semi-periphery" in the work of those influenced by Wallerstein as somehow denigrating the non-European, in fact, the history of the core-periphery model shows it to be a critical tool for analyzing the rapacious global impulses of the North Atlantic hegemonic powers, subverting in turn the Washington Consensus ideology that constructs the Global South as lagging behind and in need of evolution. In the dependency critique adapted by Wallerstein, unequal development is imposed upon the South by the North through the various instruments of global capitalist expansion and entrenchment. Such a recognition of the Washington Consensus's complicity in unequal development has the empowering potential to forge new approaches to culture, society, and history in the Global South, and the search for such approaches has long been a kind of great white whale in comparative literature's critical discourses, within which, it often seems, the more we talk of the global, the more rooted we find ourselves in Europe.[7] In other words, a historicized understanding of the core-periphery model that properly sees it as originating in the radical intellectual traditions of Latin American thought might actually have the force to reverse the problem of Eurocentric method rather than reinforcing it.

Still, translating to literary study this dependency-informed Wallersteinian model presents acute challenges. Even after acknowledging the model's roots in political economy, it is possible to criticize the move to mark the Global South as a "periphery" in so varied a set of disciplinary contexts. Indeed, the general question of how much is too much when borrowing from social sciences to understand literature is important to acknowledge here.[8] Although literature, literary influence, and culture—both high and low, mass and elite—may play an important role in the spread of global capitalism and the hegemony of global superpowers like the United States, it is unlikely that the adaptation of Western novels or Hollywood films in a Global South context can implant the same type of concrete obstacles to local agency that the political economy instruments described by development economists and social scientists can. What makes this situation particularly confusing is the way an overly direct application of the world-systems model to the global movement of literary influences has tended to produce a result that flattens out the world system, describing neutral movements of literary texts from one global context to another, with too little acknowledgment of the world's uneven landscape. In such cases, rethinking of the literary terrain according to a world-systems model becomes merely a newer version of that older banal comparativism, which inadvertently recreates the myth of global flatness—by, for example, discovering a similar narrative structure in a canonical work of metropolitan literature and a novel from a marginalized region.[9]

Thus, one of the biggest challenges in the contemporary discussion of the global—namely, acknowledging the persistent problem of uneven development over an ever more complicated landscape—is both enabled by the referencing of world-systems theory and obfuscated by the way this theoretical frame tends to be translated into specifically *literary* contexts. Literature's very literariness tends to defer such questions, at least as articulated in the current criticism. A novel, for example, can speak through multiple voices and so launch a variety of critiques simultaneously, as Mikhail Bakhtin has demonstrated. Thus, the nineteenth-century European novel simultaneously cataloged and critiqued the rise of bourgeois life in that region, so it is difficult to take an exemplary text from that era and read it in a way that performs the type of devastating critique of bourgeoisification found in the work of Marx and Engels. The similarly multivalent contemporary global novel likewise cannot usually facilitate a completely uncomplicated critique of the current state of global capitalism, although it may or may not be enlightening in thinking through such a critique. For this reason, I do not strive to ignore the polysemy of literary texts by reading them as though they were unreconstructed condemnations or uncomplicated celebrations of global empire, for I am a literary critic interested in the ways varieties of texts articulate multiple critiques. One issue here is what happens when we turn our attention to the formal qualities of a novel, film, memoir, or poem. Is this a moment when geopolitical context must necessarily be discarded in favor of technical questions? A strain of literary criticism has been arguing for some time now that literary form also has content.[10] Still challenging, however, is the search for a literary practice that enables us to read form not just as generalized content, but specifically in terms of geopolitics.

This problem stems from a larger issue with the current dynamics of global culture, especially as experienced inside what Wallerstein would call "the core," and especially related to knowledge production. Immanuel Wallerstein's work on world systems draws heavily on the work of dependency theorists who were often based in Latin America, Africa, or the Caribbean. This body of intellectual work has been largely erased in the process of incorporating the world-systems approach into contemporary critical discussions of world literature in which Wallerstein has been constructed as the heroic creator of a discourse. As my second chapter will document, a comparable erasure has been performed in our understanding of critiques of Orientalism, wherein Edward Said's broadly influential contribution becomes a beginning ex nihilo in spite of the long tradition of Arab intellectuals critiquing the link between colonial politics and Orientalist writing. Both of these discursive histories illustrate metropolitan culture's strong capacity to absorb, appropriate, and repurpose anti-imperialist global culture. This makes the task of reading global culture through imperialism particularly difficult, and as a scholar working inside the United States, with the many advantages that privileged location offers but without the earlier easy access to the Cairo bookshop, I have engaged this problem of accessing the globally antihegemonic strains in the cultures of the Global South as a particular challenge in framing this study.

I deploy two strategies with this challenge in mind. First, I have placed a particular emphasis on the way the work of global intellectuals might inform the practice of reading global literature. I have found this necessary as an antidote to the documentable willful marginalization of almost any type of intellectual work from the Global South in critical studies carried out in North Atlantic institutions. This phenomenon appears not just in the examples cited above—the diminishing of contributions by dependency theorists or Arab critics of Orientalism—but also in institutional obstacles to the translation, publication, circulation, and citation of intellectual work coming from outside the North Atlantic.[11] My emphasis here is on the relationship between institutions and intellectual production. Indeed, the tendency to see cosmopolitan academic intellectuals working in U.S. and European academies but with roots in the Global South (and this obviously includes myself) as an antidote to the problem of theory by great white men interpreting the rest of us is really only a further extension of the problem, since this method reinforces English as the language of global culture and eschews the impulse to make what institutions marginalize into an important element of the discussion. Furthermore, it typifies the tendency to resort to the identitarian—an impulse that is particularly strong in the United States.

My second key strategy is to center the influence of U.S. imperialism within an understanding of contemporary global literary culture. This is in contradistinction to the general tendency to eschew discussions of imperialism or a historically dominating American role in the most recent bibliography of critical studies of world literature.[12] World history since Bretton Woods is, in part, the history of the emergence of the United States as the world's only hyperpower. Too much scholarship has used the idiosyncratic nature of the U.S. empire as a pretext for discounting its centrality, but this is unwarranted. Certainly, there are many aspects of U.S. imperialism after World War II that suggest a rich historical particularity. America's willingness to let finance capital take the lead, its use of proxies abroad, and its emphasis on mass media and innovation all suggest a historical rupture distinguishing the later twentieth-century trajectory of American empire from the big European empires of the nineteenth century. For the nationalistic Right, these particularities evidence "American exceptionalism," whereas for a great deal of critical cultural studies, they indicate the dissolution of nationalisms in the modern world and the need to discard old-fashioned ways of thinking about imperialism.[13] Although I find academic criticism's critique of American exceptionalism valuable in many ways, this study employs a different approach. Just as postcolonial literary studies of the 1980s and '90s convincingly demonstrated a symbiotic relationship between elite cultures in Europe and the European empire-building project, I suggest that the distinctions that shape a new imperialism during the American century might be studied in their relationship to culture. In other words, I wish to focus upon these characteristics of U.S. globality not to destroy exceptionalism, but rather to emphasize U.S. imperialism by exploring it in detail.

One example of a specifically cultural and discursive phenomenon that makes U.S. imperialism unique would be its tendency to deny its own existence through an energetic commitment to cover up and erase itself. Whereas few bourgeois Englishmen would have bristled during the Victorian era upon hearing the lyrics to "Rule Britannia, Britannia rule the waves!" the tradition in the United States since World War II has usually been to insist, often against all evidence, that foreign invasions, occupations, appropriations, and assertions of power have always been acts of liberation rather than conquest. In spite of America's rhetorical claims to global benevolence, some scrutiny reveals that each stage of postwar U.S. imperial history is ushered in by a bold history-making act of militarism by the United States: the bombing of Hiroshima and Nagasaki and the conclusion of the Pacific campaign, leading directly to the Korean War and the onset of the Cold War; the invasion, long occupation, series of "carpet-bombing runs," and then finally withdrawal from Vietnam by the U.S. military, leading directly to a later, more baleful, post-McCarthy Cold War era; the American-led multinational liberation of Kuwait falling quickly on the heels of the dismantling of Soviet hegemony in Eastern Europe; and the exploitation of the September 11th attacks as a pretext to invade and occupy both Afghanistan and Iraq, marking another reshuffling of America's post–Cold War emphasis. This history of multiple stages initiated in distinct violent births may go far in explaining the contradictory discourses surrounding the United States' global implication. In this sense, world literature criticism's tendency to look away from a prominent U.S. hegemonic role has reinforced just this American tendency to cover its own figuration as imperialist.[14]

From this tendency toward self-denial in American culture, my category of domestications emerges. In its academic, media, cultural, political, and literary discourses, the United States has a powerful ability to erase its own international implications and to express itself as an autonomous domestic space.[15] Everything from the most banal discussions of the need for soccer/football to incorporate more goal scoring and advertising opportunities[16] to the most dire act of invading a foreign country with the result of displacing millions, causing the deaths of hundreds of thousands, and destabilizing a region, can be cast from inside the United States as a domestic political, social, or cultural question:

Who is winning the uninterrupted "debate between liberals and conservatives," how will this affect ratings, and what is the next newest trend?

The ways in which the tendency toward domestication affects academic criticism may be more subtle and elusive. A critic or intellectual has many tools to think beyond the discourses of cable news and public figures. At the same time, academic institutions and structures in which individuals work are far from being completely globalized in the way they produce research, nor are they particularly committed to transcending the restrictions of old-fashioned nationalism. Academic work circulates within a broader American culture. For these reasons, I have found it necessary to commit to a framing that explicitly puts American cultural production in dialectical, contrapuntal conversation with global culture—hence the importance of the moment of reading outside the United States, even drawing on voices from the outside that may be explicitly critical.[17] Indeed, part of this strategy emerges out of the extensive reading this project required of me in what this study designates as the American "Third World" novel, for in the writings of Paul Bowles, Tim O'Brien, Dave Eggers, Norman Rush, and others, one finds not only a critical consciousness regarding the global reach of the United States, but also a frustrated weariness at the futility of trying to find any alternative to the American lens. One of my responses to this situation is the persistent emphasis in this study on intellectual work originating outside of U.S. academic or cultural institutions—including by historiographer Abdallah Laroui, political theorist Abdallah Saaf, feminist thinker Fatema Mernissi (all from Morocco), political economist Samir Amin from Egypt, and literary critic Paik Nak-chung from Korea.

An embodied, gendered, thinking, geohistorically located, and globally counterhegemonic figure of the intellectual recurs in the following pages as a foil to cultures of U.S. imperialism, but it is important not to expect any study to sum up the cultures of the Global South. As a result of U.S. imperialism, American culture touches all contemporary global cultures to a greater or lesser extent. The main goal of this study is to offer tools to incorporate that reality into the critical practice of the study of global literature and thought. An important part of this aspect of my reading practice, however, is developing an ability to avoid projecting a domesticated set of American concerns onto other global cultures and to see them, instead, as including their own local historiographies that predate the coming of American hegemony or actively resist it. This book is written with an aspiration to forge a critical practice that places a premium on recapturing such erasures in the critical discourse of the global.

There is now a widely accepted understanding that the colonial enterprise was so central to the history, economy, and geopolitics of Western Europe in the post-Enlightenment era that its high culture was intimately involved in the colonizing project, as postcolonial studies have demonstrated. To have this proposition so widely ascendant among U.S.-based literary critics is no small achievement, yet, as with many revolutionary paradigm shifts, one is almost as dazzled by the alacrity of the new paradigm's containment as by the radical nature of the development itself.

Domestications is at its core an attempt to probe the containment of postcolonial theory. For that reason, the chapters of this study are organized around a set of five key words: novel, idea, perspective, gender, and space. Each of these carries its own special purchase for literary postcolonial studies, so they carry with them a discursive authority in linking high culture with imperialism within cultural studies. For this reason, they are invoked here to explore how the categories they reference look similar or distinct under the light of U.S. imperialism's historical particularity.

Chapter 1, for example, takes up the category of the *novel*. At the moment the United States became the world's most powerful global hegemon—the end of WWII—the American literary novel suddenly became interested in fiction set in the postcolonial world. American writers began to set sophisticated fiction in Africa, Asia, and Latin America, and the trend continues to the present. In important ways, Paul Bowles served as a catalyst. With his connections to older Lost Generation writers and to younger "Beat poets," he embodied the turn to the Global South for Americans. In his early work, he wrote of existentially lost bourgeois Americans who sought exotic locales through which they might critique the crushing normativity of American Cold War society. Increasingly, however, Bowles's career and his relationship to Third World space evolved, and he became in his transition toward translation and ethnography a nonfiction version of one of his characters, seeking without success to penetrate the alien culture around him. This set the tone for an American tradition of writing about this newly accessible Third World, which came to be constructed as unknowable in its atavism.

My first chapter, therefore, focuses on this striking parallel between the work and career of Bowles. Bowles's influence on later American engagements with the Other of the Global South has still not been fully appreciated, and this is largely because the notion that the Global South subject is an Other to the American abroad is resisted by U.S. imperialism's plausible deniability principle. Bowles, however, was far more aware than his contemporaries of the importance of the geohistorical place of the viewer. As an American living famously as an expatriate in the first stage of American global dominance, he labored against the prison house of the American viewpoint, first in his fiction and then in his "translations from the *Moghrabi*."

While the expat Bowles sought to understand his idea of a Moroccan essence in all its opaque primitivism, North African intellectual culture continued a parallel evolution in a different direction in its engagement with the cultural divide between the "West" and the "East." The second chapter traces this genealogy of Arab thinking about knowledge production across the East/West divide from Jamal al-Din al-Afghani in the late 1800s through contemporary Arab writers like Abdallah Laroui and Abdallah Saaf. I emphasize the strong connection made in Arab thought between Orientalist discourse and colonial politics, present for nearly a century at the time Said wrote his classic *Orientalism* (1978).[18] Arab intellectuals greatly influenced Said, but their works are usually distinguished from his classic text by the connections they make between the local situation, with its "crisis of the Arab intellectual," and Orientalist epistemologies. Said himself seemed to acknowledge the limits of reading Orientalism through a North Atlantic lens and move toward a method closer to the North African one in his subsequent works, but the influence of *Orientalism* in the United States has remained far stronger than either the late Said or the Arab intellectual work, since the former could be consumed in its U.S. context in a manner that did not disrupt the American idea of North Africa as a "no-idea-producing area."[19] For this reason, this chapter focuses on the *idea* as a marker of the dynamics of knowledge production. These dynamics appear most obviously in postcolonial theory's peculiar hesitancy to incorporate fully the heritage of the Global South intellectual into its own critical practice. This approach continued to be challenged, however, by thinkers like Laroui, who argued persistently that knowledge production is (and should be seen as) produced by bodies, bodies that are geohistorically located.

The third chapter turns directly to the category of *perspective*, continuing the call to notice the place of the reader. During the later Cold War, the Bowles vision moved to Southeast Asia, where conflict was viewed through a distinctly American lens. My reading exposes this lens by internationalizing the text of Vietnamese Cold War history. The Vietnamese concept of *dịch vận*—or persuading the enemy—presumes the opposite of the American imperial lens, namely that nationalism's "Other" is a rational creature who is accessible through human reason. This strategy undergirds the life story of Ben Aomar, aka Ahn Ma, a Moroccan syndicalist who traveled to Hanoi in the 1950s to work alongside Ho Chi Minh and Vo Nguyen Giap and assist in propaganda production directed at North Africans fighting under the authority of the French military. Just as the North African lens suggests the international horizons of Vietnamese history during the earlier Cold War, so too does the Korean narrative of fighting as proxies for American forces during the "American War" in the 1960s and '70s, as exemplified in Korean novelist and Vietnam War veteran Hwang Sok-yong's *The Shadow of Arms*. Careful attention to the functioning of narrative point of view, or focalization, allows for a contextualization of Tim O'Brien's accounts of the American Vietnam experience and the accounts in American art house cinemas against international narratives of the national history that reject the collapsing of historical experience into America's trauma. O'Brien's *Going After Cacciato* is particularly important for this argument because its critique of the U.S. war effort emerges out of an expansive story rooted in one white, middle-class American soldier's imagination—a consciousness that is able to produce not only knowledge but even a certain reality through merely dreaming. Thus, the novel critiques the war while subtly reinforcing the integrity of the structure of U.S. imperialism by allowing the American consciousness to remain the exclusive focus.

Gender analysis has been central to postcolonial theory since Said's deconstruction of Flaubert's representation of Kuchuk Hanem in *Orientalism* and Spivak's "Can the Subaltern Speak?" (1988). Similarly, women's bodies are the central text of America's self-concept regarding its global role, from the era of the Vietnam conflict through the global "War on Terror," as the world transitions out of the Cold War. In Southeast Asia, Asian women were represented as hypersexualized descendants of the geisha, readily available to comfort traumatized Western men while at the same time unleashing a threatened social anomy in their home region. In the move to the Muslim world, the stereotype was jolted in the opposite direction, constructing a picture of women that needed saving from their captivity in an oppressive society that kept them cloistered. The American norm of being sexually liberated without being oversexed became a rallying point for U.S. imperialism. In the novels of William T. Vollmann and Norman Rush, and in the discourse of *WID*, or "women in development," the traditional American skepticism around thought structures of normativity is challenged by the figure of woman, for these novels, while exhibiting many of the features of the Bowlesian narrative, express an ambivalence toward American normativity. In these narratives, it seems to still deserve condemnation in its most domestic manifestations, but then suddenly becomes subtly mobilizing vis-à-vis the global fashioning of gender roles. This discourse of international women, in its sense of itself as rooted in empiricism, is complicated by ethnographic work and feminist theory that attempt to operate within the double bind constituted by clashing critical discourses of patriarchal global forces and female agency, as I show in chapter 4, whose focus is the keyword *gender*.

Finally, chapter 5 takes up the category of *space*, specifically focusing upon the historical question of partition—much discussed in British colonial history, but broadly erased by cultural critics and historians in its U.S. Cold War manifestations. The United States in its era of global hegemony, and especially at the start of the Cold War, has been just as invested in partition as the British Empire was, but the special features of American-style partitions have received far less scrutiny from cultural studies in North America, even though the very idea of partitioning illustrates so richly the textured nature of cultures of U.S. imperialism during and after the Cold War. The Cold War partitions of Germany, Korea, Vietnam, China/Taiwan, and Yemen illustrate most immediately the straight binary thinking of the era when the United States sought to project onto the world a notion of complete irreconcilability between capitalism, democracy, and freedom, on the one hand, and communism, one-party rule, and social equality on the other. But partition also seduced American policy makers in its demonstration of the power to conceptually remake space. Yes, it had an anachronistic, old-colonial air about it, but it also appealed to the particular American impulse to construct the world imaginatively, an impulse that took on special purchase within the United States after the Cold War ended.

The domesticating force of a highly nationalistic discourse of postnationalism facilitates this particular movement. For example, in Francis Fukuyama's argument that history's ideological apex coincided with the end of the Cold War, there is a culmination of the idealist structuring of American empire. Meanwhile, counterhegemonic cultures write back to the new idealism of U.S. empire after the Cold War by rooting even fictional texts in the archive as an expression of an increasingly tenuous historical status. I explicate here the irony between the rhetoric of the global that spikes in the United States after the Cold War and the idiosyncratic way the globalized has been conceptualized in the United States. As thinkers and cultural producers inside the United States have resorted to an increasingly idealist frame in seeing the world as post-historical, globally, thinkers and writers including Paik Nak-chung, Hwang Sok-yong, and Sonallah Ibrahim have invoked a documentarian response. Part of what these authors write back against is the idealism behind the American notion of development as an economic and capitalist force that can reshape the world in a neoliberal, consumerist image. Using critical geography, with particular reference to the work of Tanoukhi, Neil Brenner, and Neil Smith, I trace this response back to intellectuals who worked from an anticolonialist base, emphasizing resources and land, and showing—contra some popularized notions of capitalist universalism—that the world has not been flattened into an ethereal realm of ideas. This bibliography, with its emphasis on uneven development, instills back into Wallersteinian paradigms the element of global capitalism's rapaciousness, which is too easily downplayed in other expressions of his analyses within world literature discourse. Furthermore, this group of thinkers can be read comparatively against the new Bowles novel, manifested in the critically acclaimed work of contemporary novelists Dave Eggers and Adam Johnson, who employ many of the tools found in the Cold War version of the American "Third World" novel but are no longer delimited by the older versions of the genre and their acerbic antinormativity.

The organization of these chapters follows a very roughly chronological path, excepting the second chapter, which serves as something of a theoretical detour that grounds the anti-imperialist challenge to globalizing Americanism as articulated by the postcolonial intellectual. Chapter 1 can be connected to the first phase of the Cold War, chapter 3 to the later Cold War, chapter 4 to the transition to the post–Cold War, and chapter 5 to the eras of "globalization" and the War on Terror. This organization is intended to emphasize certain continuities, from Bowles to Eggers, for example, and for that reason portions of a particular chapter move freely into other epochs. The sequence also downplays the real but often overstated changes in the United States' engagement with the Global South across these different periods. One important issue with this approach, however, is the way it maintains a connection to U.S. narratives even when it goes out of its way to explicitly constitute other positions from which to read—the postcolonial lens, for example. This should not be interpreted as an assertion that all globally local historiographies are shaped by U.S. imperialism, but rather merely that U.S. imperialism is a post–World War II global reality, which cultures of the world must respond to or exist alongside of, irrespective of the increasing complexity of global flows and the increasingly provincial quality of the discourse of its elected leaders.

I have fashioned the research question of this study to encourage discomfort. While I draw on important work done by literary scholars who focus on U.S. imperialism before World War II, my own emphasis is the post–World War II trajectory of U.S. imperialism in full historical flower. Studies of media, pop culture, and middlebrow writing of the post–World War II era in the United States have been invaluable to my thinking, but my choice has been to focus on elite culture, including literary fiction, academic and cultural studies, and auteur cinema. The relationship between such materials and U.S. imperialism is difficult to describe. Indeed, many of the American writers and artists in my bibliography have taken explicitly anti-imperial stands. In marking the challenge I have set for myself in this project, I want to reference a second point of origin for my work, to be paired with the moment in Cairo referred to at the start.

In March of 2003, the United States invaded Iraq. In the run-up to that moment, a surprising consensus of cultural elites took shape in support of invasion. Although there was a strong (albeit overmatched) current of opposition to the invasion inside the United States, what astonished me during that time was how many "liberal" icons—both at the level of the institution and the individual, including the *New York Times*, all the major cable news networks, a large majority of Democratic representatives, Thomas Friedman, Keith Olberman, and so on—lined up behind the idea, at least for long enough that the invasion could be carried out and the occupation begun. In a sense, this point in time marked the beginning of sustained thinking about my project, for this was indeed an amazing moment. One might observe, for example, a collection of highly educated and well-intended faculty sitting on a committee at a U.S. university and writing in a report that a junior colleague should avoid translating Arabic in order to procure time to do the important work that earns tenure, even in the same month that the invasion was taking place. It was possible at that time to read articles about the important contribution of Arab Americans or be invited to submit an essay to a special number of a journal on Arab American writing, as though to celebrate more geographically privileged, English-speaking Arabs somehow lessened the violence being visited on those far away and using a different tongue. And in a notorious case, the *New York Times*, considered by many the national paper of record, published on its front page an erroneous story of nuclear centrifuges being imported into Iraq and, thereby, fumbled its own integrity so badly that it would years later issue a formal apology. Undoubtedly, this period was characterized by its peculiarity. As a half-Egyptian, half-American English professor working in the United States, I experienced this period as highly confusing. Much of what motivates this study is a desire to understand how that milieu could have suddenly enveloped Americans and what possibilities might lurk that something similar could happen again.

CHAPTER I
Novel

The Specter of Normativity

Paul Bowles and the American "Third World" Novel

I. CONTEXTS OF THE BOWLES NOVEL

At the end of the World War II, the United States found itself suddenly at the top of the world. As one historian puts it, "The US dominance was absolute, both as a reflection of American growth and because of wartime destruction elsewhere."[1] Only a few years beyond its Great Depression, the United States was now looked to as the most powerful and prosperous nation on the planet. This brought with it responsibilities and uncertainties. Not only did the United States have the capacity to intervene in events around the world, but its willingness to actually do so seemed to escalate along with this new ability. The gradual collapse of the old European empires also fostered an ever-increasing interventionism that suddenly threatened to become the main characteristic in U.S. global relations. [2] At precisely this moment, an interest in the Global South as a physical setting gathered momentum in American cultural texts. For example, as recent scholarship has documented, American producers of American culture used North Africa as a setting after the American military campaign there in World War II,[3] made biblical epics that allegorically commented on the Arab-Israeli conflict after 1948,[4] and generally "churned out a steady stream of stories, fiction and nonfiction, that took Asia and the Pacific as their subject matter."[5] America's turn to the Global South included military activity, political machinations, tourism, art, and culture. Still, the Cold War was understood at the time (and to an extent still is today) as a northern affair, a contest between the United States and the Soviet Union that divided Europe, with the parallel contest over the "Third World" playing only a supporting role. Such a centering of the Cold War in the Global North, of course, facilitates an obfuscation of American imperialism inasmuch as it downplays the American role in the Global South.

This chapter reads American novelist Paul Bowles as the originator of a movement in literary fiction toward the Global South as a physical setting for American literature. The goal of such a move is to build on recent scholarship in showing that elite literary culture was not immune from the turn south in popular media, middlebrow writing, and American politics, even if this turn—in the case of literary culture—necessarily domesticated itself by proposing its own marginality. The idea of a Cold War of the North created by a hegemonic American discourse allowed for nonconformist Americans like Bowles to bring the Global South into American culture as an alternative to the concept taking root in the United States of white-collar work "as a form of routinized mental labor," a psychological constriction born of the office setting, which fostered a "new middle class consciousness."[6] However, that the Global South had to enter this discussion on the strict terms of an emerging counterculture in the work of a writer who proposed travel as a rebellion against routine, one who would eventually influence full-fledged countercultural actors like the Beat writers, had an impact both ironical and ideological.

A common theme in cultural texts of this moment concerns the American gaze looking out on the world with an unsteady or naive air, as though slightly surprised and taken aback by the sudden and comprehensive nature of its new global influence. Two examples of this are the title character in British author Graham Greene's *The Quiet American* and Port Moresby from Paul Bowles's *The Sheltering Sky*. Greene's Alden Pyle, who is exuberant and ambitious but also clueless and reckless, is contrasted with a wise but cynical British journalist, Thomas Fowler. A similar contrast between characters embodying old and new imperialisms occurs in chapter 19 of *The Sheltering Sky*, when Port visits a French officer in charge of an Algerian outpost to complain of his passport being stolen. The Frenchman wears the mantle of the authority figure unsteadily because he is bedridden by illness, yet manages to win his conversation with Port by referencing his superior knowledge of native psychology. Port wants badly to know Algeria, to "penetrate to the interior"[7] of it—culturally, linguistically, cognitively, and sexually. Thus, this moment represents a setback on his journey, as it also allegorizes—in a manner quite resonant with the Pyle/Fowler pairing—the United States' lack of readiness to take over global hegemony from the fading, ineffectual colonialism of old Europe.

In one of the better-known documents of the era to address globalization, Henry Luce claims in the course of his essay celebrating the "American century" that "Americans—Midwestern Americans—are today the least provincial people in the world. They have traveled the most and know more about the world than the people of any other country."[8] But intellectuals and cultural critics in the United States disagreed with Luce on this point and, as a result, generally represented the emergence of total American globalism less effusively.

The epistemic crisis that spurred this more sanguine, critical view of the "American century" resulted partly from the Global South's unwillingness to conform to an objectively knowable paradigm. Christine Klein explains a key dimension of this problem:

> Although the United States had been a world economic power since the end of the nineteenth century, and a world political and military power since the end of World War I, not until after World War II did it displace Great Britain as the world's most powerful nation. Because this was a new role, and because it required repudiating a long standing intellectual tradition (if not a political reality) of isolationism, this rise to power demanded a reworking of national self-definition. The task of national identity formation was complicated by the fact that this rise to global power took place at the very moment when nationalist leaders throughout Asia were in the process of throwing off Western domination. The political and cultural problem for Americans thus became, How can we define our nation as a non-imperial world power in the age of decolonization?[9]

The types of contradictions raised in this discussion of U.S. globalism haunt characters like Port Moresby or Alden Pyle, but historically speaking, many of American society's trends during this period of increased global influence were toward domestication, and this profound contradiction—between a sudden deep implication in the global and a turning back to the home front—laid the foundation for a large swath of American cultural and social life after World War II.

The political movement behind the House Un-American Activities Committee and the McCarthy hearings played a central role in shaping the way Americans experienced the global during this period. One consequence of the rise of McCarthyism was a domestication of the global that deferred the contradictions around questions of imperialism raised in Klein's reference to Asian (and by extension, of course, African, Caribbean, and Middle Eastern) decolonization movements. McCarthyism pitted anticommunist Americanism against a liberal Americanism that emphasized democratic freedoms.[10] This debate could be carried out within a domestic discourse that reduced the global to a planetary contest for supremacy between the United States and the Soviet Union—a contest in which the entire Global South was usually little more than a chessboard.

As direct engagement with concerns of the Global South became increasingly marginalized by the struggle around the House Un-American Activities Committee, another type of domestication came to the fore. If McCarthyism's goal was to impose ideological conformity, literary fiction and cultural criticism's engagement with the global often responded by attempting to expose conformity rather than communism as the central threat to postwar American culture. McCarthyism had its comparable conformist manifestations in Jim Crow institutions; television shows like *Father Knows Best* or *Leave It to Beaver*, which peddled a normative white middle-class ideal; the flight to the suburbs; homophobia; and a general proliferation of processing and automation. This cultural history planted the earliest seeds of Cold War counterculture in the United States, reacting against America's crushing compulsion for the hyperrational and the normative in light of the rise of the routinized professional managerial class.

Within this context, U.S. literary fiction turned its attention to the American experience of the global—with some emphasis on the Global South even early on. A general cultural milieu that surrounded the House Un-American Activities Committee drove this trend, but the idea of Europe as a refuge was less attractive to this generation of writer-intellectuals, who saw the war-ravaged continent as moribund, in stark contrast to the Lost Generation writers who collected around Paris. Yet these circumstances made it far easier for early Cold War American writers to engage with the Global South through an American lens shaped by cynicism toward domestic conformity, which bred a willful projection of difference onto the new settings of the non-West. Nothing illustrates this cultural history better than the career of Bowles, whose lifelong engagement with the Arab Maghreb began in the 1940s as a rejection of the American normativity that would haunt him over a career-long engagement with North African and other Global South settings.

Bowles was the key figure in the incorporation of more global settings into U.S. literary fiction after World War II. Because of this centrality and his sustained engagement with Arab and African themes over the course of his writing career, it is often assumed that his novels have been subjected to a thorough critique by scholars of postcolonial literary studies, but in fact the postcolonial field has never made literary fiction produced in the United States a main focus of its analysis. Neither have literary critics writing about Bowles shown a great deal of interest in either the colonial discourse analysis approach or postcolonial theory. Instead, critical discussions of Bowles have focused primarily on his gothic themes, his use of violence, his expatriate lifestyle, and questions of sexuality in his life and work. More recent studies have taken up interesting and important new questions, like the role of his fiction and his career in the emergence of a niche market for literary fiction,[11] the mapping of American racial politics onto North Africa in his novel *The Sheltering Sky*,[12] or the significance of parent figures in his novel *The Spider's House*.[13] Generally speaking, the close relationship between his work and the global spread of American hegemony seems intuitive to students and readers encountering his work for the first time, but it has not been a major topic of interest among his critics. This general absence of discussion of the rise of imperialism by critics writing about Bowles results from domestication of the concerns raised by his work.

For example, to categorize Bowles as an expat American writer in the tradition of Gertrude Stein and Ernest Hemingway is to ignore the spread of U.S. global dominance after World War II, the geohistorical particularity of North Africa, and the distinction between the U.S. relationship to that particular region and the U.S. relationship to Europe. The realities of uneven development, as well as cultural, civilizational, and religious distinctions, are never lost on Bowles or his characters, but literary critical discussions of expat literature, in their tendency to ignore these distinctions, indicate a marked domestication within their discourse that divides the world into the homeland and everywhere else.

In this criticism, Europe and North Africa seem not that different as places to which Americans might escape.

But in the fiction of Bowles, the distinction is clear. At the beginning of *The Sheltering Sky*, for example, the narrator spells out the motives of the three Americans for choosing North Africa as a travel destination in a manner that emphasizes difference from Europe:

> At this point they had crossed the Atlantic for the first time since 1939, with a great deal of luggage and the intention of keeping as far as possible from the places which had been touched by the war. For, as he claimed, another important difference between tourist and traveler is that the former accepts his civilization without question; not so the traveler who compares it with the others, and rejects those elements he finds not to his liking. And the war was one facet of the mechanized age he wanted to forget.[14]

In this description of North Africa as culturally and historically distinctive, the narrator of *The Sheltering Sky* emphasizes the geohistorical particularity of North Africa, which is pointedly absent from much expatriate discourse. In this marking off of North Africa as an alternative that is neither America nor Europe, a new American discourse of the global inheres.

The three traveling Americans in *The Sheltering Sky* share with many of Bowles's characters a white middle-class background and a deep-seated postwar ennui. (The direct influence of French existentialism in his first two novels is pronounced and unsurprising given that he first visited Morocco after a period in France and finished one of the first translations into English of Sartre's *No Exit* before writing *The Sheltering Sky*.) In search of an alternative to an American society that has become buttoned-down, conformist, militaristic, and banal, the narrative often describes their quest to capture a place, a time, and a people that are not merely distinct from Europe and the United States, but even essentially different from the conformity that has come to characterize America after the war. Critics often mention the bleakness of Bowles's stories, and this quality, I would argue, can be linked to a double bind created by the situation engaged by the narrative's quest. On the one hand, the Bowles protagonist may be so infected by the conformity with which Cold War America imbues its subjects that he (or she, in the case of Kit in *The Sheltering Sky*) may find his mindset haunted by it as he travels. These protagonists are left with the options of retreating from their attempt to escape or entering into either madness or death. On the other hand, the setting for their quests must necessarily take a particular shape that also fosters bleakness.

In *The Sheltering Sky*, for example, Port, as noted regularly, insists that the trio of American friends must seek out situations and places that are remote enough not to have been touched by Europe. The need to escape everything "Western" creates an emphasis on the atavistic and primitive, as critics have noted. A corollary to this quest for the primitive is a disdain for more politically active local cultures that subvert the essentializing idea of the place, and this includes almost every variety of "Third World" nationalism. The resulting tensions, experienced by characters and their narrators, between the point of view of the protagonists and their setting when events take place during the era of decolonization and global "Cold War" constitute a literary manifestation of the cultural tension described by Klein in the quotation above. Characters with a self-concept as a rebel against establishment normativity, in their quest to escape the site of this conformist culture, confront another rebellion, with which they feel no sympathy.

McCarthyism can be viewed as having a major influence on American writers like Bowles and his Beat Generation friends, who fled America between the end of World War II and the start of the Vietnam War.[15] This connection illuminates important themes, but it also domesticates the issue of the United States' influential confrontation with the Global South in the latter's historical moment of decolonization. Precisely in the shadow of the sudden pervasiveness of global hegemony and the Calvinistic high anxiety that this global dominance provoked in both the American cultural and political classes—as Truman returned from the Potsdam Conference (1945), first Vietnam and then Korea were partitioned (1948), the CIA began overthrowing democratically elected governments in places such as Iran (1953), Guatemala (1954), and Congo (1961), and American presidents began to assert their authority over questions of Third World nationalism (as in Eisenhower's rebuff of Britain, France, and Israel during the 1956 Suez Crisis)—canonical authors of literary fiction in the United States allowed their imaginations to immigrate from Paris, New York, and Yoknapatawpha County to the exotic locales in which the United States was suddenly implicated. Paul Bowles published *The Sheltering Sky* in 1949, barely a year after Joseph McCarthy became a senator. The confrontation with the global reflected in this novel and Bowles's subsequent career was not only shaped by the new American globalism but also left an indelible mark upon American discourses of the global.

II. LENSES ON NORTH AFRICA

An oft-repeated quotation from Norman Mailer testifies to the specific way Bowles's influence can be connected to the revolt against conformity and the beginnings of American Cold War counterculture: "Paul Bowles opened the world of Hip. He let in the murder, the drugs, the incest, the death of the square (Port Moresby), the call of the orgy, the end of civilization: he invited all of us to these themes a few years ago, and he wrote one short story, 'Pages from Cold Point' . . . , which is one of the best short stories ever written by anyone."[16] This emphasis on drug use, gothic violence, and diversity of sexual practices in Bowles's work sheds light on the way his writing responds to the restrictive nature of American thought during the Cold War and the way it made him a celebrity and an inspiration for writers, critics, and fans who came to his work, and literally came to his North African refuge from America in many cases. The iconoclasm that won him admiration among alternative artists has left him disdained by more conservative literary critics and decidedly marginal within many versions of the canon of American letters.

This connection to counterculture tends to domesticate his impact and influence by emphasizing the way issues raised by his fiction subvert the suffocating normativity within the domestic space of Cold War America without fully considering the epistemic crisis in America's new relationship to the global that his fiction dramatizes. I have referred already to the way Bowles's *The Sheltering Sky* initiates a uniquely American cultural engagement with the Global South, but of course, it also dramatizes this engagement in a manner that lends itself to domestication far more than much of his subsequent work. This is best illustrated through a return to the issue of point of view, which, as I have argued, should not be read as merely a technical or formal question in the cultural texts of American globalization, but rather as a powerful epistemic tool for constructing representations within a new global reality.

Most of the first half of *The Sheltering Sky* is narrated through the point of view of Port Moresby, albeit in third person. For example, in the previously quoted passage from chapter 2, the narrator signals Port's point of view through the phrase "as he claimed" inserted into the clause: "For, as he claimed, another important difference between tourist and traveler is that the former accepts his civilization without question." The focalizing of the text primarily through Port—less often at first Kit—facilitates the reader's understanding of the trip of the three Americans through the Algerian desert as an explicit disavowal of the values and ideologies of the post-WWII American domestic scene. The notion of Arab North Africa as an escape from the banality of bourgeois American life after the war is made every bit as explicit in Bowles's second novel, *Let It Come Down*, about an American banker named Dyar, who quits his job and moves to Tangiers as a way of dealing with his ennui. The narrative structure of *The Sheltering Sky* makes it clear and uncontroversial that Algerian life is outside the inner consciousness of the Americans and constitutes an Other against the America that Port has rejected.

But the novel never fully validates Port's scathing criticism of everything American, and it openly subverts his pretensions to achieving meaningful engagement with what he considers to be authentic Arabs.[17] The pretentions themselves are expressed by Port in the opening pages when he discourses on the distinction between tourist and traveler. "The difference is partly one of time, he would explain. Whereas the tourist generally hurries back home at the end of a few weeks or months, the traveler, belonging no more to one place than the next, moves slowly, over periods of years, from one part of the earth to another."[18] Subsequent events, however, reveal that Port is not so unfettered a citizen of the world. For example, just after arriving in Algeria, Port finds himself caught in a regrettable trap by a local thief who uses a prostitute to lure him away from his hotel, his wife, and his American friend. Port initially resists the con artist's overtures, but in the end, he meets the prostitute Marhnia, escapes an attempt by the two locals to rob him, and reappears disheveled and distraught at his hotel room after daybreak the following day. Joseph Boone's description of the Western male subject's encounter with the Arab East applies to Port's behavior in this initiating experience: "[Foreign] encounters . . . may precipitate unsettling anxieties of masculinity for male travelers and artists who find both their manhood and desires unexpectedly called into question. Insofar as gender identity is constitutive of individual subjectivity, this denaturalization of masculinity—regardless of the subject's sexual orientation—may also trigger a larger crisis of identity itself."[19] Subtle evidence of Port's disorientation in the Algerian milieu mounts as the journey proceeds. After leaving the more urban and Europeanized port city of Oran and moving into the Algerian interior, Port is excited to procure an invitation to tea from a local named Abdeslam ben Hadj Chaoui, but the get-together goes badly. Monsieur Chaoui begins the conversation by discoursing on his love for the magical dream city of New York, which the couple is escaping, and when Kit offends him by suggesting that they leave early, Port has no culturally translatable social skills to call on to smooth over the offense. In the end, the scene describes without comment an Arab host and American guests that are completely at odds in their values and viewpoints, and Port's pretensions to connections with his surroundings are exposed as a result.

Still later comes the scene I have already mentioned, in which Port is shown up by the French colonial officer, Lieutenant d'Armagnac. Here again, Port proves lacking in his knowledge of the local environment. D'Armagnac is ill and, before meeting Port, fears being dominated by the American coming to visit him, even imagining that because Port is American, he must be enormous, inarticulate, and heavily armed. Meeting the real Port disabuses him of these stereotypes, and in the end, he manages to gain the upper hand, in spite of his illness, through a superior sense of the proper way to read local behaviors and motivations. The issue at hand is the loss of Port's passport, which Port blames on the Arab proprietor of his hotel. Lieutenant d'Armagnac takes it upon himself to tutor the American in local ways:

> "To me it seems just the kind of thing that would not have been done by a native."
>
> Port was taken aback. "Ah, really?" he said. "Why? Why do you say that?"
>
> The lieutenant said: "I have been with the Arabs a good many years. Of course they steal. And Frenchmen steal. And in America you have gangsters, I believe?" He smiled archly. Port was impassive: "That was a long time ago, the era of gangsters," he said. But the lieutenant was not discouraged. "Yes, everywhere people steal. And here as well. However, the native here," he spoke more slowly emphasizing his words, "takes only money or an object he wants for himself. He would never take anything so complicated as a passport."[20]

In this scene, Bowles has created a highly suggestive exchange in which two round, psychologically complex characters manage to represent a moment of historical transition. The French officer, who embodies the old colonialism, lies sick in bed for the entirety of the meeting, suggesting the powerlessness of European colonial regimes after the war. Still, the American in the scene, even this polyglot world traveler, who has far more interest in "natives" than his two American companions, is exposed as naive and culturally ignorant. This sense of Port's limits is enhanced by the novel's sudden jump to Lieutenant d'Armagnac's perspective in the preceding chapter. By focalizing this scene and the previous one through a non-American and allowing someone other than a countryman to frame Port, a sense of our protagonist as limited within this environment comes to the fore in a new way. Subsequent events reinforce these representations, as the passport turns out to have been stolen by Lyle, an English hotel guest, who wants to sell it to legionnaires to pay for more extensive African travels. Port's charge against the Arab Abdel Kader proves erroneous, as d'Armagnac suggested it would. At the moment the reader is introduced to the French officer, he is very ill and unhappy and thus seems to represent the postwar ossification of European colonial presence in the region. But in the end, it is the American Port who comes off as not really ready for the new life in Africa to which he aspires.

The final narrative subversion of Port's pretenses is his death from typhoid, which surprises many first-time readers by coming only two-thirds of the way through the text. What seems like the story of a knowing American's ambitious encounter with the exotic must become something else, as its main character is exposed as inadequately prepared for the milieu into which he has dragged his reluctant companions. Since most of the novel has been focalized through a character that is summarily expunged, the novel's textual economy receives a jolt as well. A new formula for narrating must emerge. This shift has the effect of invalidating much of Port's pontificating about how to interact with the North African setting.

But the novel's killing off of Port does not result in a call for Americans to go back home and conform; rather the problem of how to transcend the strictures of American conformity outlives Port through his (up to that point) skeptical wife. The moment Port dies, Kit becomes the exclusive source of the novel's focus. Faced with a crisis, she immediately gives up her suspicions of the binarism of her husband's worldview and, in running away from Tunner into the open desert, attempts to recapture what she's lost by following an even more radical path toward the embrace of the Algerian Other that her husband had promoted.

This ostensibly radical shift in the novel's subject matter and style has been prepared through representations of Kit's interiority throughout. Unlike Port, she at first misses the comforts of New York and Paris. In a scene near the end of part 1, she finds herself cornered on a long train ride by the quintessentially normative American Tunner. At one point, she encounters the least bourgeois group of locals on a walk back through the third-class train car. This experience repels her, and she retreats into Tunner's arms, even though she has shown a marked distaste for him up to that point. Later, at the tea, she is annoyed with the local host that Port arranged, and she argues regularly with her husband about the banal conversations and interactions they are having on the trip.

As Port becomes ill and the novel directs its discourse increasingly through her point of view, Kit's attitude toward her surroundings starts to change. This becomes most obvious on the bus trip into the interior during which Port first reveals how ill he feels. As Port sleeps constantly, already becoming effectively absent, her imagination turns more directly to her surroundings. At one point, she surveys the landscape around them and the camel caravans they pass: "For the first time she felt a faint thrill of excitement. 'It is rather wonderful,' she thought, 'to be riding past such people in the atomic age.'"[21] This is a transitional moment between two distinct mindsets that Kit occupies over the course of her psychological journey from the person who walks with revulsion through the third-class car in part 1 to the person who rejects Tunner and seeks out a connection with the nomadic tribesman Belqassim after Port's death in part 3. Regarding this latter Kit, the style of the novel also transitions. Dialogue is eliminated, as is Port's predominant point of view, and a free indirect style focalized tightly around Kit's point of view plays out events.

Brian Edwards has made a useful connection between Kit's voluntary sexual enslavement by the African trader Belqassim in the last section of the novel and the institution of Jim Crow with its unqualified official stance against interracial sex. By the end of the novel, Kit's very body performs the rejection of American Cold War values that provided the rational motivation for Port's conception of the trip. Her bodily engagement with the African continent channels Port's desire to possess the African landscape sexually—as exemplified in his encounter with the prostitute Marhnia or his willful giving of offense to another set of Algerian friends in an almost maniacal attempt to have them procure for him a liaison with a blind singer. While Port's attempts at penetrating the culture through sexual penetration seem not to be fully actualized, Kit enters into a relationship with Belqassim that is almost purely physical. Their lack of a shared language and their active sex life make their relationship the direct converse of what her extremely verbal and never physical marriage to Port was.

All of this points back to the Janus-faced position of Bowles's novel vis-à-vis American empire. *The Sheltering Sky* critiques American bourgeois Cold War values through the words and actions of its characters, but at the same time, it domesticates its situations so that the sexual union between Kit and Belqassim, for example, collapses into the issue of civil rights within the borders of the nation-state. Geopolitical questions, such as the balance of power between America and the old colonial powers, are raised ever so fleetingly, as in the scene between Port and Lieutenant d'Armagnac, but with Port's death the novel casts aside such issues to turn even more definitively to its focus on the psychology of the Western subject in the liberal context of the individual's argument with American society. In this sense, the novel's final shift from Port's perspective to Kit's is comparable to the drift in American liberal thought of the early Cold War as described by Thomas Hill Schaub: "In fact, within the binary assumptions of cold war thought, global confrontation and psychoanalysis tended to blur into a psychopolitics that affirmed anxiety and conflict as realistic and inevitable consequences of sustaining freedom."[22]

Kit's embrace of Belqassim goes beyond Port's initial rejection of American imperial bourgeois culture. Whereas Port is only able to project the rejection cognitively, Kit throws her whole body into it. At the same time, her reliance on intuition, "nature," and spontaneity exacts a critique of everything that is objectionable about American culture to its renegade expatriates of the South—its hyperrationalism, militarism, mechanization, artificiality, and hypocrisy, as embodied in its antimiscegenation laws. Still, there are several levels at which this moment in the novel participates in American imperial culture in complicated ways. Belqassim is systematically reduced to a penis by the novel's entrenchment in Kit's point of view. As I have suggested, Port is the narrative voice's main focalizer through parts 1 and 2, but with diversions from this lens in passages that describe Kit's feelings, follow her train ride with Tunner during which Port is not present, or skip to the French point of view of d'Armagnac, for example. From the beginning of part 3 until the short, epilogue-like final chapter, however, Kit's perspective commands the narration with exclusivity. Since she does not speak with

Belqassim, his voice is never heard, and he is represented mostly through his facial expressions and by Kit's response to their sex life. This response is wholly positive: "But since she lived now solely for those few fiery hours spent each day beside Belqassim, she could not bear to think of warning him to be less prodigal of his love with her."[23] If their ardor reinforces the Jim Crow subtext, the subtext in turn strips Belqassim of his Arabness. By serving as an object to be acted upon by Kit's body, her consciousness, and in general, her agency, Belqassim is transformed, first into blackness, then into that particular blackness that haunts America, is exceptional to it, and is in the process of being domesticated away from the colonial/imperial scene. This erasure of the African part of Belqassim's identity dramatizes Mahmood Mamdani's claim that "the will to separate foreign from domestic policy is characteristic of imperial democracies and was one of the key legacies of the Cold War."[24] In the same vein, Belqassim's absorption into American domestic policy (not in the narrative itself, but at the level of its interpretive understanding) can be said to prefigure what McAlister reads as the deploying of U.S. multiculturalism to valorize American forces during the first Gulf War, because in both cases American multiculturalism displaces and defers questions of any locatable agency within that Arab/African who has been constructed as Other.

III. THE LENS AS LIMIT AFTER *THE SHELTERING SKY*

Because Bowles's novels sought out the Global South as an antidote to American conformism, the issue of point of view in them became increasingly vexed. Structure becomes ever more attached to questions of cultural and historical difference over the course of his four novels: from *The Sheltering Sky* in 1949, which narrates exclusively from the point of view of its American characters except for the brief scenes focalized through the French officer, to his next two North African novels, *Let It Come Down* (1952) and *The Spider's House* (1955), which experiment increasingly with Arab points of view, to his final novel, *Up above the World* (1967), set in Central America and turning specifically on withholding local points of view until the very end. Whereas the reader experiences Belqassim exclusively through the focalizing lens of Kit, later Bowles fiction attempts to move beyond this incarceration within an alienated bourgeois American point of view. Critic Allen Hibbard has provided a helpful mechanism for understanding this trajectory in his short essay on

The Spider's House, which focuses on "decisions the writer makes with respect to methods of narration."[25] Twice in his very brief discussion of the novel, Hibbard favorably compares Bowles's organizing of narrative point of view to the structures found in Hemingway's travel book *Green Hills of Africa* and Conrad's *Heart of Darkness*. For Hibbard, Bowles's predecessors demonstrate the way "perceptions of the foreign environment can be filtered or screened by the colonial narrator."[26] Hibbard rightly asserts that something more complicated is going on in Bowles's fiction, and he also correctly asserts that Bowles's long 1955 novel of the Moroccan revolution is the most productive text for considering the distinctiveness of Bowles's narrative techniques.

More generally, the arc of Bowles's use of narrative "filters" in his first three novels, published from 1949 to 1955 and all set in Arab North Africa, is also worth considering. In *The Sheltering Sky*, Bowles scrupulously adheres to a narrative point of view delimited by the thoughts and perceptions of the American characters. Bowles's second novel, *Let It Come Down*, published in 1952, repeats a deep structure present in *The Sheltering Sky*, but with several noteworthy variations. Although the setting has shifted to Tangier from Algeria, the main character, Nelson Dyar, an American fleeing the banality of his life in New York to create a new one in Morocco, performs essentially the same function in the novel's textual economy as Port and Kit. The pressures of Cold War conformism in the United States form the impetus once again for the bored American clerk and card-carrying member of the new professional/managerial class, for whom Morocco represents licentious sex, drugs, and international intrigue. The novel focalizes primarily through Dyar, but also seeks to present a collection of characters of diverse nationalities in order that it might be read as a portrait of society in the Moroccan International Zone at the end of the colonial era. This spatial shift leads it beyond the more limited uses of point of view in *The Sheltering Sky*. The thoughts and perceptions of several characters are narrated using free indirect discourse, although Dyar's perceptions occupy most of the novel. Among the other characters whose points of view are narrated—who act as filters, in Hibbard's terminology—are two Arab Moroccans: a young woman named Hadija, who is briefly Dyar's consort, and a man named Thami, the second most important character in the novel. Of these two, Hadija does not radically alter the narrative value system set up by Bowles in his previous novel. Although *Let It Come Down* does narrate one short scene from her point of view, in most of the scenes in which she appears, she is viewed from under

Dyar's distressed gaze, and he finds her as utterly impenetrable psychologically as she is willing sexually.

The character of Thami, however, represents Bowles's move beyond the perspectival limits of his first novel and toward the narrative strategy of *The Spider's House*. Thami is the first Arab character in a Bowles novel with the beginnings of a complex psychology. He is from an elite family and has made the decision to abandon his familial standing by marrying a lower-class woman. Eunice Goode, an American expatriate, describes him thus: "Outwardly Europeanized but inwardly conscious that the desired metamorphosis would remain forever unaccomplished, and therefore defiant, on the offensive to conceal his defeat."[27] Surely, Thami's very Europeanness is what allows Bowles to feel comfortable with a richer representation of his character. We learn, from seeing Tangier through Thami's perspective, of his frustration with his domestic life and his alienation from both his in-laws (who are inveterately provincial) and his own family, who are elitist and hypocritically enamored with empty ideas—like (in the novel's economy of value) Arab nationalism.

Yet, in the end, the novel most urgently wants to represent the psyche of Dyar and not Thami. Just as Kit rejects American idealism by abandoning Tunner in *The Sheltering Sky*, Dyar rejects American entrepreneurism by stealing from his American employer and the employer's British client. Dyar declares himself nonaligned in the Cold War by stealing from the Russian agent, who attempts to recruit him as well, and finally, just as Kit leaves behind every societal structure that she has ever lived with by escaping into the desert, Dyar escapes from the International Zone and heads for Spanish Morocco, using *kif* and *majoun* to push himself to his existential limit. At the end of the novel, he proves that he's reached an existential point of no return by killing an Arab, as did Camus's hero in *L'étranger*. Dyar deserves comparison to both Camus's Meursault and *Sheltering*'s Kit. Part 3 of *The Sheltering Sky* is introduced with a quotation attributed to Kafka: "From a certain point onward there is no longer any turning back. That is the point that must be reached." As an epigraph for the final leg of Kit's journey, and by extension that of Dyar, the statement connotes the double bind of the rebel confronting Cold War conformity. Both cases seem to suggest that the strictures of middle-class American life can follow one abroad and that the foreign space is only useful in pushing the bourgeois individual toward a definitive break with the normative. Thami is a round character in a way that the nameless Arab of *L'étranger* is not, but the key issue in both novels remains the dilemma posed by being forced to choose between conformity and madness. In snuffing out Thami, Dyar puts a definitive end to the suggestion of the Arab as producer of discourse.

Bowles's third novel, *The Spider's House*, published in 1955, is even bolder in its experimentation with moving toward a structure that attempts to incorporate an Arab perspective. Another subtle but significant shift in setting is also enacted, as events take place in Fez, the most traditional of Moroccan cities, at the time of the revolution against French colonial rule. The move in setting from the international city of Tangier (in *Let It Come Down*) to Fez is suggestive of the novel's themes. Fez is home to a more ancient, imperial, and Islamic history within the region, in short, a physical grounding of Bowles's conception of local authenticity. But it is also the birthplace of the Istiqlal Party, which began the fight for Moroccan independence from French colonial rule. Herein lies the symbolic contradiction embodied by setting, since the nationalist movement represents (somewhat ironically) Europeanization in Bowles's conception of Moroccan authenticity.

The Spider's House begins with a brief prologue, which uses free indirect discourse to present the perspective of an American writer living in the city—a character who shares much with Bowles himself. The American, Stenham, is visiting Moroccans at the beginning of the novel. To his surprise, they insist on sending a young local home with him, leading to much reflection on his part regarding the mystery of Arab ways. This prologue serves to suggest that something about Fez is not right from a Euro-American perspective.

Book 1 of the novel is narrated entirely from the point of view of Amar, a young, illiterate Moroccan, whose family belongs to the religiously elite Chorfa group. In his family, however, Amar is something of a disappointment, having dropped out of school while still young and finding it difficult to hold down a job. The first two books follow Amar's life in Fez, presenting the story from his point of view. The third book reintroduces Stenham and brings him together with another American, Polly Burroughs, with whom he begins a complicated and highly unsatisfactory relationship. At the end of book 3, Stenham, Burroughs, and Amar all are brought together by the chaos of the unrest, and the last hundred pages follow their flight together from the troubles in Fez, shifting among the three points of view as the narrative moves from chapter to chapter. It ends with the two Americans resolving their differences, abandoning Amar, and speeding away together while the Moroccan youth runs after them.

In *The Spider's House*, Bowles deemphasizes the forthrightly existentialist resonances of his two earlier novels, with their at times pronounced references to the writings of Sartre and Camus, to write what he himself describes with a touch of disdain in a 1981 preface as a "political book." But the novel's attitude toward Morocco and Moroccans is more complicated than my reference to the final image might imply. Bowles uses Amar's point of view to suggest that "authentic" Moroccans are at odds with the *hezb al istiqlal*, which represents (for Bowles) a kind of corruption of the essential Moroccan character. One of Amar's functions in the text is to expose the corruption and inauthenticity of the independence movement. This visceral dislike of *hezb al istiqlal* apparently shared by author and character, partly inspired the writer Mohamed Choukri to comment (with *The Spider's House* in particular in mind) that "Paul Bowles loves Morocco, but he does not love Moroccans."[28] Indeed, disdain for politically active, anticolonial Moroccans can even be said to form a point of union between the otherwise disparate points of view of the American Stenham and the "authentic" Moroccan Amar.

Hibbard's distinction between this novel's use of perspective and the more typical and simple pattern found in Conrad and Hemingway deserves more consideration. Praising Bowles's narrative arrangement, he suggests that "Stenham, like Bowles himself, is a fine interpreter of the local culture,"[29] and he concludes that through characters like Amar, Bowles enables us "to transcend the confines of our own experience."[30] Several other critics who have worked on Bowles have valorized his sustained efforts as a chronicler of the Moroccan subaltern. *The Spider's House* is one starting point for this trend, with Amar, an illiterate, unemployed, religious Arab Muslim the earliest fully developed example of such a figure in his work.

Hibbard accurately calls attention to innovations that Bowles introduces after the publication of his first novel. In the case of Amar, however, the character's ability to function in the text as a disruption to American representational norming is somewhat limited by Stenham's tendency to constantly interpret him. Another limitation is the thoroughgoing essentialism in the portrayal of Arabs in Bowles's fiction, which goes disturbingly unacknowledged by critics. Early in *The Spider's House*, for example, Amar is followed and then interrogated by an acquaintance that he has rightly deduced is a follower of Istiqlal. In an attempt to confuse his interrogator, Amar adopts the ingenuous strategy of telling him the truth. The narrator explains to us that this will work because it was well known that Moroccans "always judiciously mixed in false statements with the true, the game being to tell which were which."[31]

Essentialism is more subtly manifested, however, in Amar's experience with the Istiqlal Party. At first he is taken in by their apparent kindness, but he is soon turned off by their lack of devotion to Islam, their drinking of alcohol, and their disrespect for local festivals. By the end of the novel, he finds them utterly alien and not at all Moroccan, their habits being those he associates strictly with the hated French. What we seem to have in Amar is a rigid, unimaginative, and prudish Arab subaltern, when compared, for example, to working- and peasant-class Moroccans in stories by Arab authors translated by Bowles. Whereas Bowles's Amar shows no interest in politics, alcohol, or anything that he perceives as tainted by the West, peasant-class characters in Choukri's *For Bread Alone* form opinions about social and political ideas that are complex, fluid, and capable of absorbing and engaging multiple influences. In *The Spider's House*, it is not just Amar who finds the Arab nationalists insufficiently Moroccan. Stenham, his British friend Moss, the Moroccan maid at the hotel, and even Bowles himself (in his 1982 preface to the novel) all declare that the nationalists are blind ideologues with no appreciation of local custom and no qualities to make them preferable to the French. Indeed, both this preface and the one Bowles wrote for *Let It Come Down* invoke the theme that the old Morocco depicted in the novels no longer exists and that independence has destroyed the best of the country. In opening up a new world through his experiments with perspective, Bowles also manages to close off—or more precisely, to keep closed—the possibility of the Arab as a historical, modern subject with political agency inside his fictional world. One legacy of Bowles's project is a continued struggle with the problem of the Arab individual as a political agent in both the geopolitical and cultural realms of America's contemporary foreign relations.

Another legacy is a particular blindness inscribed in Bowles's novelistic discourse. Throughout *The Spider's House*, Stenham insists on distinguishing himself from the French, who oppress the Moroccan people. Bowles declares in the preface that when he surveyed the conflict he was "finding it impossible to adopt either side's point of view." Like many cultural theorists of empire, he sees the American position as essentially distinct from those of the old colonial powers, yet in his own narrative of the conflict, his American characters are regularly looked down upon by Moroccans or presumed by them to be complicit with the French. Ultimately, Bowles's narrative pattern creates a value system that enables him to suppress American complicity in maintaining a colonial deep structure in North Africa after the Second World War. Here Stenham performs the problem of U.S. hegemony in the Global South during the era of decolonization. He enjoys white Western privilege and even asserts power over Amar, but his privilege has a particular character, coming as it does with an insistence that the revolution in Morocco is between two equally bankrupt forces—French colonialism and *istiqlal*—and that he has managed to maintain a complete and benevolent independence from both.

IV. NO EXIT THROUGH TRANSLATION

In the character of Amar, the young, illiterate, somewhat Oedipal, deeply religious inhabitant of Fez's old city in *The Spider's House*, Paul Bowles has created a hauntingly problematic representation of the Moroccan subaltern that has fascinated his American readers. He is caught up in global and regional forces in the novel that are presented as mostly rapacious and callous: French police, Moroccan independence leaders, his despotic father, and clueless Americans. Francine Prose anachronistically jumbles decolonization and the War on Terror to interpret Bowles's Amar as a prophetic guide to understanding the Muslim subject's sense of grievance against the West. Greg Bevan sees him as shaped by family cruelty in a way that the young Paul Bowles would have understood. In Allen Hibbard's judicious reading, Amar represents a disruption of the patriarchal gaze that monopolizes older colonial discourse fiction, so commonly filtered through white male subjects untethered in exotic lands.[32] In this sense, Amar is also an innovation in the technique that shaped Bowles's narrative structure, as I have suggested. Stenham, the former communist, expatriate American writer, is part authorial alter ego, part extension of the white male protagonists in Bowles's best-known North African narratives, "A Distant Episode," *The Sheltering Sky*, and *Let It Come Down*. By pitting Stenham's point of view against Amar's in the novel's narrative structure, Bowles offers the most ambitious effort in his fictional work to transcend an American episteme.

What critics have not yet explicitly connected is the synchronicity between Bowles's composition of *The Spider's House* and the beginnings of his movement toward translation of oral Moroccan folk narrative. The topic of Bowles's translations has drawn increasing interest from critics since Mary Martin Rountree first attempted to summarize his efforts in this area as part of a special issue on Bowles's work in *Twentieth-Century Literature* in 1986, with important statements on aspects of his translations published since Rountree by Nirvana Tanoukhi, Mustafa Ettobi, Brian Edwards, and Mona El-Sherif. None of this criticism particularly emphasizes the connection between the translations and Bowles's fiction, yet critics and biographers have documented that Bowles's interest in translating stories by illiterate Moroccans first crystallized in the early 1950s, around the time he was writing *The Spider's House*. Rountree cites 1952 as the point when he first had the idea of translating stories told by his Moroccan friend (with whom he is believed to have been romantic), the painter Ahmad Yacoubi.[33] *The Spider's House* is set in 1954 and was published in 1955, and Amar, the main Moroccan in the novel, shares a similar family background with Yacoubi, who was eighteen and living in his hometown of Fez when Bowles first met him in 1947.

Paul's complex relationship with his wife, Jane, has been regularly referenced as an instrumental force in his gradual move toward translation, although most scholarship suggests that she was far from encouraging of her husband's translation projects. After her first major stroke in 1957, Bowles devoted more time to her care and speaks of the translation of oral stories as a practical substitute for sustained writing projects that would have distracted him more from caring for Jane.[34] By the 1960s, however, Bowles had come to consider translation central to his project, and he had collected a group of younger Moroccan men who narrated to him. Rountree comments, "If, as Mohammed Mrabet [one of Paul's best-known story-telling Moroccan friends] suggests, Jane Bowles did indeed resent her husband's working as a translator at the expense of his fiction, she would surely have been alarmed by his absorption in the Moghrebi translations after her death in 1973."[35] Although critics always characterize Jane's resistance to Paul's interest in translation as a manifestation of her sense that his own writing should be prioritized, some scholarship also suggests the couple had diverging attitudes toward the Arabic language. Whereas Jane achieved a respectable acumen in the reading, writing, and speaking of Arabic in a relatively short time, Paul never showed any interest in written Arabic, devoting himself instead to Moroccan dialect, or *darija*, which he called "Moghrabi," and even then finding it difficult to keep up with his culturally absorptive wife.[36] This distinction suggests that it could as easily have been the type of translations Bowles was undertaking that garnered Jane's objection as much as the fact of devoting time to translation.

Orality, however, was a key component in Paul's practice of translation. Indeed, his translations rendered stories that had been told to him, and he often introduced translation collections by acknowledging that he could neither read nor write standard Arabic. The resort to the oral was more than a product of his linguistic circumstances, however. Rather, he asserted that when it came to choosing a storyteller worthy of translation, "I'm inclined to believe that illiteracy is a prerequisite."[37] In such statements, as well as in the "translations from the Moghrebi" project in general, Bowles reinforces key aspects of the representation of Moroccan society that emerge from much of his fiction—especially *The Spider's House*, in which Amar's illiteracy gives him innocence, insight, and attractiveness. These qualities initially draw Stenham to him, but ultimately, Stenham is too cynical and corrupted by modern rationalism to connect fully. What Stenham fails to pull off in *The Spider's House*'s poignant ending, becomes the author Paul Bowles's quest in his translations, each featuring an illiterate or semiliterate younger Moroccan man heavily invested in some aspect of traditional Moroccan culture.[38]

Some Bowles scholarship has compared his affinity for taking nonelite Moroccans as subject matter with Gayatri Chakravorty Spivak's famous essay shining light upon the absence of subaltern voices in Western scholarship about postcolonial societies, but Spivak's purpose was to expose the way well-intentioned Western scholarship, by setting itself up as mediator, obfuscates direct access to nonhegemonic discourses.[39] The mediating role played by Bowles the translator is far more prominent than was acknowledged by early Bowles critics. The more critical discussion has turned to the translations themselves, the more Bowles's role as a mediator carefully shaping these representations of Morocco has come into focus.

For example, Bowles admits that he selects the authors he will translate based on their class background and level of education, so that the initial principle of selection must be seen as a highly considered aspect of mediation. There is a rank economics to this exercise of power that pervaded the earliest writing about Bowles's translations. In Rountree's 1986 article, for example, money operates as an understated leitmotif. Of one of Bowles's first ventures into translation, with a watchman who published under the pen name Driss Ben Hamed Charhadi, for example, she writes, "After Bowles had successfully translated and published a few of Charhadi's anecdotes, Charhadi, elated by the money he made, and eager to continue this odd kind of 'work,' began to record almost daily with Bowles."[40] Indeed, the ability to enrich those he translated, reinforced by Bowles's choice of marginalized communities in an unequally developed postcolonial state, gave Bowles an unusual agency over the embodied authors. More than a translator, Bowles offered his authors a path to hard currency unattainable in the normal course of life for most Moroccan members of the social class in question. Thus, in the case of Bowles's longest, most successful, and most important translator/author relationship, with Mohammed Mrabet, the initial motivation for the endeavor is consistent: "When Mrabet [was] assured that Larbi made enough money from the book [that Bowles translated] to get married, Mrabet declare[d] that he too ha[d] stories to tell."[41]

The actual process of translation and what role it may play in mediating postcolonial voices has been a topic of intense discussion among literary critics.[42] Here again, the idiosyncrasy of Bowles's translation practice is suggestive of the translator's power over the author because no original text can be accessed to measure the particularities of the translator's politics and stylistics. The target language text effectively becomes the only indicator of the source text. In the one exception, Bowles's role as assertive representative comes into even sharper focus.

Mohamed Choukri grew up poor in northern Morocco but eventually educated himself and established a name as an important—albeit distinctive and controversial—literary figure in Morocco before his death in 2003. By the time he met Bowles in Tangier in the early 1970s, he had begun writing stories and poems. Bowles had set off on his career translating orally recounted, heavily autobiographical tales by poor Moroccan men, and he promoted the idea of having Choukri become one of his authors, although Choukri had achieved the full literacy of an educated Arab years earlier. When Bowles includes stories by Choukri in a collection of tales by Moroccan folklorists, the Choukri stories stand out as having a different sensibility from the others, in Rountree's early assessment. Even more significantly, in the case of *For Bread Alone*, an autobiographical narrative by Choukri translated by Bowles and highly reminiscent of other life-based narratives in his translations, an original Arabic version eventually appeared, providing evidence of the kind of oral-based agenda that shaped Bowles's practice of translation.

Choukri has stated that when he first agreed to the project that would become *For Bread Alone*, he falsely told Bowles, upon the latter's suggestion that they produce an autobiography, that he had already written one. The two began to sit together in sessions in which Choukri narrated the book to Bowles as he was writing it himself. At the time *For Bread Alone* appeared in English, the Arabic manuscript, *Al Khubz al Hafi*, did not immediately attract any interest from Moroccan publishers. By the time it did appear, Bowles's translation had become one of his most successful. Scholarship has since shown that Bowles constructed an English text that conformed to the patterns set up in earlier examples, such as Charhadi's *A Life Full of Holes*. The poverty and sexuality of the young protagonist are sensationalized and the rise of his nationalist consciousness and his drive to become literate are downplayed or made haphazard. Ettobi makes the case by looking at the word choice of specific passages, while Tanoukhi focuses particularly on Arabic passages that Bowles omits in English, using these omissions as a clue to the translator's agenda; both critics come to similar conclusions. Tanoukhi sums up the result of the translator's efforts as follows: "A comparison of the Arabic and English versions shows that Bowles's translation suppresses Choukri's investment in a literate, rational, and modern nation by presenting *Al Khubz Al-Hafi* as a celebration of the oral, irrational, and primitive."[43]

Initially, Paul Bowles's translation projects were an extension of his experiments with point of view in his own fiction. Both attempted to use specifically literary practices of form and language to move beyond a basic problem in the politics of representation faced by an expatriate writer working in an unequally developed former colony, but not faced by one haunting Paris's brasseries. For Bowles, this problem was also part of the problem of being a middle-class white American trying to live in the world during the early Cold War. The oppressiveness of mainstream McCarthy-era conformity followed his characters all the way to North Africa, threatening to block their sincere aspirations for engagement with the Other. But a new conformity ultimately haunted this new project, as the Choukri case makes clear. Even though his concept of the local subject originated in his attempts to flee the American mindset, a rigid structure governed Bowles's notion of the primitive and authentic Moroccan, thus allowing the Western rationalism that he hoped he might transcend to encircle his global vision with even more resilience.

V. CONCLUSION: THE TRANSNATIONAL AS HORIZON

Bowles's career suggests that the literary discourse of America in the world started off at the Cold War's beginning as a discourse of an unreachable epistemological horizon. In *The Sheltering Sky*, Americans are pictured traversing an Arabian desert in search of a mythical authentic Arab essence. Later, in his less commercially successful 1950s novels, he tries to portray some Arabs as characters with consciousness and even as focalizers. Still later, Bowles virtually gives up writing novels and devotes himself increasingly to translation projects—what he imagines are unfiltered transcriptions of authentic Arab voices. As scholarship has shown, however, his efforts at translation yielded anything but an unfiltered capturing of a counteressential voice of the Other. Rather, through a principle of selection that gave voice only to a particular type of Moroccan and a translation practice that allowed his own prejudices about what constitutes Moroccan authenticity to come to the fore in each text, Bowles produced a body of work that—among other things—demonstrated the near impossibility of trying to go beyond the narrow limits of the American Cold War mindset. Indeed, his career might be seen as a lifelong struggle to transcend such limits, to capture something truly different.

To compare this project with the best-known narratives of colonial discourse from the historical high point of the British, French, and other European empires—that is, the works of Kipling, Haggard, Conrad, Forster, Dinesen, Gide, and others—proves complicated. Some of the shapers of literary colonial discourse spent almost as much time in the spaces they wrote about as Bowles did, and perhaps came to know aspects of their local settings even better than Bowles, whose sense of Morocco seemed open in some ways but quite restricted in others, as my discussion has suggested. In the search for sharp distinctions that mark American writing about its empire, the plausible deniability thesis comes again to the fore. The notion that America is not an imperial power at all allows for a unique type of critical discourse. The local setting in Bowles's work offers an occasion to criticize a U.S. domestic normativity that has a culturally suffocating effect back on American soil. Few Europeans—perhaps not even Conrad—felt so compelled to critique the idea of Europe when they found themselves in an "exotic" locale. The influence of this American way of writing about the Global South can be seen in a few examples of fiction that came shortly after the main Bowles novels. The Jane Bowles story "Everything Is Nice," the Saul Bellow novel *Henderson the Rain King*, and Thomas Pynchon's debut *V.* each take a different part of the African continent as a setting—in whole, largely, and in small part, respectively. The styles and forms of these three works differ radically, but each uses the African setting as part of a textual critique of bourgeois Cold War American norms.

The interpretation of Bowles's project as a predecessor to American counterculture illustrates the way American literary writing about the Global South might be distinguished from British colonial discourse. This unique American invention—counterculture—proves a mechanism among American writers who followed Bowles to the Global South, allowing them to turn the problem back to the domestic scene and away from a "Third World" that seemed unruly and opaque. At the same time, the overlap between Bowles and earlier literature of colonialism is distinguishable. For example, his ethnographic impulse varies only slightly from the more admirable of the British officers portrayed in Kipling's work, just as his rejection of individuals that he associated with Arab nationalism suggests a rich connection to the same author's mocking presentation of the Indian babus created by the British Empire. Ultimately, the distinctions and the continuities are equally significant, since the discourse of American imperialism is both a variation on older imperialisms and a continuing historical theme.

What came after Bowles is also a variation on a theme that he set forward in American literary fiction. At the time of the surprisingly successful publication of Bowles's *The Sheltering Sky*, literary fiction that took Latin America, Africa, or Asia as a setting had not been particularly common among American writers. Since Bowles appeared on the scene, American literary fiction that takes place in the South has appeared with more and more frequency. A preliminary catalog of the trend would include some of these novels and perhaps many others: Saul Bellow, *Henderson the Rain King* (1959), William Burroughs, *Naked Lunch* (1959), Thomas Pynchon, *V* (1961), Katherine Anne Porter, *Ship of Fools* (1962), Walter Abish, *Alphabetical Africa* (1974), Tim O'Brien, *Going After Cacciato* (1978), John Updike, *The Coup* (1978) and *Brazil* (1994), Kathy Acker, *Blood and Guts in High School* (1978) and *Kathy Goes to Haiti* (1978), Russell Banks, *The Book of Jamaica* (1980) and *Continental Drift* (1985), Robert Stone, *A Flag for Sunrise* (1981), Alice Walker, *The Color Purple* (1982) and *The Temple of My Familiar* (1989), Don DeLillo, *The Names* (1982), Paul Theroux, *The Mosquito Coast* (1982), Robert Olen Butler, *A Good Scent from a Strange Mountain* (1989) and *The Deep Green Sea* (1992), Reginald McKnight, *I Get on the Bus* (1990), Norman Rush, *Mating* (1991) and *Mortals* (2003), Mona Simpson, *The Lost Father* (1992), Bob Shacochis, *Swimming in the Volcano* (1993), William T. Vollmann, *Butterfly Stories* (1993) and *The Atlas* (1997), Stephen Wright, *Going Native* (1995), Cormac McCarthy's "border novels," Barbara Kingsolver, *The Poisonwood Bible*

(1998), Patricia Henley, *The Hummingbird House* (1999), Ann Patchett, *Bel Canto* (2000) and *State of Wonder* (2011), Denis Johnson, *Tree of Smoke* (2007), Adam Johnson, *The Orphan Master's Son* (2012), Dave Eggers, *A Hologram for the King* (2012), and Vendela Vida, *The Diver's Clothes Lie Empty* (2015), with no doubt many more important novels that have escaped this author's notice or have not been produced yet as these pages are being written. In chapters 3–5 of this study, I will discuss a few of these titles in more detail. For now, the long list of titles is significant for several reasons.

For one thing, the list suggests the influential nature of the types of narrative fashioned by Bowles. If Bowles has been traditionally categorized as an off-beat cult figure with a complex relationship to the high canon of American letters, this can be ascribed at least in part to an unwillingness to think the literary in terms of setting—and this unwillingness characterizes both his fans and detractors. The Bowles novel—and particularly *The Sheltering Sky*—made settings outside Europe and North Africa interesting to American writers. The sense of the Global South as a place of escape and difference runs through this bibliography, often in ways that echo Bowles's disdain for the conformity of America's white middle class. The central consciousness in the novel is almost always a liberal or antiestablishment one in conflict with the crushing normativity that pervaded bourgeois American life during the Cold War period. The action is most often focalized through the consciousness of the alienated American subject. Thus, while the story takes place primarily in the Third World, the setting is usually a pretext for the critique of American bourgeois normativity. The not completely logical corollary, in the Bowles project, to his fictional characters' desire to throw off the constraints of American normativity is his disdain for Third World nationalist movements or, indeed, any type of local politics. This dismissal of local histories and their response to geopolitics runs through the bibliography of the American "Third World" novel listed here. In general, American literary fiction prefers a more docile, consumable, and folkloric face for its Third World. The tension that inheres in this tendency stems from the authorization of anticonformity within the U.S. domestic space, which simultaneously seeks out a highly normativized idea of the foreign in its Global South setting. There is a sense in which this dynamic in the text can be understood as a critique of two bourgeoisies, the one domestic, the other foreign. Yet this attempt at making the text's divergent attitudes toward domestic and foreign normativities ignores all geopolitics, stemming as it does from an unwillingness to acknowledge directly what the American stake is in the foreign scene. In this sense, the American writer Stenham in *The Spider's House*, who sees himself as above the fray but is equated by most Moroccans with the European civilization that rules over them, is more of a synecdoche for generations of American writers than a mere character in one novel by Bowles. This tension between divergent attitudes toward the two conformities performs within the literary text the very tension described by Klein as a dilemma for American thought vis-à-vis the Third World during the Cold War: how to think of yourself as an anticolonial global power.

Another reason for a brief inventory of the American "Third World" novel as it evolves after Bowles is to make clear the correlation between the rise of interest in the Global South within American letters and the emergence of the United States as a global superpower. This correlation, widely accepted by postcolonial scholars analyzing the nineteenth-century British canon, is still highly elusive on the American side of the Atlantic. Literary criticism dealing with contemporary fiction in the United States, once highly limited by the tendency for critics to write as fans of the famous authors they admired, has become exponentially more sophisticated over the course of a generation. Particularly noteworthy as examples that demonstrate the new possibilities for rigorous discussions of contemporary writings are Kathleen Fitzpatrick's study of television's influence on American novelists, Lawrence Hogue's analysis of the postmodern conception of language in contemporary American fiction, Rachel Smith's artful examination of post-9/11 narratives through the lens of affect theory, and Mark McGurl's authoritative study of the reshaping of American aesthetics by creative writing programs.[44] Each of these studies has in its own way done much to advance the critical possibilities for discussing contemporary writing. These studies prove definitively that the study of contemporary fiction has come to show every bit as much sophistication as studies of classics.

What remains largely absent from the work of critics dealing with contemporary U.S. literature, as well as those thinking in terms of the links between canonical literature and imperialism, is an examination of the connections between the emergence of the United States as a globalized superpower and its elite literary culture. This topic's relative neglect is yet another way in which America's superpower status retains a semblance of plausible deniability.

CHAPTER 2

Idea

Other Moroccos

Representation, Historicism, and the North African Lens

In 1994, the academic journal *Ariel* published what it called "an extensive interview/debate" with Paul Bowles conducted by the Moroccan Abdelhak Elghandor. The year is significant in that it represents a moment when Bowles's fame, bolstered by the Bernardo Bertolucci film adaptation of his novel *The Sheltering Sky* in 1992, was once again ascendant in the United States and Europe, even while *Moroccan* interest in the expatriate writer was beginning to gather momentum. Significantly, the mid-1990s represent the moment when postcolonial studies, the critique of colonial discourse, and the deconstruction of "Orientalism" emerged as powerfully influential critical discourses. Indeed, Elghandor refers several times to both Bowles's Moroccan critics and the critique of Orientalist discourse during the interview, which is framed by *Ariel*'s editors and Elghandor as follows: "The first of its kind between a latter-day American Orientalist and an 'educated Moroccan,' the representative of a class that Bowles, in his cultural bias for atavism and primitivism, avoids and even despises." The editor's note continues: "The purpose of this interview is to hear a non-European voice debating Paul Bowles on some pertinent, cultural questions that have always been left unasked by all previous interviewers of Bowles."[1]

Such a framing promises much more than an impassive, journalistic transcription of Bowles's responses, and in fact, what unfolds is unmistakably combative. The aging Bowles, already in his mideighties, only five years from his passing and no doubt disoriented by the rough treatment by his interlocutor, sounds at certain moments like a dyspeptic crank, suggesting, for example, that an atom bomb be used to destroy New York City and later calling for the "extermination" of all religious people, including the pope and the archbishop of Canterbury.[2] At the same time, Bowles's Moroccan questioner does not always come across as a balanced and knowing student of the art of fiction, although he has clearly read Bowles's writings fairly comprehensively. For example, he has no compunction about suggesting a crude rewrite of the novel *The Spider's House*, forty years after its publication, in which the American protagonist Stenham meets and debates the Moroccan nationalist leader Allal El Fassi as a way of incorporating the discourse of literate Moroccans into the work.[3]

In its agonistic tone, the interview pithily reflects the deep divide in discourses around Bowles in the United States between those interested in alternative trends in twentieth-century American letters and those interested in North Africa as a region, with its complex histories, cultural discourse, language, and social life. Although there is a growing body of insightful literary criticism of Bowles's work in the United States, by far most of the commentary on Bowles as a fiction writer tends to have a fan-like tone that subverts the potential for insightful criticism. It has been common even years after his death to find Bowles listed in the acknowledgments of books of criticism about him or even appearing next to the author in the photograph on the dust jacket. Experts in Arab or North African studies, on the other hand, tend to ignore Bowles's work in their writing and may also speak disdainfully of him in conversation.[4] Within Morocco, the emergence of a local critical discourse around Bowles's fiction has produced a still small body of critical commentary, but one that regularly shows more range, nuance, and potential for navigating between the poles of Arabist Bowles bashers and literary critics who are also fan/celebrants. At least the full diversity of opinions and positions regarding the importation of the American expat writer phenomenon to the Global South are represented in everything from Mohamed Choukri's gossipy attack on the person, *Bul Bulz wa-'uzlat Tanjah* (Paul Bowles and the solitude of Tangier), to Ibrahim Khatib's short study of the fiction, which focuses meticulously on the texts and thematically connects the readings through their movement between

Moroccan cities.[5] Thus, it would be false to imply that Moroccan native informants offer a tight consensus around the meaning of Bowles's expatriate life in Morocco and his literary and translational representations of Moroccans. While Bowles translated Choukri's previous works into English, as I discussed in chapter 1, Khatib worked on the other side of the translation machine as one of the first to translate samples of Bowles's fiction into Arabic. Thus, their respective books about Bowles represent the complicated cultural implications of Bowles's lifelong striving toward a constructed notion of North African authenticity.

Within this transnational bibliography, the *Ariel* interview stands out as a not entirely successful but unmistakably noteworthy encounter between pro-Bowles and anti-Bowles discourses. Bowles sometimes strikes his usual essentialist note, as when he declares in response to a question about modernizing trends in Morocco, "I don't approve of any hybridization, naturally."[6] Still, to try to reduce Bowles's projects to this series of reactionary statements made in the midst of a confrontational interview is unsatisfying, and one feels that Elghandor might have created something even more interesting through attentiveness to both the generic particularities of works of fiction and the distinctions in the historical moment that produced Bowles compared to that of the high Orientalists of the British and French empires that were so scrutinized by postcolonial criticism in the early 1990s. Even so, one is impressed by the insightful reading of certain blindnesses in Bowles's discourse that come out of the interview in spite of the fact that as an interviewer/interlocutor Elghandor is not really at liberty to proffer and elaborate thoroughly his claims and readings.

Particularly interesting is Elghandor's line of questioning, which deconstructs the way Bowles's striving toward the voice of the subaltern Moroccan subject results in the production of an imagined Morocco, which appears in his work as a "no-idea-producing area."[7] Early in the interview, Elghandor sets the tone: "Your ignoring of Arabo-Islamic institutional, written culture—its poetry, its prose, its philosophy, and its scripturalist theology, and your exclusive concentration on the oral, the folkloric, the visual, the mystic, the intuitive, and cult orders have created in your writings a biased, incomplete, sometimes even a lopsided and erroneous view of Arabo-Islamic culture."[8] In response, Bowles resorts once again to his notion of essential authenticity, arguing that Morocco is at its heart Berber and that attention to the long list of cultural discourses cited in the question would merely obscure that fact, but the question succeeds in calling attention to the incompleteness of Bowles's representation of North Africa, even for all its complications. And even for all the distinctions one must make between an American later twentieth-century writer of literary fiction and the older Orientalisms of Edward Lane, Richard Burton, and Ernest Renan, Elghandor's critique also points to a consistent erasure of ideas that answer back to the hegemonizing project of Western Europe and the United States in the tricontinental regions. The challenge in reading Bowles's representation of North Africa, therefore, lies not merely in disrupting the American critics' celebratory discussions of Bowles's oeuvre via attention to what has been written about him by Moroccan critics. Once we see Bowles as the creator of a discourse, it is necessary to place the politically implicated idiosyncrasies of his representation of non-Europe in conversation with Arab intellectual discourses, attention to which challenges not only Bowles's essentialism but also the enduring presumption of the "no-idea-producing area" that travels from Orientalist discourse through the American "Third World" novel and even infiltrates strains of postcolonial theory itself.

The Moroccan historian, philosopher, and novelist Abdallah Laroui (b. 1933) and the richly complicated body of work he has produced, for example, might be proposed as a counterpoint that challenges the imagined North Africa portrayed in Bowles's representations. Laroui and Bowles share certain places of residence and life experiences, but their projects as writers do not obviously connect.[9] As an individual and scholar, Laroui's reception in the United States, where he spent several complicatedly significant years teaching at UCLA in the 1970s, reenacts some of the erasures performed by Bowles's fiction and challenged by Elghandor in his interview. Laroui is prominently and consistently cited in the major critical work of Said, and specialists with a particular interest in North Africa or the Arabic-speaking region often closely associate the two, as indeed does Elghandor while interviewing Bowles. But Laroui, when read at all in the United States, is seen as a subject for those working in area studies or focused on the Middle East, with none of the significance as a theorist or global public intellectual that Said's justifiably and extensively influential work accrues. Although attempting to compare the global reception of intellectuals and theorists requires care and attentiveness,[10] Laroui, who wrote in Arabic and French and spent most of his career working in Moroccan institutions like Muhammad V University in Rabat, where he was a professor for much of his career, represents just the sort of figure that proves an affront to the constructed "no-idea-producing area," as seen so often from American institutions. Had he spent his entire career in a North American or Western European institution and published less in Arabic and more in English, he would be far more likely to be read as a theorist instead of as a symptomatic figure from a no-idea-producing area, of interest only to regional specialists. His full oeuvre includes works of critical theory, historical studies, historiography, novels, and memoirs, encompassing some work published originally in French and other work in Arabic. Over the course of his career, his critical and theoretical writing has returned repeatedly to the interlocking themes of historicism, the intellectual, and orientalism.

These three critical emphases are components of Laroui's evolving theory of the materialist component to processes and systems of representation. Intellectuals create systems of representation, according to Laroui's writings, so it is imperative that one inventory their particular ideological allegiances and geopolitical contexts. Such an inventory exposes historical writing as an act of representation, and consequently exposes both the responsibility of historians toward a narratological approach to their praxis and that of literary critics toward a sense of the geohistorically implicated nature of the literary text. In many ways, the Orientalist is the example par excellence of geohistorically implicated representation. The Arab intellectual's critique of Orientalism also exemplifies this phenomenon, but it does so with an awareness of its subject position that is usually lacking in Orientalist discourse. In this chapter, I hope to trace a genealogy of the North African and West Asian critique of Orientalism, with its focus on geohistorical location, from the late nineteenth century through Laroui, Edward Said, and the Saidean turn in Arab intellectual discourse. This approach is designed to clarify Laroui's complex model, to eschew the portrayal of his intellectual production as a historical accident or exception that proves the rule of the no-idea-producing area, and to reinsert the Arab intellectual into the debate around imperial representations of the global. This reinsertion, then, strikes at the heart of the processes of domestication in the post-Bowles moment of American hegemony.

I. AL-AFGHANI, HAYKAL, AND THE ORIGINS OF THE ARABO-ISLAMIC CRITIQUE OF ORIENTALISM

By now, the history of Said's influence on our thinking regarding representation is directly accessible and should be familiar. Remember that

Orientalism opens with Marx's famous quotation about representation from *The Eighteenth Brumaire of Louis Bonaparte* regarding the mid-nineteenth-century French peasantry, to the effect that "they cannot represent themselves. They must be represented." Over the course of his now classic and immensely influential study, Said applied this statement to the situation of Western representations of the Arab and Muslim in post-Enlightenment Europe and the United States, showing how, through a method that was citational and self-reinforcing, Orientalists created a convenient image of the Arab as passive, silent, and supine. In the aftermath of *Orientalism*'s publication, critics pointed out that Said's strategy of employing Michel Foucault's notion of a discourse to read Western Orientalist writing through the lens of "colonial discourse analysis" reinforced this very aspect of the Orientalists' representation of their subject matter, since it left discourses emerging from the Arab world unexamined, indeed unnoticed. A good summary of this critique of Said's *Orientalism* can be found in Bart Moore-Gilbert's comment that "*Orientalism* generally promotes an idea of the colonized subject as passive, silent and incapable of resistance. [It] seem[s] to accept at face value the power relations inscribed in the colonialist trope of 'surveying as if from a peculiarly suited vantage point the passive, sensual, feminine, even silent and supine East' (Said, *Orientalism,* 138)."[11] These criticisms do not stick as well to the later work of Said, as his American readers know. Less familiar to us, however, is a particular silencing that is reinforced by the criticism itself. In fact, Arab intellectuals had been linking Orientalist discourse with colonial politics in their writings for several generations before the publication of Said's study, and this extensive bibliography includes both writers cited by Said, like Laroui and his contemporary and regional colleague, Egyptian Anouar Abdel Malek, and writers not emphasized by Said, including Egyptian Muhammad Hussein Haykal and Palestinian Abdul Latif Tibawi. Perhaps precedent setting within this discussion is the peripatetic Persian pamphleteer, polemicist, activist, and teacher Sayyid Jamal al-Din al-Afghani (b. ca. 1838, Asadabad, Iran—d. 1897, Istanbul, Turkey).[12]

Strikingly, al-Afghani is regularly classified as a key figure in the modern renaissance of intellectual movements around West Asia and North Africa, even though his writings consist primarily of scattered articles and letters. The physical person of al-Afghani plays an unusually strong role for a nineteenth-century intellectual in establishing his legacy. Al-Afghani was a peripatetic activist, teacher, and journalist with life experiences and intellectual networks in India, Egypt, Turkey, Iran, and

France. His travels also took him to Russia, England, and Afghanistan, among other locales. In addition, contradictions proliferate in his life narrative. Apparently, al-Afghani constructed during his life an image of himself as a Farsi-speaking Afghan to camouflage his connection to Shiite Iran and thus reinforce ties to the Sunni strain of Islam, which he believed would be more practical as a tool to unite the geographically diverse Muslim communities under siege from European—particularly British—colonialism in the middle of the nineteenth century. This motive seems to have been instilled from an early formative experience. Although little is known of his early life in western Iran, historians have concluded that the first of his many trips abroad was probably an excursion to India as a teenager—precisely during the events of the 1857 "mutiny."[13] If al-Afghani was indeed an eyewitness to this influential and particularly bloody historical turn in British colonial practice within the North African / West Asian belt, the experience must have played a decisive role in his lifelong opposition to the spread of British hegemony. As a result of this opposition, historian Wilfred C. Smith is able to argue that al-Afghani is the first Muslim thinker "to stress the Islam-West antinomy,"[14] and novelist and essayist Pankaj Mishra is able to rank him alongside the Indian Rabindrinath Tagore and the Chinese Liang Qichao as one of the three intellectuals who led "the revolt against the West" and facilitated "the remaking of Asia."[15]

As Mishra emphasizes, al-Afghani's style of resistance was rooted in an intellectual project, but also in this dimension of his life contradictions proliferate. A key paradox that scholars focusing on al-Afghani's writings struggle with is the apparent contradiction in the way his two best-known works, "The Refutation of the Materialists" and "The Answer to Renan," deal with Islam and its relationship to modernity. Al-Afghani's "The Refutation of the Materialists" was written in Persian during a stay in India that encompassed the early 1880s. In it, al-Afghani polemicizes against a group of Indian "naturalists," led by Sayyid Ahmad Khan, whose enthusiasm for nineteenth-century Anglo-European rationalism was subverting the intellectual cohesion and political solidarity of the Muslim community, according to al-Afghani's argument. While "The Refutation of the Materialists" seems to take a stand in favor of traditional Islamic thinking against the westernization of intellectual culture, the "Answer to Renan," published in a French translation[16] in France in May 1883 in response to a lecture by the famous essayist and skeptic Ernest Renan, seems to take a contradictory position. In this piece, al-Afghani concedes that scientific learning in Europe has indeed far surpassed such inquiry within the Muslim world, but this is simply a matter of Islam's newness compared to the two major religions of Europe, which have had time to evolve and reform in ways that Islam is only just experiencing. In making this distinction, al-Afghani seeks to refute directly Renan's racialist thesis that the Arab mind is uniquely incapable of scientific, philosophical achievement. While the particular goals of each work are clear enough, the question remains: Does al-Afghani take directly contradictory positions on the accomplishments of European science and learning in his two most important essays?

The history of the scholarly reception of this apparent contradiction is interesting in itself. Albert Hourani, a Lebanese-British historian and probably the most influential figure among English speakers on the intellectual history of the twentieth-century Arabs, takes it for granted that al-Afghani was a religious Muslim who adopted a performance of rationalism in his "Answer to Renan" as a strategy to seduce his French audience:

> Al-Afghani was understating his case. He not only believed that Islam was as true or as false as other religions, but that it was the one true, complete and perfect religion, which could satisfy all the desires of the human spirit. Like other Muslim thinkers of his day, he was willing to accept the judgment on Christianity given by European free thought: it was unreasonable, it was the enemy of science and progress. But he wished to show that these criticisms did not apply to Islam; on the contrary, Islam was in harmony with principles discovered by scientific reason, was indeed the religion demanded by reason.[17]

But Nikki Keddie downplays the connection between al-Afghani and traditionalist thinking vis-à-vis Islam. In her reading, al-Afghani was a thoroughgoing utilitarian whose main goal was the political unification of the Muslim community, for which any type of theological claims or confessionalist stances toward religion served as a mere instrument: "The political unification and strengthening of the Islamic world and the ending of western incursions there were his primary goals, while the reform of Islam was secondary."[18] In Keddie's formulation, positions regarding Islamic thought in "The Refutation of the Materialists" are at least as calculated to appeal to that document's Asian Muslim audience as the "Answer to Renan" is designed to appeal to Europeans, and the contradiction is resolved through framing both essays within al-Afghani's political goals, which trump anything he has to say about actual ideas.

In her extensive biography of al-Afghani, Keddie fleetingly offers a distinctive understanding of the connection between these two and others of his essays. In her discussion of the basic argument of the "Answer to Renan," she notes at one point that "Afghani is thus pessimistic about the ultimate triumph of the pure freedom of investigation."[19] This particular formulation articulates a consistent stance toward ideas and discourse that runs through al-Afghani's various writings, albeit one that is deemphasized in the commentary around al-Afghani. Indeed, this very lack of emphasis by al-Afghani experts is what allows historians and commentators to figure his thought as contradictory at its core in the first place. If al-Afghani's point has been deemphasized, this cannot be attributed to its subtlety, because the second page of the "Answer to Renan" frames the argument emphatically:

> M. Renan's talk covered two principal points. The eminent philosopher applied himself to proving that the Muslim religion was by its very essence opposed to the development of science, and that the Arab people, by their nature, do not like either metaphysical sciences or philosophy. This precious plant, M. Renan seems to say, dried up in their hands as if burnt up by the breath of the desert wind. But after reading this talk one cannot refrain from asking oneself if these obstacles come uniquely from the Muslim religion itself or from the manner in which it was propagated on the world; from the character, manners, and aptitudes of the peoples who adopted this religion, or of those on whose nations it was imposed by force.[20]

Although Renan has no compunction about assuming thought can be objective and untainted in certain geographies (namely, in Europe), al-Afghani takes a clear and consistently oppositional position: "I will say that no nation at its origin is capable of letting itself be guided by pure reason."[21] For purposes of later writing by more recent Arab thinkers on the topic, it is highly significant that the true nature of al-Afghani's critique of free investigation and universal knowledge comes to the fore in a short essay refuting a famous French Orientalist, for it was precisely al-Afghani's anticolonial predilections that led him to his insightful connection between politics and knowledge making, which would later have such a rich history among Arab thinkers and essayists. In other words, a study of the later trajectory of this idea in North Africa and West Asia suggests an amendment to Keddie's formulation: not only was al-Afghani engaged in a critique of the myth of pure knowledge, but his specific target was the way geopolitics was masked whenever appeals to pure knowledge were fashioned by Europeans or Asian Europhiles.

Al-Afghani's pivotal role in the development of an engaged intellectual history in Asia and North Africa has been acknowledged by writers and historians from Hourani to Mishra. Those historians focusing on the Arabic-speaking region note his years in Egypt and his decades-long mentoring of the Egyptian Muhammad Abdu, an intellectual influence on both liberals and conservatives in early twentieth-century Egypt and a former sheikh of Al-Azhar University in Cairo. Al-Afghani and Abdu mark a starting point for the Arab *Nahdah*, or awakening, a late nineteenth- and early twentieth-century intellectual, cultural, and political movement that would eventually yield ground to a more overtly political discourse of anticolonial nationalism after World War II. A prominent figure from the end of the *Nahdah* is the Egyptian Muhammad Husayn Haykal, who wrote the first Egyptian novel to receive widespread critical attention, produced a plethora of varied and influential essays over his career, and also engaged in party politics, especially in the years before and after World War II. Haykal acknowledges being influenced by the writings of al-Afghani and Abdu.[22] Also, he shared with al-Afghani, Abdu, and his more famous contemporary, Taha Husayn, the experience of an influential sojourn in France that shaped much of his thinking about modern trends in global thought. Scholars of Egyptian intellectual history in Europe and North America, however, have historically found the shift to an interest in Islamic topics on the part of both Taha Husayn and Haykal in the 1920s and '30s a curious contradiction to their espousal of liberal European secular humanist ideas in their earlier writings, since one thing that seemed to distinguish this generation of the *Nahdah* was a much more fervent embrace of European Enlightenment thought.

For example, Haykal's *Hayat Muhammad*, a book on the life of the Prophet that was first published in 1935, is often misread as a reactionary turn to soft Islamism. Charles Smith, the historian who has produced the most extensive scholarship in English on Haykal, challenges the notion that Haykal's later Islamic writings marked a distinctive ideological shift. Rather, he tries to demonstrate how changed political circumstances within Egypt engendered an adjustment in Haykal's emphases. Smith does acknowledge that another motivation for the shift was external: "[Haykal] called for increasing attention to Islamic history, in part because of Western intellectual interest in Eastern culture."[23]

What critics have not noted, however, is the way Haykal's biography of the Prophet represents a culmination in a series of critical statements in his nonfiction. These statements date to well before the turn to Islamic subjects and connect Haykal to al-Afghani's early claims regarding the geohistorical location of knowledge production. In this light, *Hayat Muhammad* should more properly be read as part of a critique of Orientalist discourse, an outgrowth of texts like *Tarajim misriya wa gharbiya* (Western and Egyptian travels, 1929) and *Thawrat al Adab* (The revolution of literature, 1933, collecting in book form essays from the 1920s). After visiting Hungary and Bosnia in the 1920s, Haykal concluded his report on the difficulties of the Muslim minorities in Europe with the following comment on an exemplary case of Europe's Orientalism: "I wrote several years ago of a book published by a group of Western thinkers called 'The Face of Islam.' This book sets out to explore the extent in the various Islamic countries of Muslim desire to escape from their own Islamic high principles in favor of embracing those of the West in the present day. This book is nothing more than an image of the West's attitude toward the issue of Islam. Their line of thinking is natural. For dominant civilizations in every age have always been anxious to convert the peoples they conquer, no matter what original religious affiliations the conquered may hold."[24] Here Haykal connects Orientalism with political power and the colonial project, as he does with even more specificity in a pivotal chapter of his best-known work of criticism, *Thawrat al adab*. In a chapter dealing with the "causes for lagging behind of the [Arabic] narrative," Haykal addresses directly and critically the work of Hamilton Gibb. Haykal concludes that Gibb's value judgments about Arabic literature are self-interested and self-fulfilling prophecies. Moreover, they cross the line between scholarship and politically motivated rhetoric. In the end, "such authors dress themselves in the scientific and historical researcher's clothing while the work reinforces what many Western political leaders call for along the lines that the fates have thrown upon them the burden of conquering and civilizing the states of the East. In fact, it is their own ambition that has thrown upon them the burden of oppressing the states of the East and dictating to them their affairs."[25] The consistency of statements by Haykal linking the conclusions drawn by Western Orientalists with political power and colonial ambition in Europe through the various genres of travel writing, literary criticism, and religious writing suggest a partially formed but nevertheless profound critique of Western metaphysics that must be accounted for in understanding the intellectual origins of later studies of the same topic. This broadly unacknowledged strain in Haykal's thinking not only connects with al-Afghani's program of intellectual resistance through contextualization of knowledge production, but also constitutes a disruption to the most common manner by which historians read early twentieth-century Arab thinkers, exemplified in Hourani's statement that "it was generally accepted that European civilization was the highest in the world. . . . In a sense too the moral judgement of Europe was accepted."[26]

II. DECOLONIZATION AND ORIENTALISM: ABDEL-MALEK AND LAROUI

When Anouar Abdel-Malek published his essay "Orientalism in Crisis" in 1963, he forged a more cogent and systematic summary of the critique of politically motivated knowledge production that had preceded him in Arabo-Islamic writing, while at the same time evolving the critique in the direction of Said's discourse analysis approach. The essay appeared in the "Notes and Comments" section of *Diogenes*, an international academic social science journal with Third World liberationist leanings, which included Léopold Senghor, for example, on its editorial committee at the time. Abdel-Malek, by then a prominent Egyptian intellectual, published his argument in English[27] in an international journal at a time when the Nasser regime in Egypt was engaged in a harsh crackdown on both communists and Islamists inside the country, a historical reality that could have influenced the author's choice of an international venue instead of an Egyptian, Arabic one.

The essay begins by reinforcing the connection between knowledge production and geopolitics: "One will note with interest that the real impetus of Oriental studies in the two key sectors, that of the Arab world and the Far East, dates essentially from the period of colonial establishment, but, above all, from the domination of the 'forgotten continents' by European imperialisms (middle and second half of the twentieth century)."[28] Abdel-Malek continues by linking the anticipated decline of Oriental studies to geopolitics as well: specifically, the emergence of movements of decolonization, challenging Western Europe and the United States at the level of culture and ideas and not just politically and/or administratively. Decolonization movements have for Abdel-Malek exposed the methodological insufficiency of the Orientalist approach, relying as it does on a scrupulous eschewing of any sources produced by scholars and intellectuals from the regions under study. The emergence of anticolonial independence movements provides Abdel-Malek with a historical context distinctive from that of al-Afghani and Haykal, but he also puts a greater emphasis in his critique on the conception of the problem as rooted in social scientific method. That is, his references suggest a heightened attention to epistemology in his version of the critique.

Some of the specific claims that anchor Abdel-Malek's discussion presciently foreshadow the arguments Said will make fifteen years later—for example, his strong critique of essentialism: "[The] two schools of traditional orientalism . . . consider the Orient and Orientals as an 'object' of study, stamped with an otherness—as all that is different, whether it be 'subject' or 'object'—but of a constitutive otherness, of an essentialist character, as we shall see."[29] One of the traits of the Orientalist method that facilitates this alterity is a scrupulous avoidance of any scholarship from the Arab world. On this point, Abdel-Malek suggests a problem with the echo chamber of Orientalist scholarship that Said develops more fully into colonial discourse analysis. Finally, some of the specific tropes within Orientalist scholarship, including the decadence, passivity, and irrationality of the so-called Oriental, reappear in Said's more elaborate version of the argument.

It is important to clarify that I am not arguing here, as others have attempted to do, that Said merely repeated points made previously by Arab scholars.[30] In fact, Said's study covers material and formulates a method that was genuinely innovative and fully justified its substantial influence. Rather, my point is that most readers of Said, by obliterating the preceding North African and West Asian intellectual bibliography upon which Said was drawing in part have stunted the potential of his work to suggest a theory for reading representational politics across politically contested geographical spaces.

In the specific case of Abdel-Malek, the Arab thinker who was probably closest to Said in point of view and research focus, one must also note distinctions between himself and Said, as well as similarities and differences with the Arab and Islamic critics of Orientalism that preceded him. Abdel-Malek's argument offered a language for the critique that made al-Afghani's polemics more comprehensible within academic discourse. Through his emphasis upon methods of research, access to primary texts, and bibliographical sources, Abdel-Malek managed to maintain the politically engaged character of al-Afghani's critique of universalizing epistemologies while expressing it in terms acceptable for social science researchers.

Another characteristic of Abdel-Malek's study that distinguishes him from both the liberal Haykal before him and the radical humanist Said after him is the open commitment to Third World Marxist liberationist thought. His direct engagement with such movements, laid out in the second half of the essay, appears in the form of a distinction not found in any other discussion of European Orientalism that I have looked at, namely, a difference—noted at the height of the Cold War's political division of the two Europes—between Western European Orientalism and Eastern European Orientalism. This characteristic of the study is consistent with the main claim that epistemology cannot be disconnected from geopolitics, and it allows for a comparatist generalization of the problem across the Global South, to China and Latin America, for example, in a way that Haykal's use of the life of Muhammad as an entry point cannot manage because of its religious orientation, which would not be shared in all parts of the "tricontinental" region.[31] At the same time, Abdel-Malek's approach verges upon collapsing an important distinction between Eastern European and Soviet Marxism on the one hand, and the Third World liberationist Marxist-influenced school on the other. The latter approach, which I have called the Mariátegui tradition in another context,[32] can be read as distinctive in multiple ways, but principal among them is the argument for historical difference, which is crucial to the sort of antiessentialist materialist approach I am trying to delineate.

Perhaps the most sophisticated proponent of this approach in the Arabic-speaking regions is Abdel-Malek's contemporary, the Moroccan Abdallah Laroui. Laroui is yet another pivotal figure in the genealogy of the Arab critical discourse of geopolitically located knowledge production that I am tracing here. Although Bowles's combative interlocutor Elghandor lists him alongside Said and Abdel-Malek as part of a triumvirate of prodigious critics of Orientalism, in fact, Laroui's critique of the Orientalist project emerges out of a series of studies grappling with the linked questions of historicism, the intellectual, and the crisis of Arab society. In this sense, he shares with Haykal a more impressionistic approach to Orientalist discourse per se, using a series of readings embedded within studies of more general topics, as opposed to a single critique, like Said's book or Abdel-Malek's article.

In a period from the early 1960s through the late 70s, Laroui moved from his native Morocco to Egypt, where he served as cultural attaché, to France, where he completed his doctoral dissertation, back to Morocco, from where he was invited to join the faculty at UCLA in Los Angeles, and finally, back to Morocco as professor of history at Mohammad V University. Three studies published over that period on multiple continents established his reputation as one of the premier critical thinkers in North Africa. The first of these, a critical study of Arab intellectual culture, provoked, at least in part, by his experiences in Egypt in the early 1960s, appeared originally in French as *L'idéologie arabe contemporaine* in 1967. Translated into Arabic more than once, most recently by the author, the book has not appeared in an English version. In it, Laroui makes his first attempt to describe the way the European colonialism that most historians of the Arab awakening credit for inspiring Arab thought actually suffocated the local production of knowledge, instilling an intellectual culture unresponsive to the dynamics of the region and marked by dependency on the colonial powers. Classifying contemporary Arab intellectuals in three categories—sheikh, or promoter of a religious ideology; politician, or advocate of democracy; and technocrat, or proponent of science and technology—Laroui reads each category as a manifestation of a culture that is subservient and nondialectical in its relationship with Western scholarship.

In 1970, Laroui published *L'histoire du Maghreb: Un essai de synthèse*, based on his earlier dissertation research. As the book's rather dialogic titles—on the one hand a history, on the other a thought piece—suggest, this study seems to have evolved into something other than what the author set out to produce. While the main body of the book surveys historical development of the Maghreb region from the earliest times to the near present, the narrative is overlaid with a polemic against the colonial discourse that shapes the academic bibliography making up the historical discussion at the time of the book's writing, including the "no-idea-producing area" assertion. As a result of his encounter with this scholarship, Laroui writes the introduction after the tradition of radical historiography that one might find in works by C. L. R. James or Walter Rodney, critiquing the existing bibliography that has written the history through a colonialist frame as the results of the research are presented. His connection to anticolonial historiography is evident, for example, when he claims that the study of the ancient period in the Maghreb has been "directly influenced by the general ideology of colonialism,"[33] or when—like Abdel-Malek—he prefigures Said, in his analysis of the self-referentiality of Orientalist scholarship: "All these historians refer the reader back to each other and invoke each other's authority."[34] The emperor's historians, he insists, have no clothes.

In *The Crisis of the Arab Intellectual: Traditionalism or Historicism?* Laroui extends the line of thought first put forth in *L'idéologie arabe contemporaine*. In this later group of essays, traditionalism constitutes a societal obstacle to progressive historicist thinking among the region's intellectual class. These essays make a radical, counterintuitive link between the style of thinking that produces the sheikh and the bourgeois nationalism of the Nasserist and Baathist orthodoxies in the region at the time. They argue for historicism as method with the potential to break from this ossified political orthodoxy, but the great challenge in producing a truly historicist vision for Arab thinkers at that moment was the thoroughgoing interweaving of contemporary Arab ideology—even in its nationalist and traditionalist manifestations—with Western metaphysics and the colonial historiography that correlates to it.

Although all three of these books are critical of Orientalist discourse and its connection with colonial politics, *The Crisis of the Arab Intellectual* is the first to present a free-standing essay directly addressing Orientalist practice, in a chapter titled "The Arabs and Cultural Anthropology: Notes on the Method of Gustave von Grunebaum." Laroui's reading of the Austrian von Grunebaum's career emphasizes the somewhat contradictory features of his European training. On the one hand, he studied and worked in Vienna, which had become a cosmopolitan center of intellectual culture by the middle of the twentieth century, thus putting him "in a position to benefit from other schools of European thought: French, English, Italian, Russian." At the same time, the European Orientalist tradition in which he worked took a highly traditional philological approach to methodological issues, and in this context, von Grunebaum trained as a "philologist and specialist in classical Arabic poetry."[35] Laroui, however, marks von Grunebaum's move to the United States during World War II as the starting point of a new direction in the scholar's methodological approach. As he shifted positions from the Asia Institute in New York City to the University of Chicago after the war to UCLA in the 1950s, von Grunebaum moved in the direction of cultural anthropologist of the Islamic world and, later, upon being promoted up through the administrative ranks, general expert in Islam. Laroui clearly implies that American academic institutions encouraged the scholar to become a generalist and to work at the level of generalization. It is also interesting that the events of World War II play a role in the transition from European philologist Orientalist in the tradition of Renan to American commentator in the era of new American global hegemony.

Within the genealogy of Arab critics of Orientalism, Laroui is distinguished by his emphasis on questions of method, but placing his early writing alongside the older work of al-Afghani, Haykal, and Abdel-Malek reveals other distinctions. For example, the American context emerges as a distinct semantic field in the work of Laroui for the first time among these critics. This is true in his discussion of von Grunebaum, but also in other analyses, as, for example, in this passage from *History of the Maghreb*: "When we think of the medievalists who are neither archeologists nor classical scholars and of the present-day writers on the Maghreb (Americans in particular) who are neither Arabic scholars nor classical scholars nor historians, and whose sole access to their subject is through the sweeping generalizations of the popularizers, we see what ravages can result from the slightest carelessness in the formation of an opinion."[36]

Also, Laroui's critique of von Grunebaum appears in the middle of a series of essays critiquing the traditionalism and intellectual dependency of *Arab* intellectuals. By being the first to link his deconstruction of Orientalist discourse and method with the crisis of Arab intellectuals, Laroui suggests a "contrapuntalism" (a term later coined by Said while writing *Culture and Imperialism* to facilitate his critique of *Orientalism*'s inadequacies) that might operate at the level of method. In this dialectic, the intellectual and the Orientalist are yoked, and a progressive method can be formulated by the former only within the context of a consciousness about the politically motivated nature of the writings of the latter. At the same time, an agonistic, hermetic attack on Orientalism that does not simultaneously engage in self-critique will not advance the possibilities of historicist method in Arab intellectual culture, and as such, it will accomplish little, if anything.

Laroui makes an explicit statement of his commitment to historicism, but what remains implicit, albeit consistently present and unmistakable, is the place of the intellectual in the biopolitics of knowledge production. In later writings, this aspect of Larouian epistemology will become even more explicit, but even in these earlier writings the unmistakable concern with the intellectual as not merely a social phenomenon but also a necessary component in the process of knowledge production is evident. That Laroui links his critique of Orientalists with a parallel critique of the Arab intellectual adds a new dimension to the geopolitics of knowledge production that I am tracing here. The embodied intellectual, for Laroui, cannot blithely transcend her or his geohistorical location, and neither can the theorist or the creator of a method write away the intellectual's body.

Perhaps on this point, the discourse in and of Paul Bowles and Morocco is most clearly distinguished from Larouian thought. Several of the Bowles scholars I have cited mention in passing that Laroui criticizes Bowles's essentialism in *L'idéologie arabe contemporaine*. What is never acknowledged, however, is that this discussion focuses exclusively on the later translational turn toward constructing Moroccan authenticity through capturing the voice of the illiterate peasant in Bowles's work. Indeed, Laroui's contrastive view finds it untenable to approach a society as though knowledge production were innocent and unnecessary to mark off. A few years later, Laroui reinforces this critique of Bowles's *translations* in the expanded Arabic version of *Crisis*, entitled *al-'Arab wa al fikr al-tarikhi (The Arabs and Historical Thought)*. Interestingly, Laroui's revisiting here of his critique of the Bowles translations in the late 1970s emphasizes this particular aspect of the American's work as a popularizing, American phenomenon that overemphasizes one particular dimension of Moroccan reality.

III. EDWARD SAID AND THE PARADIGM SHIFT

Said's *Orientalism*, first published in 1978, has become one of the most influential works of critical theory of its time, with its primary impact coming to force in the English-speaking world, but an influence also profoundly felt in the Arabic-speaking world, and indeed globally. Unlike other texts mentioned so far, it was authored originally in English, was published in New York, and focused (along with only Abdel-Malek's article) exclusively on the epistemological and political concerns growing out of the work of Orientalists. By deploying a method informed and shaped by European antifoundationalist thought in the traditions of Freud, Marx, and Foucault, Said was able to do much more than expose the hypocrisy of Western Orientalist practice. He also depicted the epistemological traditions of Europe and the United States as a house divided between critical theorists on one hand and Orientalists and those they influenced on the other. Said's ethos also distinguished him from Arab world critics who had preceded him. He wrote with great authority about Western texts; indeed, his sensitivity to the stature and artistry of writers like Flaubert and Massignon, not to mention his keen perception of discursive and aesthetic detail in all the authors he discussed, distinguishes his text in a way that has often been erased by the polemical atmosphere of its reception. That is, although Said was careful to distinguish the variety of characteristics in what he called "manifest Orientalism" and often wrote about European travelers and scholars with a great deal of admiration, he was very often interpreted—by both advocates and antagonists—as "condemning the West."

Reading Said's *Orientalism* in the context of a genealogy of North African and West Asian critiques of Orientalist thought allows for an interesting framing of this already very familiar text. There is no question that Said's systematic approach represents a break with what came before him. While his argument is similar to some earlier anticolonial thinkers, he draws on a distinct set of sources and writes for a distinct audience compared with Haykal or Abdel-Malek. While there is no question that Said was aware that his topic had been much discussed by Arab intellectuals, several of whom he cites, it is highly doubtful that he ever did any systematic review of Arabic thought on the topic, not only because he does not cite or mention many of the thinkers within this tradition, but also because his carefully delineated research parameters do not include these texts, as he makes clear in his introduction: "There were—and are—cultures and nations whose location is in the East, and their lives, histories, and customs have a brute reality obviously greater than anything that could be said about them in the West. About that fact this study of Orientalism has very little to contribute, except to acknowledge it tacitly. But the phenomenon of Orientalism as I study it here deals principally, not with a correspondence between Orientalism and Orient, but with the internal consistency of Orientalism and its ideas about the Orient (the East as career) despite or beyond any correspondence, or lack thereof, with a 'real' Orient."[37]

This statement summarizes the study's unique approach, which would foster an enduring methodological trend in cultural studies research known as colonial discourse analysis. This aspect of the text represented a break with the strategy of works like *Hayat Muhammad* or *The Crisis of the Arab Intellectual*. In its moment, it allowed Said to preempt an Orientalizing reading of his study, forcing its English-language readers in the United States or England to turn their attention back on their own critical tradition and the central role played in it by the objectification of a constructed Other. The method employed both captured the zeitgeist of a moment in which U.S. literary criticism was on the verge of a definitive break from the overly long hegemony of the by then thoroughly ossified New Critical approach, and also may have reassured many North American critics that they could take radical positions vis-à-vis the Arabs or the Third World without having to do sustained research that attended to the cultural, linguistic, and historical realities of those regions.[38]

Focusing exclusively on colonial discourse allowed Said to treat the historical trajectory of Orientalist rhetoric with a breadth that far outstripped the work done up to that moment by other Arab critics. Al-Afghani and Abdel-Malek had each devoted an essay to the topic, while Haykal and Laroui had scattered throughout several works observations that constituted a critique of Orientalist thought. Of this group, Laroui focused the most on discontinuities within the Orientalist tradition, especially as it migrated to the United States. Said, however, was able to make transitions and an interplay between continuity and discontinuity central to his study as a result of his far more expansive breadth. Thus, transitions—from representations of the East in antiquity to the era of European Christendom, from the eighteenth to the nineteenth centuries, from European colonial discourse to the reign of U.S. pundit culture after World War II—appear everywhere in his sprawling genealogy of Euro-American Orientalist discourse.

The importance of transitions and discontinuities in Said's study were easily overlooked because of the subtlety of his notion of the latent/manifest divide. The following passage dealing with the emergence of European Orientalists who were also colonial administrators illustrates the problem: "Orientalism assumed an unchanging Orient, absolutely different (*the reasons change from epoch to epoch*) from the West. And Orientalism, *in its post-eighteenth-century form*, could never revise itself. All this makes Cromer and Balfour, as observers and administrators of the Orient inevitable."[39] I have added emphasis to two different moments in the quotation, both incorporated as grammatical afterthoughts, a parenthetical clause and an appositive phrase, respectively. Also, the passage itself is about a continuity within Orientalist discourse. Still, the subtle parenthetical ruptures in the passage mirror the construction of the larger work, which moves dialectically between the continuities in the outward gaze of European Orientalist discourse and its epochal particularities.

Said's attention to particularity within continuity resulted in a far more systematic treatment of Orientalist discourse than those of his Arab-world predecessors, but this reality does not erase the debt his study owes to a century of critical writing about the Orientalist approach. At its core, Said's study constitutes a detailed critique of the possibility of disinterested knowledge production, and this strain in the argument especially comes to light when reading Said against the North African and West Asian critical discourse that preceded him. If al-Afghani pronounced with clarity his position that "no nation at its origin is capable of letting itself be guided by pure reason," Said was no less emphatic: "No scholar, not even a Massignon, can resist the pressure on him of his nation or of the scholarly tradition in which he works."[40]

Although Said is participating in a long tradition of critical writing about Orientalism that aims at the larger issue of knowledge production, as I have shown, one must also acknowledge that he demonstrates the connection with unprecedented force. For example, in a discussion of Flaubert's *Bouvard et Pécuchet*, an unfinished novel about two aging bureaucrats who construct a quixotic plan to retire to a bucolic life in the French countryside that would not immediately jump to mind as a text participating in Orientalist discourse, Said broadens his subject from Orientalism to epistemology in his comment that Flaubert "frames the specifically modern structures of Orientalism, which after all is one discipline among the secular (and quasi-religious) faiths of nineteenth century European thought."[41] In several earlier passages, Said has linked Orientalism with knowledge production, including when he states that "Orientalism is better grasped as a series of constraints upon and limitations of thought than it is simply as a positive doctrine."[42] A nice summary of this prominent motif in the study is found in the following passage, which discusses the need for a certain type of knowledge production as an expression of superiority, expressed here specifically in terms of domestication: "On the one hand, Orientalism acquired the Orient as literally and as widely as possible; on the other, it domesticated this knowledge to the West, filtering it through regulatory codes, classifications, specimen cases, periodical reviews, dictionaries, grammars, commentaries, editions, translations, all of which together formed a simulacrum of the Orient and reproduced it materially in the West, for the West."[43] Appropriately enough, this quotation introduces a discussion on travel writing, which can be understood in this context as a means to transmit domesticating knowledge of that which is strange, making it familiar and asserting knowledge, authority, and power over other geographies.

In his cast of characters, Said collates many of the discussions that have preceded him. Laroui's reading of von Grunebaum is analyzed in

Orientalism's conclusion, as is the same Hamilton Gibb taken on by Haykal, and the Louis Massignon critiqued by Abdel-Malek. In a particularly brilliant long section in the middle of the study, Said reads Ernest Renan's place in the Orientalist canon[44] (without mentioning al-Afghani's "Response," an omission at least partially justified by the book's aforementioned research parameters and later corrected in *Culture and Imperialism*). Said is most interested in Renan the philologist, touching only briefly on the skeptic emphasized by French studies and working more slowly toward the polemicist taken on by al-Afghani. For Said, Renan's resort to philological approaches to Semitic studies is more than a rationalist critique of traditional religion. It is also a nationalistic assertion of the civilizational gains of the Enlightenment that have caused Europe to surpass the lands of ancient civilizations that are now stagnant. This strain in Said's reading is evident in the following passage from near the end of this section: "If in what I have so far said I have insisted so much on Renan's comparatively forgotten study of the Semitic languages, it has been for several important reasons. Semitic was the scientific study to which Renan turned right after the loss of his Christian faith; I described above how he came to see the study of Semitic as replacing his faith and enabling a critical future relation with it."[45] Here the word *ricochet* comes to mind. Renan sets out to debunk a certain type of traditional French orthodoxy; out of this impulse grows a pronounced critique of France's constructed Other. Distinctions of historical specificity and style notwithstanding, this very buttoned-down moment in the French Orientalist tradition lends itself to comparison with the origins of the American "Third World" novel. Paul Bowles also set out to critique the suffocating bourgeois normativity of U.S. Cold War life, and in doing so, produced a representation of North African society deeply invested in an essentializing primitivism.

Said acknowledges in a famous passage in the introduction that his emphasis on this elaborate cast of individual writers who participate in Orientalist practice constitutes a break with the Foucauldian method that he sets out to deploy: "Yet unlike Michel Foucault, to whose work I am greatly indebted, I do believe in the determining imprint of individual writers upon the otherwise anonymous collective body of texts constituting a discursive formation like Orientalism."[46] This distinction raises a crucial issue. Said here recognizes that he is out of step with the turn of critical theory in France, England, and the United States in his focus on the author's role in questions of knowledge production. Indeed, on this point, he is much closer to the historicizing impulse that studies authors as producers of knowledge, exemplified in the work of the Arab thinkers discussed in this chapter. If a "split" has opened up between two types of literary figures in the United States, those who produce theory and criticism and attend the Modern Language Association on the one hand, and those who produce "fine writing" and attend the Association of Writers and Writing Programs on the other, an interesting convergence occurs around the bibliography of globalization. The American "Third World" novel, following Bowles, marginalizes, erases, mocks, and/or circumvents the producer of discourse in the postcolonial world. Meanwhile, critical theoretical studies promote the myth of the disembodied producer of knowledge in the form of the transcendent theoretician. On this point, Said's study dissents from much of the critical work that it inspired in the United States.

IV. ARAB THEORY AFTER SAID

In the years following the publication of *Orientalism*, the impact of Said's argument gathered momentum and *Orientalism* increasingly became an influential and much-discussed text in the Arab world. Sabry Hafez makes the claim that at the time *Orientalism* was published in English, its author "was entirely unknown in the Arab world."[47] This changed, however, as word spread among the intellectual class regarding the book's argument and the sequels that followed closely after it and functioned as case studies, *The Question of Palestine* (1979) and *Covering Islam* (1981). English-speaking intellectuals in the region made important statements about the text within a few years of its appearance. It was soon translated, somewhat controversially, into Arabic by Kamal Abu Dib in 1981. (In 2006, it was retranslated by Muhammad al-Enani.) Circulating as it did at a time when Arab nationalist thought was in decline and increasingly regressive versions of Islamism were gaining momentum in most cross-sections of Arab civil society, the antiessentialist impulse in Said's study was broadly ignored, and the hermetic, self-reflexive critique of Western Europe and the United States was translated into an argument that the region's many problems were all the fault of the West. Hafez describes a general trend in the Arab reception of Said's work: "Thus, instead of seeing Said's seminal work as exposing (and undermining) the basis and motivation of the Orientalist discourse, they considered it the latest in a series of diatribes against the misrepresentation of Islam in European discourse. In the process, they completely overlooked Said's most persuasive argument—about the dialectics of knowledge and power, the complicity of discourse in the dynamics of hegemony and imperialism, and the fabrication of an inferior Orient as justification for its subjugation and conquest."[48]

Hafez calls Syrian critic Sadik Jalal al-'Azm the "main exception" to this line of misinterpretation.[49] First published in 1981 and reissued and collected several times thereafter, al-'Azm's review essay, "Orientalism and Orientalism in Reverse," may be the best-known response to Said from an Arab intellectual working in the region. The essay participates in a critique that reappears among Marxian critics steeped in the history of the Arab region when it argues that Said's text does not sufficiently distinguish premodern forms of European Orientalist discourse from those post-Enlightenment forms more directly implicated in colonial politics and global capitalism,[50] a critique of Said also made by Samir Amin and Maxime Rodinson. Al-'Azm also takes issue with Said's characterization of Marx as subservient to European Orientalist frames of thought, an argument that would later be elaborated by Aijaz Ahmed, and he argues that in the Arab region, Orientalist ways of understanding the self have proliferated among intellectuals who have been too willing to characterize their own culture as distinct from Europe's, particularly in its Islamic foundation.

On this latter point, which is somewhat confusing to any reader who takes seriously the role of geopolitical power in Said's original argument, al-'Azm manages to tie his critique of Said to his most famous work of criticism, *Naqd al-fikr al-dīnī* (*The Critique of Religious Thought*, 1969). Consistently over the course of several decades, al-'Azm was one of the region's most outspoken critics of religious modes of thinking. Thus, his reading of Said not only breaks with the soft Islamism of many regional readings of Said's text; he goes on to make Islamism the issue, essentially arguing that the main problem with Said's text is its inability to provide tools that will utterly dismantle regional Islamist thinking. In this sense, al-'Azm refused to accept the research parameters that Said set for himself.

In placing al-'Azm's critique next to the pro-essentialist regional misreadings of Said's work, the general influence of Said's more elaborate and systematic study in the Arab region becomes clear. Whether thinkers in the Arab world agreed, disagreed, or mistakenly believed themselves to agree or disagree with Said, the issues of Orientalist discourse, colonial politics, and the politics of representation, and the reformulation of all these questions in the context of neocolonialism and globalization all became problems that they filtered more often than not through what was perceived to be a Saidean lens. As a result, the Laroui school of representation theory became a regionally delimited discussion. Within this northwest African bibliography, issues of representation, historicism, the intellectual, and Arab identity came to the fore within a semantic field shaped by Europe, the United States, and the regional intellectual.

For example, in the year that *Orientalism* was first published in English, Tunisian Hichem Djaït published the original French version of his *L'Europe et l'Islam*, in which he addresses many of the same issues raised in Said's study, but does so with a Laroui-like attention to the dialectic of power and discourse between the Arab intellectual and the Orientalist. From the start, Djaït frames the issue ambitiously and in terms of method: "[Europe] cannot be compared, we are told, with any other civilization, past or present, except perhaps that of the Neolithic period."[51] The issue of comparatism sets in motion a dialectic between Orientalists and Arab intellectuals that is examined over the course of the study. On the one hand, the anticomparativist tendency toward universalism that Djaït studies in Europe delimits the possibilities of an effective historicist European lens: "Western intellectuals fall into ethnocentrism even when they think they are questioning it, since they think that they alone are qualified to define universal values."[52] On the other hand, Djaït also recognizes a crisis in Arab intellectual culture, one that explains for him the rise of Orientalism itself, which he claims "filled the gap" during a period (1860–1960) when Islam "lacked the intellectual and scholarly resources to examine itself."[53] In this manner, Djait connects something similar to Said's analysis of Europe's colonial discourse with his own version of a crisis in Arab intellectual culture. The two are inextricably connected and can only be read through a historicist approach to theories of representation that locate the individual theorist geohistorically. "The past is by definition infinite, while the present is limited by its finitude. And history in the past is beset by history in the present, which excludes objectivity, demands meaning, and challenges every cultural consensus, however broad."[54]

Djaït references Laroui in his introduction, but for the most renowned Moroccan thinkers of his generation, Laroui's ideas were often even more central and overt. Abdelkebir Khatibi (Moroccan, 1938–2009), for example, took on Laroui directly and by name, arguing that the latter had asked the right questions in his studies of how the Arabs were represented, and had even properly diagnosed Arab nationalism's role in mystifying representations of the region. But he broke definitively with his contemporary on the question of historicism. Influenced greatly by the reading strategies of his friends Roland Barthes and Jacques Derrida, Khatibi found in radical philosophies of difference the only possibility for the demythologization of the Arab nationalist consensus within the North African intellectual class. Historicism struck him as particularly unpromising as a tool to critique nationalism. Khatibi distinguishes his own position from Laroui's in the following passage: "Quand nous critiquons les tentatives comme celle de Laroui, ce n'est pas par souci polémique, mais c'est qu'il nous est possible (d'ailleurs très aisément) de montrer que cette vérité de l'historicisme n'est qu'un artifice théologique sous une forme idéologique."[55] Laroui's historicism—of which Khatibi bases his understanding on a reading of *L'idéologie arabe contemporaine*—is, as far as he is concerned, just another ideological trope that does not go far enough beyond the faith-based methods of the traditionalists. Khatibi seeks to emphasize "difference," expecting this engagement to produce a more penetrating portrayal of the diversity of Arab and Maghrebi experience, a portrait of a "maghreb pluriel." Although he sees himself as exposing Laroui's positivism, like Laroui, he sees Arab nationalism as the great obstacle: "Cette unité est donc, pour nous, du passé, à analyser dans son insistance imaginaire. Et d'ailleurs, cette prétendue unité tant réclamée englobe non seulement ses marges spécifiques (berbères, coptes, kurdes . . . et marge des marges le féminin), mais elle couvre aussi la division du monde arabe en pays, en peuples, en sectes, en classes; et de division en division, jusqu'à la souffrance de l'individu, déserté par l'espérance de son dieu, à tout jamais invisible."[56]

Intellectual historian Hisham Sharabi wrote in 1988 that he saw Khatibi as the most radical in his generation of Arab critics.[57] Today this judgment seems overstated because Khatibi's language seems so much of that particular moment—and even of that particular moment in France. Khatibi's critique of Laroui owes a great deal to Derrida's critiques of Marx and Althusser. In Morocco, the most prominent of the younger generation of critics, Abdelfattah Kilito, has been framed as a critic of Khatibi by Kilito's perceptive translator Wail Hassan in the latter's introduction to his translation of Kilito's *Thou Shalt Not Speak My Language*. Kilito's work shows that the Arab intellectual—even when circumventing Laroui's emphasis on historicism—cannot avoid the question of the uneven world that has been bequeathed to the North African writer by the Orientalists.[58] Such critiques notwithstanding, in a regional context, Khatibi's work calls attention to the difficulty of a representational strategy that is open to particularity and progressive but also generative. Appropriately, for Khatibi the precise distinctions inhering in theories of difference applied to the Maghreb offer the most effective subversion of that type of Orientalist reduction, present in trace elements in the representational strategies of the American "Third World" novel, which sees the Other through an arbitrarily isolated essence.

If a main difference between the Laroui of *The Crisis of the Arab Intellectual* and the Said of *Orientalism* is the former's insistence that the problems of knowledge production in the North Atlantic and North Africa are inextricably linked, Khatibi appears an important figure in the Larouian genealogy in spite of his criticisms of his fellow Moroccan. This becomes particularly clear in Olivia Harrison's recent study of the way the Palestine problem is represented as the anticolonial struggle par excellence for cultural producers from the Maghreb. In the specific case of Khatibi, his concept of double critique is fashioned in part to deal with the double bind faced by the Maghrebi intellectual who must critique the myth of national unity—in support of which the cause of Palestine is so regularly deployed—while simultaneously critiquing the neocolonial structures that produced the Palestinian problem in the first place. Thus, "Palestine represents the possibility of what Khatibi calls 'double critique'—a critical-distance taking from both colonial culture and a purportedly originary Arab-Islamic culture often articulated with reference to the Mashriq."[59] The axis between "colonial culture" and "originary Arab-Islamic culture" parallels the dynamic of linked crises in knowledge production excavated in the work of Laroui.

The second of Laroui's most prominent Moroccan contemporaries is Mohamed Abed al-Jabiri (1936–2010). Primarily writing in Arabic (and thus, far less well known outside his region than Khatibi and Laroui), al-Jabiri also addresses the problem of the overgeneralization of Moroccan and Arab realities, but where Khatibi's radical metaphysics produces the notion of "le pluriel" as a counter to essentialism, al-Jabiri suggests an alternative historiography that subverts the contemporary prejudices against philosophy and precolonial history in deriving his argument for "*al khususiya* [الخصوصية]" in readings of the region. In another context, I have written about the way al-Jabiri's notion of *al khususiya* in his reading of northwest African intellectual history constitutes a revision of Hourani's narrative of Arabic thought during the *Nahdah*.[60] In this discussion, *al khususiya*'s function as a reinscription of historicism in Moroccan intellectual discourse after Khatibi's critique is more relevant. Al-Jabiri's main analytical goal is to critique the binary opposition between traditional and modern that so dominates historiographical thought and writing about the Arab region. His focus is intellectuals and their evolution in the region through space and time. The most disruptive aspect of his narrative is the introduction of geographies of scale into the historicizing of the intellectual. Al-Jabiri sees the Maghreb region as distinct in its intellectual cultural formation from the Mashriq region, whose intellectuals tend to dominate discussions by historians. The various historical particularities that characterize the former region decouple in al-Jabiri's reading the binary between modern European and traditional Arabo-Islamic. The geohistorical specifics that facilitate this decoupling include the absence of the following historical factors in the Maghreb: Ottoman influence, a substantial Christian minority playing a particularly important role in intellectual life, and a more prominent influence from Europe due to the Anglo-French rivalry, among other reasons.

In al-Jabiri's narrative of Moroccan *khususiya*, or particularity, the intellectual (contra Bowles) plays a decisive role in defining cultural specificity. The breakdown of the divide between traditional and modern undercuts much Orientalist scholarship. Unlike Khatibi, his attention to particular cultural questions does not force upon him a rejection of historicism. Rather, the geohistorical emerges as a methodological category that furthers the goals of historicizing against Orientalizing without accepting the received wisdom of nationalist discourse.

Although it is not entirely clear the extent to which Laroui's Moroccan contemporaries influence his practice, because he does not mention them, his revisiting of the problems of historicism and representation in *Mafhum al Tarikh* (*The Concept of History*, 1992) broadly addresses critiques launched by Khatibi and al-Jabiri. Published as part of a series authored by Laroui in Arabic in the 1980s and '90s, which treats key categories in the form of book-length definitional arguments, *Mafhum* is Laroui's attempt to survey the major concepts and schools of thought related to the study and practice of history, taking into account each of the regions where he has lived and worked. The text begins with and sustains a marked emphasis on the individual creator of history with the contexts, stimuli, institutions, and pathologies that shape the work product of this creator. In this sense, the study, whose tone and structure at times take on an encyclopedic and almost pedantic air, resonates with the emphasis on the embodied creator of a discourse that one finds from al-Afghani to Said and throughout the bibliography of critiques of Orientalism. In its emphasis on the milieu that shapes the historian,

Laroui's overview participates in the new turn toward the geohistorical. For example, he distinguishes early on between cultural conceptions of history that put more or less emphasis on narrative versus those that put more or less emphasis on the documentary. The book's introduction concludes with a statement quite consistent with the discursive trend I have been tracing: "In one sense, history is a general phenomenon (every subject is a historical subject); but in another sense, one does not find general history. Rather, there are only particular histories."[61]

Two aspects of Laroui's wide-ranging study speak directly to the concerns of this chapter. First, Laroui specifies the character of the American scene, which he finds overly invested in data, econometrics, and the quantitative.[62] This critique of U.S. intellectual discourse resonates strongly with Bowles's rejection of post–World War II suffocating American normativity. Directly at odds with Bowles, however, is the equal weight given here to the historiography of decolonization in Africa, Asia, and the Arab world. Laroui by no means centers anticolonial historiography, given his critiques—elaborated in his early work—of its tendency toward nationalism and the predicament of traditionalist forms. Still, where the liberatory aspirations of anticolonial historiography appear as a source of mockery not only in Bowles but also in American "Third World" novels by John Updike, Saul Bellow, Joan Didion, and many others, here they are an unreached horizon whose unrealized possibilities must be considered alongside their legacy of inadequacies and disappointments.

Two important points should be emphasized about Arab theories of representation during the period after Said's *Orientalism*. First, while the Saidean turn in Arabic critical discourse broadly marginalized Laroui-inflected historiographic critique, the two discourses were far from separate. Although Laroui only mentions Said's work when specifically requested to do so, several of his Moroccan interlocutors cite Said as a direct influence. This is true of philosophy professor, novelist, and former Moroccan minister of culture Bensalem Himmich, whose survey of Orientalist discourse, published in Arabic in 1991 under the title "Orientalism in Its Closed Horizons," takes inspiration from Said's study, even as it tries to distance itself from what it calls his "oversensitiveness"[63] by, for example, emphasizing the authority accorded to Arabic philosophical discourse by Europeans prior to the Enlightenment period. The other important example is al-Jabiri. In *Mas'alat al-huwīyah: Al-'Urūbah wa-al-Islām wa-al-Gharb* (The issue of identity: Arab-ness, Islam, and the West, 1995), he begins by attempting to construct a theory of cultural identity through two overlapping frames. The diachronic frame is the evolution of the idea of the future through time, traced from the ancient world, through Judaism, Christianity, and Islam, through the European Enlightenment and forward to the present day. The synchronic axis is the Arab versus the Other. In this second dimension, the history of Orientalism, its style of representing Arabs, its implication in geopolitics, and its contemporary perseverance are reexamined with Said's inspiration openly acknowledged. In this study, the Arabs' future problem comes from the post–World War II regime of American-led global capitalist development. The Arab is behind and must catch up—that is, economically underdeveloped and politically backward under the onus of dictatorial regimes, and in its emphasis on religion and the foreignness of its language and culture, generally speaking behind. In her/his awareness of these realities, the Arab is filled with anxiety vis-à-vis the future. The European and U.S. Others also feel anxiety about the future with respect to Arabs and Muslims, since they represent the newest, greatest threat and global adversary, which satisfies the need for a futuristic narrative involving good guys, bad guys, crises, and some hope of denouement. In this study, al-Jabiri offers a method that allows for a historicized reading of Islam, viewing Islamic civilization and multiple Islamic identities as geohistorically located. In this sense, the study reinforces the anti-Orientalism and anti-essentialism of the Laroui-influenced strain of thought. Furthermore, he directly connects the problem of the Arabs, their history, their identity, and their discourse with their representation by their Other. The two critiques are inextricable and mutually dependent, as, indeed, they were in Laroui's *The Crisis of the Arab Intellectual.*

The second and most surprising point to be made about this stage is that Said himself belongs not in the Saidean camp, but rather in the distinctively Laroui-inspired discourse. Said revisited *Orientalism*'s central questions and its methods throughout the rest of his career. He wrote two case studies—*Covering Islam* and *The Question of Palestine*—around the same time, then he addressed critics and respondents and suggested revisions and elaborations in "Orientalism Revisited" (1985), "Afterword" (1994), and "Preface to the Twenty-Fifth Anniversary Edition" (2003). Intriguingly, in the second in this triumvirate of essays, Said refers to his own ambitious 1993 study *Culture and Imperialism* as *Orientalism*'s "sequel,"[64] a reference that opens up the possibility of reading most of what comes after 1978 as revision of the study that generated so much response. A main distinction between Said's initial critique of Orientalism and that found in Laroui's early work is the former's exclusive focus on a discursive history within Western writing, where the latter's historiography read Orientalist discourse as intimately tied to the dynamics within Arab intellectual culture. In his later criticism of his book's reception in the Arab world in the 1994 "Afterword," and even more in his elaboration of "contrapuntalism" as a specific method for reading through cultures of colonialism, Said moved away from the Europe-focused postcolonial discourse that his initial study engendered. The readings in *Culture and Imperialism* also emphasize geographies of scale and the role of the intellectual.[65] Thus, in multiple ways, the later directions of Said's critique moved increasingly toward a congruity with an important strain of radical North African theories of representation, even though the author-function that his most famous work participated in creating has been regularly directed toward a different set of methodological strategies.

V. REPRESENTATION IN THE WORLD

Near the end of *Orientalism*, in the course of a reading of Louis Massignon's work, Said pauses to make a general point: "The real issue is whether indeed there can be a true representation of anything, or whether any and all representations, because they *are* representations, are embedded first in language and then in the culture, institutions, and political ambience of the representer. If the latter alternative is the correct one (as I believe it is), then we must be prepared to accept the fact that a representation is *eo ipso* implicated, intertwined, embedded, interwoven with a great many other things besides the 'truth,' which is itself a representation."[66] Said's position suggests that a portrait of Morocco that emphasizes the destitute lives of the illiterate and the marginalized, centering "atavism" and "primitivism" in its version of Moroccan realities, should not necessarily be dismissed for its falsity. Indeed, such emphases may be considered very much in line with some of the most progressive and important trends in historiography and cultural studies within the "Western" academy, particularly those influenced by the South Asian subaltern studies group.

Furthermore, although I have suggested that many large movements in Said's work have become domesticated within critical theory discussions in the United States, broadly speaking, his position on theories and processes of representation as expressed in the Massignon passage would find many adherents among practitioners of literary criticism and cultural studies. For example, when W. J. T. Mitchell, in an essay about representation theory, writes, "Every representation exacts some cost, in the form of lost immediacy, presence, or truth, in the form of a gap between intention and realization, original and copy,"[67] he not only reinforces Said's call to account for contingency in representation theory, but he also suggests a strategy for dealing with a politics of portrayal that centers the primitive. A strategy of presenting subaltern lives can begin as radical but end up as mainstream through its influence, revision, and reception, with the result that a special place has been created for the Other's subaltern, one that reinforces a telescoped view of the Other's social reality.

Critics of Orientalism in North Africa and the Middle East—from al-Afghani to al-Jabiri—place a particular emphasis on the role, the person, and the milieu of the representer, and this also (albeit less frequently) finds some resonance in contemporary theories by U.S. scholars. Anna Gibbs, for example, writing about "mimesis," a much-favored topic of Said's, begins her discussion with the claim, "Rather than privileging one view over another, the task of theory may then be to know through which optic it is most productive to look at any given moment. Or—perhaps more difficult—to learn how to oscillate between these views, neither of which can be simply discarded."[68] Here again, the representer has been brought to the fore, but equally importantly, the process of making a representation is given special purchase.

Generally speaking, it is certainly fairly unusual to refer to the Arab thinkers referenced in this chapter as makers of "theory." As a result, when discussing in an American context a figure like Abdallah Laroui as a maker of a discourse, a critic like myself may feel a special burden to make explicit "what is new," "what is different," or "what makes this *theory*" (all three questions that I have heard from U.S. academic colleagues when sharing work of this type). Gibbs's stand offers an implicit rebuttal to the critical desire to erase all non-Saidean Arab critiques of Orientalism. Also, I have tried to demonstrate that reincorporating such critiques carries potential to expose those aspects of the bibliography of representation theory that Said himself inspired, which have "exacted a cost" in the form of self-referencing critical discourses that leave North African and Arab realities unacknowledged, or acknowledged only via monolithic representations that eschew what Khatibi would call the *pluriel*.

The intellectual—as subject, object, and creator of discourse—plays a special role in this dynamic as a potential force for disruption in U.S. domesticating discourse. A pincer movement from academic theory that centers Europe and the United States, on one side, and from the literary novel, which may use a critique of American bourgeois normativity as cover for an erasure of "Third World" action and thought, on the other, renders the decolonizing intellectual immobile. Spivak's ground-breaking essay "Can the Subaltern Speak?" raises precisely these issues with respect to academic theory in its opening section. The section includes a by now well-known breakdown of distinctive—but not exclusive—categories of representation as found in Marx. Since the specific passage from Marx that Spivak wants to rescue from its more familiar classical positivist interpretation is the same section from which Said takes the epigraph for *Orientalism*, it opens the possibility of reading the essay as a collegial critique of Said's approach to the colonial discourse issue. But the end of the section eschews this possibility, emphasizing instead Said's distinction from the semantic field of U.S. theory: "Curiously enough, Paul Bové faults Said for emphasizing the importance of the intellectual, whereas 'Foucault's project is essentially a challenge to the leading role of both hegemonic and oppositional intellectuals' (Bové 44). I have suggested that this 'challenge' is deceptive precisely because it ignores what Said emphasizes—the critic's institutional responsibility."[69]

This genealogy of an Arab intellectual critique of Orientalism has suggested that any worthy theory about representation, as well as any worthy representational practice, will place extra weight on inventorying the representer. Such an inventory, furthermore, should go beyond rehearsing an abstract exercise by incorporating at some level an understanding of the representer's milieu, and specifically that context as both a product and expression of a particular geohistorical—and geopolitical—location. My claim is that contemporary U.S. culture—at multiple levels of expression—proves particularly averse to such an inventory in its dealings with the Global South, whose oppositional intellectuals represent an offense to the American idea of these spaces as backward. To acknowledge the figure of the intellectual is to turn away from the U.S. race toward its future of innovation, globalization, incorporation, advancement, and development—precisely what this study of domestications has undertaken to do.

CHAPTER 3
Perspective

Domestication and Eastern Asia

America Imagines the World

Over the course of a few years in the mid-1960s, American involvement in the turbulent history of Vietnamese revolutionary nationalism accelerated dramatically. First, the U.S. Congress passed the Gulf of Tonkin Resolution in August of 1964, then Lyndon Johnson won election as president in November of the same year. American bombings of the North began in 1965 just before the arrival of the first American troops, and finally, a full commitment of ground troops had forty thousand Americans stationed in the South by the end of 1966. In the summer of that year, Paul Bowles traveled to nearby Thailand on a commission from the publisher Little, Brown to write a travel book about Bangkok, a place he admitted he had never seen.[1] While the book project seems to have been doomed nearly from the start, the various notes, letters, and a single short story that come out of Bowles's experiences in Thailand from September 1966 to January 1967 interpolate in an East Asian context the major themes of the author's project to imagine the Third World, and thus prefigure his continuing influence as manifested in the discourse of the American "Third World" novel.

In early notes, when Bowles is still considering writing the Bangkok book, one finds generalizing platitudes like "Buddhism is a simple philosophy designed to foster an attitude productive of contentment."[2] But

Bowles's acumen as a writer, essayist, and theorist of setting had evolved beyond trying to build anything on such generalizations, and as a result, the tone of his letters moves away from such attempts at cultural generalization and toward the impossibility of writing a book, his personal discomfort, criticisms of the locals and the local environment, visa problems, and finally, other writing projects with no relation to Thailand. Bowles's relatively quick dispatching of the book idea that had brought him to Thailand can be attributed to the experienced traveler's ability to know what he does not know: "Bangkok is a big surprise to me"; "I've never seen such an aimless and haphazard city."[3] Although his travels have taken him by the 1960s to Europe, Central America, North Africa, and South Asia, what evolves over the decades is an adroit ability to portray the epistemological limits of the American point of view, and this literary skill characterizes the documentary fragments that make up his encounter with Southeast Asia. In North Africa in particular, he had already worked through a set of problems from the American consciousness's drive to break free from its own culturally delimited epistemological possibilities, as dramatized in *The Sheltering Sky*, and evolved to a stage in which his main literary energy was directed at the translation of subaltern, often illiterate, North African autobiographical stories. Having crossed over to translational epistemology in this way, he could not return so effortlessly to depicting the American experience in a completely new and unfamiliar place. As a result, he settled for using his letters and notes to complain, analogize, and mock, before acknowledging the futility of the Thailand book project and moving on.

Upon arrival, his expression of disorientation runs through his notes and letters in a manner that calls to mind another characteristic of his fiction set in North Africa: Bowles's aversion to the nationalisms, histories, and agencies of the Global South that disrupt his American dissident worldview and so must be domesticated. In this case, this discourse has an ugly face that manifests in persistent mocking of local speech and behavior: "The Mystelious East. Scleam, scleam! No one will heal you. Dilectly beneath loom is glotto full of hungly lats."[4] A slightly more benign expression of this disorientation takes the form of persistent emphasis on the American gaze outward with its propensity toward—and even willful insistence upon—misreading the local.

This leitmotif in Bowles's Thai notes and letters culminates in his short story set in Thailand, based on a day trip to the countryside that he took with his American friend Oliver Evans and some Thai acquaintances. In "You Have Left Your Lotus Pods on the Bus," Evans is renamed Brooks, and the narrator, based on Bowles, is never given a name. The main plot of the story follows the two Americans on a trip outside Bangkok to view temples. They are accompanied by three native informants: an older Buddhist monk in orange robes, who enjoins the narrator in tortured conversation, and two younger understudies who never speak. The Thai characters, in their monastic piety and linguistic limitations, are reminiscent of the "authentics" who inhabit Bowles's North African fiction, putatively untouched (or, at least, less corrupted) by westernization. But the story has none of the persistent gothic touches or occasional melodramatic gestures that mark Bowles's earlier fiction.[5] Instead, the plot serves as a substratum to the main focus of the narrative, which is the interaction between the narrator and the setting, and between the narrator and the older monk, Yamyong. Each exchange between the two reinforces their cultural distance and their inability to know each other. Yamyong is surprised by the luxury of the narrator's hotel room; the narrator and Brooks produce an overdetermined reading of Yamyong's tattoo; Yamyong returns the favor by reading too much into the narrator's necktie; and the Americans and the monks experience uncomfortable moments of dissonance over the former eating in front of the latter during the fasting period. The story culminates in a bus journey back to Bangkok that the narrator endures with a dry cynicism, as though he were revising out the romantic tone of voice that afflicted the narration of Port and Kit's bus ride to El Ga'a in *The Sheltering Sky*. Again, the final point of emphasis in "Lotus Pods" is incomprehension. The most memorable feature of the bus trip is a screaming man in the back.

> "God, why don't they throw him off?" Brooks was beginning to be annoyed.
>
> "They don't even hear him," I said bitterly. People who can tolerate noise inspire me with envy and rage. Finally, I leaned over to Yamyong and said, "That poor man back there! It's incredible!"[6]

But by this point in the story, the Americans and monks have fallen too deeply into mutual incomprehension for anything to be cleared up with a mere question. A series of exchanges occurs, but these only resolve the issue after they have arrived and disembarked in Bangkok, where Yamyong is finally able to clarify the story of the screaming man being ignored by all the other passengers through an act of translation:

> "Oh, he was saying: 'Go into second gear,' or 'We are coming to a bridge,' or 'Be careful, people in the road.' Whatever he saw."
>
> Since neither Brooks nor I appeared to have understood, he went on, "All the buses must have a driver's assistant. He watches the road and tells the driver how to drive. It is hard work because he must shout loud enough for the driver to hear him."[7]

Thus, Yamyong reveals the direct relationship between the Americans' ignorance of Thai language and the impossibility of their reading the Thai milieu.

Incomprehension plays the role of protagonist in this story, and as with Bowles's North African and Latin American fiction, point of view is the main device that dramatizes the challenges of understanding across cultural barriers. In this sense, "You have Left Your Lotus Pods on the Bus" recalls the narrative structuring of prototypically American points of view in not only *The Sheltering Sky* but also "A Distant Episode," the early chapters of *Let It Come Down*, *Up above the World*, and several other works. Furthermore, as I have tried to show in chapter 1, this culturally hermetic perspectival structure is exactly what *The Spider's House* and the translations attempt to disrupt. Mark McGurl, in his wide-ranging study of the emergence of creative writing programs and their influence on twentieth-century American letters, has made a helpful observation that could easily describe the shift that Bowles's writing provoked, even among a more sedentary collection of American writers: "The signature preoccupation of modernist fiction with the technical problem of 'point of view' in narration finds new meaning when it is transferred to an institutional environment engaged on many levels with the problem and promise of cultural difference."[8] Although the observation is helpful, I would argue that the shift to an American gaze emerging out of pure imagination results more from the domestication of American imperial hegemony within the U.S. cultural imaginary than it does from the creative writing professor's sedentary lifestyle.

Bowles's experiences in Thailand suggest as much. The notes, letters, and "Lotus Pods" all reinforce the futility of transcending cultural barriers through travel. In them, the writer is hot and frustrated and constantly calls attention to his own limited understanding of his surroundings. A common (perhaps intentionally self-deprecating) strategy in the letters is to make analogies. To Jane, he writes that Bangkok is "almost as big as Paris" and "a little like Colombo."[9] To Herbert Machiz, he complains that "it's vast, huge, endless. . . . Like Los Angeles,"[10] and in what is apparently a particularly derogatory comparison, he grouses to John Goodwin that "Bangkok is like Houston, Texas, swarming with G.I.s and their floozies, all of whom wear magenta slacks, with very high-heeled gold shoes."[11]

American soldiers appear regularly in the letters, always referred to with unadulterated disdain. They are portrayed as noisy troglodytes crowding the hotel lobby, subverting the possibility of decent service and disrupting Bowles's already tenuous attempts at connecting across cultures. The technical problem of point of view as an engagement with another culture manifests itself here as a series of complexities: the soldiers violate the Asianness of Bangkok for Bowles, and they perform the travesty of the foreign presence that does not acknowledge its epistemological limits as Bowles does.[12] But they also confront Bowles with a harshly militarized American nationalism that has taken on a crude, violent form in the various countries of Southeast Asia during his self-exile in Tangier. In this sense, they embody a stage in American imperial culture that threatens to overwhelm the possibilities of postmodern irony. Specifically, the strategy of point of view combining with setting to fashion a critique of U.S. bourgeois normativity edges toward a reductio ad absurdum in its Asian narratives, challenging the constructive possibilities of irony and the total marginalization of "Third World" nationalisms and other global expressions of political and cultural agency.

After World War II, U.S. hegemony suddenly expanded in the eastern regions of Asia to absorb much of the area that had been until then either European colonies, Japanese spheres of influence, or some combination of both. Southeast Asia in the 1960s and '70s was a particularly contested space upon which this expansion of U.S. hegemony was written. Many Americans were about as disgusted with U.S. policy in the region as Bowles's letters from Thailand suggest he was, and these expressions of disgust took many forms, becoming their own cultural narrative of America in the sixties. As the case of Bowles demonstrates, however, these dissident narratives managed to remain thoroughly American. "History" could be invoked, but the geographically located, multilateral historicism that emerges out of the Laroui-Khatibi-Jabiri discussion plays no role in shaping this American lens. The mechanism of perspective—precisely as McGurl identifies it—subverts any possibility of a Vietnamese, Korean, or Filipino narrative marked by the historical particularity, or *khasusiya*, described by al-Jabiri. Through point of view, the Vietnam experience in particular has become infinitely absorbable by American voices, whose domesticating narratives display an almost infinite power to redirect the gaze of any non-U.S. point of view. This chapter focuses on a series of narratives chosen for their potential to disrupt the post–World War II history of Southeast Asia as centered in an American perspective on the American war that treats Asian historical particularities as an unreachable moment of the sublime, before revisiting the American "Third World" novel of Vietnamese setting in the new context of these disruptions.

I. VIETNAM AND THE MOROCCAN PERSPECTIVE

Within the Larouian tradition of Moroccan intellectual writing, the individual most closely associated with the Cold War in East Asia is Abdallah Saaf. Public intellectual, historian of ideas, political scientist, university professor, for a brief time education minister, and most recently, novelist, Saaf began as an essayist interested in the possibilities of a syncretized North African Marxism made particular to regional concerns. In his early work *Savoir et politique au Maroc*, he describes the relationship between the specific history of the nation-state and intellectual culture, taking as his prime examples the writings of Laroui and Khatibi, as well as Paul Pascone, a Marxist Moroccan sociologist of French origin. In a sense, the study can be understood as an extension of al-Afghani's claim that "no nation at its origin is capable of letting itself be guided by pure reason." In Saaf's study, the local political culture of postcolonial Morocco forms a delimiting context, which its great thinkers wage a continuous struggle to transcend. For example, his section on Laroui focuses primarily on the metacritical dimension of the Laroui project, the main ideas that recur in his writing, and his substantial influence throughout the Arab-speaking regions.[13] But Saaf's overview also incorporates references to Laroui's bleak experience with electoral politics and the generally uncertain relationship with the Moroccan state that he experiences in common with much of Morocco's intellectual class, a relationship that was particularly burdensome during the acutely oppressive "years of lead" (from approximately the mid-1960s until about the publication date of *Savoir*, 1992) under King Hassan II.[14]

Shortly after *Savoir*, Saaf published *Histoire d'Anh Ma*, which reconstructed the life story of Mohamed Ben Aomar Lahrech, aka Anh Ma, a Moroccan syndicalist who traveled to Vietnam in 1949 to assist the political leadership of the Viet Minh in breaking the bonds of loyalty to French colonial forces among North African soldiers. In piecing together this narrative of Moroccan-Vietnamese solidarity, Saaf attempts to recuperate active popular forces written out of history. His narrative strategy is to foreground the holes in the story instead of making them invisible, and in this, he writes against an Orientalist approach that presumes to make what is distant easily accessible, whole, and cohesive. This revisionist history also illustrates the notion of particularity propounded initially by al-Jabiri: North Africa and Southeast Asia are not essentially the same, but they share enough in their culture and history for acts of solidarity to come to fruition. Their main historical tie is a shared history with French settler colonialism, bleeding into U.S. hegemony during the period of the Ho Chi Minh / Ben Aomar collaboration. Finally, Saaf's account bears the marked characteristics of a history-from-below approach, looking for the forgotten agents and movements that compelled historical change but did not receive the attention that political leaders, potentates, and generals regularly would.

The outline of the life reconstructed by Saaf's text begins humbly in a mining area of the Moroccan Atlas Mountains, known for its phosphate deposits. Ben Aomar's formative experiences took place while working alongside Moroccan miners around Khouribga and fighting with French forces during World War II. These two influences directed him toward the syndicalist movement in Morocco after the war because the unions took the side of the mine workers during the social upheaval that preceded decolonization. At the same time, his experiences in the French army and his subsequent fluency in French prepared him for contact with the French Communist Party, which inevitably followed his rise through the ranks of Moroccan labor unions. In fact, Saaf speculates that time fighting alongside French forces in Italy during the war may have been crucial in his ideological formation as a communist, since the Italian Communist Party was a powerful force within that milieu.[15] In 1949, Ben Aomar was still a young bachelor, who had joined the Moroccan Communist Party, holding the position of an officer in one of the rural branches. He had begun writing articles in defense of a worker- and peasant-centered approach to decolonization. He had been imprisoned for the bold positions he had taken,[16] and his activity had captured the notice of party leaders, who had transferred him to the metropolitan centers to work with its high command, first in Casablanca and then, just before leaving for Vietnam, in Rabat. All of this positioned Ben Aomar well to respond to Ho Chi Minh's request for a North African comrade to make the journey to North Vietnam and work alongside the pro-independence Vietnamese nationalists, who were fighting a colonial army that had incorporated a substantial percentage of North African conscripts.

The chapters in which Saaf describes Ben Aomar's time in Vietnam include multiple gaps and jump cuts. Based primarily on interviews corroborated by a smattering of documents, including letters and postcards, the narrative of the Moroccan's trip across Europe, with the help of a network of European communists, through the Soviet Union, and finally to Vietnam, where he spent approximately a decade, leaves many gaps. Ben Aomar arrived in Vietnam around 1950 and immediately began to work with the leadership of the Viet Minh in their fight against the colonial forces. His duties included writing pamphlets in Arabic that were distributed among the North Africans, but he was also asked to serve a similar persuasive role with North African prisoners. Influenced by his own experiences as a prisoner in Moroccan French colonial jails, he began to play an advocacy role for the prisoners with Vietnamese officials, whose trust he gained almost instantly. (Ho Chi Minh is said to have given him the nom de guerre of Anh Ma; later reference is made to languorous chess matches with the renowned army general Vo Nguyen Giap in the comparatively calm years after the Viet Minh victory at Dien Bien Phu.) Other reports indicated that Ben Aomar played a military role as well, fighting alongside Viet Minh forces in important battles.

The Moroccan leader of the Viet Minh seems to have taken on a legendary quality among the North African fighters, according to Saaf's interviews, but his life among the Vietnamese had its own substance, even though it is at times difficult for Saaf to document. At some point in his time there, Ben Aomar married Camilia, a Euro-Asian friend of Giap's wife, who gave birth to the first of their three children soon after they married. After the French forces were finally defeated, Ben Aomar and his family lived a modest life near Hanoi, supported by the government of North Vietnam. Though he continued to work for the Vietnamese as a representative of North Africans, his workload seems to have diminished dramatically and reference is made to both his passion for the leisure activity of hunting and his general boredom cum homesickness. Around 1959, Ben Aomar left Vietnam and brought his family back to Morocco. Saaf also suggests that he may have fallen out of favor with the Viet Minh's leadership.

The last ten years of his life did not rise to the same level of eventfulness as the period of the great Vietnamese victory over the French. Instead, he suffered under the Moroccan regime's oppression of communists for most of the 1960s before being expelled and joining the Algiers-based Moroccan resistance. He lived out the final years of his life in Algiers, suffering from poor health and economic hardship before his death on May 7, 1971, the anniversary of the fall of French forces at Dien Bien Phu.

A striking aspect of Saaf's *Histoire* is its reversal of the point of view that narrates better-known Vietnamese histories as focalized through European and American lenses. A reference to Ben Aomar's possible "origine paysanne"[17] and the general portrait of his upbringing in circumstances of poverty and marginalization, for example, are tied directly to his concern for peasants and workers. This forms a context for a lifelong political commitment to socialist causes, which prove challenging for Ben Aomar during the post–World War II period, as bourgeois nationalist calls for Moroccan independence dominated the public sphere. Also, Saaf begins by underlining the importance of a life that spans continents and cultures in the fight for colonized subaltern classes, ending the first paragraph of the book by calling attention to the threat of monological historiographies: "Il m'était difficile de comprendre qu'un tel personnage ait pu passer jusque là inaperçu et soit à peine signalé, de manière fugitive, par la presse du pays."[18]

Perhaps partially due to his limited sources, Saaf writes in a way that can suggest a collective North African point of view on the history of Vietnam in the late French colonial era. For example, he relies on interviews with Moroccan veterans of the conflict, not only to offer insight into the reputation of Ben Aomar, but also to portray the experience of moving from a geographically, culturally, linguistically, and religiously distinct French colony in North Africa to a completely foreign Asian French settler colony in which one's main job is to combat locals. An initial collection of direct testimony from Moroccan veterans appears in the text between the passages describing Ben Aomar's arrival in Vietnam and later descriptions of his accomplishments there.[19] These short testimonials by Moroccan veterans not only dramatize the gap in the documentary record around the mysterious period of Ben Aomar's arrival and initial integration into the Viet Minh power structure, but they do so in a manner that simultaneously suggests the legends that grew around the Viet Minh's Moroccan general and reinforces the Moroccan lens through which the text is organized—even when Ben Aomar himself moves momentarily off the stage.

The issue of perspective in the text might be further illustrated around the passages that deal with the first communications between the Viet Minh and the Moroccan communists, when the summons was received that would eventually lead to Ben Aomar's departure for Vietnam.[20] Saaf puts special emphasis on the relative ignorance of Moroccan communists vis-à-vis Southeast Asia, suggesting that the full knowledge of the Moroccans was encompassed by a few articles in the party magazine, *Espoir*. While the Viet Minh's difficulties in striking the correct balance between nationalist/anticolonial goals and the goals of socialism were familiar to Moroccan communists as well, Saaf admits that this solitary parallel hardly formed the basis for a Moroccan organic intellectual's integration into Vietnamese culture.

In fact, even before his arrival in Vietnam, Ben Aomar had barely left Morocco when he found himself confronted by the issue of cultural difference, as the following passage suggests: "Upon his arrival in Paris, he was given lodging by a French communist couple who, before Ben Aomar's arrival, had imagined Moroccans as primitives. As they sat down at the dinner table they began to explain to him how to use a knife and fork. Ben Aomar with a touch of maliciousness played along with the part, later recounting the story while laughing until he cried."[21] In the anecdote, Ben Aomar's point of view sets in relief the simultaneously comic and pathetic portrait of the French couple. Also, in this instance, the issue of French "metropolitan (?)" cluelessness goes directly to a larger concern with historical difference, because the couple comes into contact with Ben Aomar through an ostensible ideological solidarity. Their material support of Ben Aomar remains invaluable but does not completely make up for the effects of their orientalizing gaze that their sense of cultural superiority forces upon him.

A contrastive narrative point of view could be easily found in English-language histories of "the first Indochina War." A highly regarded example of the latter would be Bernard Fall's *Hell in a Very Small Place: The Siege of Dien Bien Phu*. This text is an immaculately detailed account (perhaps three or four times longer than *Histoire d'Anh Ma*) of the central battle that led to the collapse of French colonial rule in Vietnam. The author was a U.S.-based journalist of Franco-Austrian descent, who fought with the French Resistance against the Nazi occupation as a teenager. He was commissioned to write the book as part of a series called "the Great Battles in History," and in accordance with the conventions of *military* history, the text relies on the careful weighing of voluminous documentary evidence and detailed descriptions of strategy, movements, and material. Fall, whose language expertise and experience had made him a prominent authority while still quite young, does not take a hawkish position in his narrative, even though his rhetorical situation is partially defined by military culture. Rather, he writes the history of the mid-1950s as a warning regarding developments in the late 1960s, when the book appeared. Still, the patina of objectivity that overlays the rhetoric of the book leaves evident its unmistakable focalized lens.[22]

Fall's incredibly detailed and fulsomely documented narrative pauses on occasion for miniportraits of the main French officers who played a role in the battle, and these asides are one instance where the focalization of the text comes into clearer relief. No such humanizing touches are ever afforded to Vietnamese or North African players in the drama. Another obvious indication of the perspectival structure is the semiregular passages that step out of the battlefield to portray domestic political debates going on back in France or Washington around the events taking place in the Muong Thanh Valley. In contrast, the narrative provides only a hint that parallel debates might have been taking place simultaneously among the Vietnamese political leadership, and there is barely any reference to French colonialism in North Africa, in spite of the prominent role in the battle played by North Africans, which Fall fully acknowledges.

Taking *Hell in a Very Small Place* on its own terms, the main payoffs of the extensive research it collates are that the fall of Dien Bien Phu represented "the end of the Indochina War . . . [t]he end of France as a colonial power"[23] and that "air power on a more massive scale . . . would have saved Dien Bien Phu."[24] The text also argues in brief that the United States was insufficiently engaged with the major significance of events involving its French ally, which it had promised to prop up, consuming itself, for example, with the McCarthy hearings just at the moment when the French fort was about to be lost to the Vietnamese forces,[25] and in this sense, a small aspect of Fall's larger argument can be read as adding to the picture that I have been elaborating of the processes of domestication that characterize the comprehension of U.S. imperial engagements within American culture.

Reading *Hell in a Very Small Place* against *Histoire d'Ahn Ma*, however, engages the structural issue of focalization particularly pointedly around the North African soldiers at Dien Bien Phu. According to a table in Fall's appendix, about a fourth of the soldiers fighting to defend the French fort were North African. Of this group, something like one in six could be categorized as having gone "missing" between mid-March and mid-May of 1954. In Saaf's account of Ben Aomar's activities, the psychological influence he was able to exert over Moroccans and Algerians played a crucial role at Dien Bien Phu.[26] This narrative fills in gaps in Fall's account, which makes only belated mention of the effectiveness of Viet Minh propaganda in the North African ranks. Initially, Fall claims that "the Moroccans had acquired a solid reputation as 'road openers,'"[27] and their *in*vulnerability to Viet Minh propaganda is contrasted with the Vietnamese fighting to defend the fort, the latter having "to be 'sandwiched' between the Moroccans and the [French] paratroopers . . . to be kept in line."[28] But the final chapters of Fall's history make direct reference to the influence of the Viet Minh propaganda campaign on Moroccan and Algerian soldiers,[29] with special emphasis placed on the long-term effects of "North Vietnamese brain washing methods" as soldiers returned to their home countries and joined the resistance against French colonialism. A gap in Fall's history is the role of Ben Aomar, which is made central by the narrative that Saaf constructs.

The distinction between these two narratives then illustrates Saaf's emphasis on historiography and epistemology in his first paragraph. I have already quoted the opening expression of surprise that Ben Aomar's story has never been chronicled, but the point can be developed. Saaf's entire first chapter is devoted to the research obstacles that confront the project of detailing Ben Aomar's transcontinental existence. The author's foregrounding of his difficulties accords with the Laroui tradition's methods of foregrounding the geohistorical location of the historian. The narrative is not about Saaf in any way, but neither does he attempt to downplay the obstructions, gaps, and uncertainties that inhere in the process of knowledge production. The difficulties in reconstructing the narrative of Ben Aomar include matters more and less benign. Fairly innocent, for example, seems Ben Aomar's tendency to tell tall tales, which imposes upon the author who collates his stories an added degree of vigilance as he gathers them second hand. But the general disinterest in the fate of Moroccan and Algerian soldiers on the part of French scholars studying the French Indochinese war constitutes a more considered problem.[30] Still less innocent and more complex is "la sensibilité [sensitivity] du suject,"[31] mentioned as a significant obstacle to the attempt to document Ben Aomar's life. Read retrospectively, this opening phrase encompasses a great deal. The subsequent narrative deals with contentiousness between communists and bourgeois nationalists in Morocco and illustrates the victory of the latter group through Ben Aomar's difficulties upon his return to North Africa around the beginning of the "years of lead." For the author of *Savoir et politique au Maroc*, the difficulty of reconstituting the life of an individual like Ben Aomar would certainly connect directly to the victory of a nationalism and dictatorship that aspired to rehistoricize the colonial period and its aftermath in a manner that conformed to the state's broad geopolitical alignment with the U.S.-led industrialized Western powers.

A final illuminating comparison—regarding both the emphasis of Saaf's narrative and the general phenomenon that Ben Aomar embodies—would be between *Histoire d'Anh Ma* and the U.S.-based historian of Vietnam Marc Jason Gilbert's "Persuading the Enemy: Vietnamese Appeals to Non-White Forces of Occupation, 1945–1975." In Gilbert's essay, the method of using appeals to solidarity among colonized peoples extends back in the cultural history of Vietnamese military engagement, in which *địch vận*, or persuading the enemy, appears as a strategy of war as early as the fifteenth century. The focus of the essay, however, is specifically on the way Vietnamese communist anticolonialism used the practice to break the solidarity of occupying armies that included South Asians, North and western Africans, and African Americans during the period between the end of Japanese occupation and the fall of Saigon and reunification of the North and the South. Within this narrative, a discursive footnote, citing a French source, is devoted to Mohamed Ben Aomar Lahrach, "a member of the Moroccan communist central committee . . . deputed to Vietnam, where he called upon members of the 1/4 Moroccan Rifles and the 4th Tabor of Moroccan Goumiers . . . to desert, and aided in the political education of North Africans who had rallied to the cause of the Viet Minh."[32] This emplotment of the Ben Aomar narrative within a more general trajectory of Vietnamese persuasion strategy suggests another connection between *Histoire d'Anh Ma* and the Laroui tradition examined in the preceding chapter, out of which, I am arguing, Saaf operates. If there is a general motif in American representations of the Global South that constructs them as no-idea-producing areas where political and humanistic agency is pictured as degraded, venal, or silly, albeit often useful for critiquing U.S. bourgeois normativity, the generalized Viet Minh construction of the rest of the world is the opposite, tending toward historicism and eschewing the presumption that the Other is a lesser and hostile figure. That is, the Vietnamese presumption of a Ben Aomar, before Ben Aomar ever becomes "Anh Ma," as a Vietnamese cultural stance, constitutes the converse of a U.S. narrative that erases or covers the "Third World" intellectual as it looks abroad. In other words, by taking the Ben Aomar of Saaf's text and putting him into a Vietnamese historical tradition, Gilbert's essay portrays a historical Vietnamese attitude toward the problem of epistemology and culture that directly clashes with a tradition built on contrasting assumptions in the United States.

II. THE CALCULATED FORGETTING OF THE "FORGOTTEN WAR"

The cease-fire that halted the Korean War on July 27, 1953, and codified the partition of the Korean Peninsula along ideological lines between North and South was signed a matter of months before the beginning of the battle of Dien Bien Phu, and it is de rigueur for American historians of Vietnam to reference the Korean experience as influencing decisions made by all the major outside parties during the Indochina War. For example, Fall writes that on May 8, 1954, a day after the fall of Dien Bien Phu to the Viet Minh, "after having ineffectually debated about the reunification of Korea for over two weeks while Dien Bien Phu was agonizing, the West was now ready to meet the Communist bloc on the matter of peace in Indochina."[33] The histories suggest that the ill-begotten idea of a temporary partition of Vietnam (which the U.S. would try and ultimately fail to make permanent) between a communist North and a capitalist and pro-Western South emerged as an offshoot of the Korean armistice. In this sense, the histories of the two Asian countries constitute a move in U.S. foreign policy toward a neocolonial interest in partitioning, creating a new model that strategically used the partitioning of national groups according to ideology in distinction from the Anglo-imperial partitions based on sectarianism, as I will discuss in more detail in chapter 5. The important point in this context is that the "forgetting" of the Korean conflict—often referred to in the United States as "the forgotten war"—facilitated the historical covering of partition as a postcolonial instrument in U.S. foreign relations.

Like Bernard Fall, Stanley Karnow's history of Vietnam emphasizes the roots of American policy in its Korean experience. He refers repeatedly to Lyndon Johnson's policy as being haunted and shaped by Johnson's perceptions of the American experience in Korea. These American histories are detailed and thoroughly researched, but they present, and may even subtly reinforce, a U.S. public sphere discourse that generalizes Asia and the U.S. involvement in it. Histories of American hegemony from other points of view, however, are more commonly marked by historical particularity, whereby Asian and African postcolonial subjects are pluralistic within their own nations and regions. The South Korean anticommunist fighters who would eventually be incorporated into the defense of South Vietnam by the United States are arguably to the U.S. forces in the American War what the North Africans were to the French during their Indochine War.[34] But the available historical research on Korean fighters in Vietnam emphasizes not their vulnerability to persuasion by the North Vietnamese propaganda machine, but rather their ruthlessness as fighters, extending as far as alleged war crimes that have never been fully excavated.[35]

None of the sources cited in the previous section, including Gilbert's essay on persuasion of soldiers of color by Vietnamese anticolonial communists, make any reference to either noticeable levels of defection among Korean fighters or extensive efforts by the North Vietnamese government to persuade Koreans to their side. The vituperative nature of Cold War polarization on the Korean Peninsula, the American skill at camouflaging its hegemonic ambitions behind local proxies, a caste mentality among some Koreans, and divisions within global Marxism (in particular, the breakdown of relations between China and the Soviet Union during the time between the Indochine and American wars in Vietnam) would have each played a role in the distinctive cultural situation represented by the Republic of Korea (ROK) forces fighting in South Vietnam. In the large histories of the war in Vietnam by American historians, the Korean troops appear, if at all, as statistics.

In American literary culture more generally, with some exceptions, the Korean War and Korean bodies are both distinguished by a marked and active marginalization. A typical reference arises in passing in John Updike's *Rabbit, Run* (1960), when a kind older widow, employing the down-and-out Rabbit to perform lawn care and listen to her extensive monologues, tells him, "This was before the war. I don't suppose when I say 'the war' you know which one I mean. You probably think of that Korean thing as the war."[36] Another reference to Korean/U.S. implication, made at an equally ephemeral level, occurs in Tim O'Brien's early memoir of his experiences in Vietnam, when a Korean stripper flits across the stage at a show for U.S. GIs.[37] William Styron's novella of the Korean War, *The Long March* (1952), never leaves the continental United States.[38]

If the American lens has shown a broad disinterest in cultural explications of its Korean experience compared to a proliferation of texts that treat U.S. engagement in Vietnam, American writers—whether academic, literary, or journalistic—have been even more uniform in ignoring the profound connection between the two wars represented by the deployment of ROK forces to fight on the side of the Americans and the South Vietnamese government in the 1960s. For some time, Korean writers also resisted the topic as Cold War sensitivities endured on the peninsula, but with the collapse of dictatorial rule in the ROK in the later 1980s, the topic of Korea's Vietnam increasingly became a focus for various cultural producers.[39] These narratives not only defy resistance from patriotic nationalists within the ROK who would try to suppress such discussions but also serve as powerful documents that disrupt the U.S.-centered narrative of the Vietnamese experience with partition and reunification in the 1960s and early '70s. For these disruptive Korean narratives, Vietnam's historical experience shares the challenge of blatant American hegemony extending out from the Korean Peninsula as a site of the brutal—if "forgotten"—initiation of Cold War binary thinking. The Korean critic Paik Nak-chung has elaborated the concept of the "division system" as a way of understanding the post–Cold War history of the Korean Peninsula. Preliminarily, the division system can be described in Paik's conception as constituting a historical trajectory whereby the dynamic of the ideologically partitioned peninsula shapes its geohistorical implication but also defines its historical particularity.[40] Comparing Korea with other ideologically partitioned states that the United States participated in dividing during the Cold War, including not only Vietnam, but also Germany, China/Taiwan, and Yemen, Paik has observed that the Korean experience represents a departure from the type of partition visited upon the Germanys after the war. Whereas Germany was partitioned in the aftermath of a national history of military expansionism and ethnic cleansing, Korea was partitioned after being the *primary victim* of Japanese fascist, expansionist militarism.[41] The equivalent in Europe would be for Poland to have been partitioned at the end of World War II as punishment for its having been invaded and occupied by Germany. In this sense, Korea sets a precedent that shapes the newly globally hegemonic United States' distinctive approach to dealings with "non-Europe."

It is within the context of division system discourse, then, that Paik frames the fiction of Korean writer Hwang Sok-yong, Vietnam war veteran and, for a time, a dissident jailed in the ROK. In introducing the most ambitious of Hwang's fiction dealing with Koreans in Vietnam, his sprawling novel *The Shadow of Arms*, Paik emphasizes the parallel histories of partition in the two Asian countries: "The crucial default, for a Korean novel of the 1980s, concerns the question of the nature and degree of the relevance of the anti-imperialist struggle in Vietnam to the aspirations of its Korean readers for their own reunification and genuine autonomy."[42] Hwang is a prominent fiction writer and political activist born as World War II was drawing to a close and shaped by Korea's turbulent Cold War history of partition and dictatorship. Among the concerns of his fiction are the discontinuities visited upon modern Korean history by the legacy of the Korean War. He has focused on impoverished Koreans as well and has fashioned a public profile distinctive in its contradictions between celebrated literary awards and time in prison for political activity. As a young man, Hwang fought on the side of the American and South Vietnamese forces waging war against North Vietnam in the late 1960s, and he has revisited those experiences in his fiction. Critic Jinim Park sees him as a central figure in a movement of the late 1970s and '80s that revisited the Korean experience of the Vietnam War as a means to create a social dimension in contemporary fiction from the ROK, where social concerns had been quite rare previously: "They viewed the war as an American colonial war: Americans as the colonizers and Vietnamese as the colonized. In that context, Koreans found themselves awkwardly situated. Korean narratives often displayed strong sympathies toward the Vietnamese, and Koreans vacillated between two conflicting views of themselves: one as American allies, and one as the same Asian 'gooks' as the Vietnamese, a combination that frequently resulted in a sense of loss as 'in-between' beings."[43]

In Hwang's early short story, "The Pagoda," the first-person narration of a Korean soldier sent with a small band of compatriots to defend a shrine said to be significant for the morale of a South Vietnamese village under threat from the People's Liberation Front, establishes a lens that presents the soldierly experience as one of alienation without lapsing into the simultaneously universalizing and highly personalized American accounts of Vietnam experiences that tend to erase the complexity and historical agency of Asian realities. The narrator's voice is uncertain in its strongest moments and feels distanced from the Vietnamese people by the barriers of his language and his office, but he also incorporates moments of feeling a higher level of solidarity with the Vietnamese around him compared to the American GIs that he has come to reinforce. A good frame for the tenor of the story is the phrase used by the narrator to describe the coastline, as he disembarks from his transport ship on the first page: "Unfamiliar, yet Asian."[44]

Hwang's narrator, Private Oh, often expresses an alienation familiar in autobiographical fictional accounts of soldiering. He bristles at his superior's maintenance of military protocol in spite of extreme conditions and is incredulous at the absurdity of the mission: to preserve a small stone pagoda that is the only thing left standing from a Buddhist temple that has been destroyed by excessive bombing. But over the course of the story, the eponymous symbol takes on significance for the narrator. "When I inspected the upper part more closely, I gradually realized that it was not so crude. Near the top was a relief of a seated Buddha surrounded by dancers' flowing robes; this section appeared to be original, while the remainder seemed to have been added later. . . . The Buddha, I suppose, was the object of the love and attachment of the village people."[45] In subsequent internal musings, the narrator considers what the propaganda value of the Buddha must be, both to potential National Liberation Front incursions and to the villagers. And in these connotations, he again marks off a third perspective on the Vietnamese scene that is distinct from both citizens and Americans. He is surprised at the level of religious fervor he sees among Buddhist Vietnamese in the countryside, but he is at least able to acknowledge it and amend his expectations. As this example suggests, his perspective marks the diversity of Asian identities, even as it acknowledges historical difference from the cultural presence constituted by the American invaders.

Americans appear at the very beginning and very end of the story. The moment Private Oh comes onshore at the beginning, he gets lost, only to be helped by an American "fair-haired sentry," who makes phone calls to find out where the narrator should go, then offers him a seat in an office and a ham sandwich. "He said something in English when he handed me part of his sandwich, and I managed to make out the word 'lonely.'"[46] But this initial moment of potential connection—already marked with uncertainty by a substantial language barrier—has dissipated by the end of the story. The narrator's alienation at the end has evolved to incorporate an even stronger bond with his Korean compatriots and the Vietnamese villagers around them. When the Americans reappear at the end, it is with the goal of destroying the pagoda that the Korean troop has been engaged in a lethal battle to defend. This closing incident is presented initially as a misunderstanding, but the disagreement between American and Korean allied forces interestingly evolves into a dispute rooted in distinctive perceptions, opposing points of view, and American Orientalist presumptions. "I didn't want to, but I tried to explain the relation between Buddhism, the villagers, and the psychological war tactics of our superiors. I began to realize that we had been only pawns in the game. Whose pagoda was it, anyway? Before I finished, as soon as I mentioned the word 'Buddhism,' this simple Western friend nodded knowingly."[47] The last few paragraphs of the story continue the back-and-forth between the American platoon sent in to "bring progress"[48] and their Korean counterparts, with the Americans' generalizing projection of Oriental essence onto the situation becoming more and more pronounced: "The fat American sergeant jumped down from the bulldozer muttering, 'Can't understand those yellows.'"[49] The pagoda is destroyed, but in the story's final sentence, the language of the narrator seems to develop the theme of the misunderstanding between Korean and American allies into a consideration of the question of perception itself: "Our field of vision was blocked by the dust behind the accelerating truck."[50]

The main Korean character in Hwang's novel *The Shadow of Arms*, Sergeant Ahn Yong Kyu seems substantially older and more cynical than Private Oh of the earlier "The Pagoda." Yong Kyu devotes his time in the novel to nurturing a business in redirecting American provisions to the Vietnamese black market to ensure that he will return to Korea from his tour having been rewarded economically. Comparing him to Private Oh suggests the possibilities offered by the literary manipulation of point of view. The two have markedly different attitudes and experience levels, yet even though both fight against and kill Vietnamese communists, the stories focalized through their perspectives manage to portray the conflict in a manner that most readers see as having "manifested the greatest sympathy"[51] for the cause of the Marxist army of liberation. One mechanism for this textual politics is the trajectory of the cynic Yong Kyu's attitude toward his American colleagues, which proves highly comparable to that of Private Oh in "The Pagoda," since both evolve toward a critical view of the generalizing nature of the American lens, which erases particularity. So Yong Kyu seems confused but also vaguely complimented at the beginning of the novel when an American officer explains to him that although Koreans "working for investigation" are allowed into an American army club where the best strippers in Danang can be found, the club will not admit as patrons "Gooks," a term that confuses Yong Kyu until he is told that it means Vietnamese. "They are really filthy but you are like us,"[52] the American explains. By the later part of the novel, Yong Kyu's consciousness has been raised enough to deliver an indignant monologue to an American deserter with whom he has become friends:

> "As I work with Americans, the one thing I hate most is to listen to you people say how alike we are, how I'm no different from an American and other garbage like that. In the same breath, I hear you guys whispering how filthy the Vietnamese gooks are. 'Gook' is the label American soldiers picked up in the Korean War from the word 'Hanguk,' mispronouncing it 'Han-goook.' Americans used it to make fun of us. But I tell you, it is the Vietnamese that I am like."[53]

Although this speech shows the evolution of Yong Kyu's mental picture of who the Americans are and what they represent, it sits against a backdrop of his general lack of concern with questions related to nationalism, culture, or history.

Yong Kyu's position within the textual economy of the novel is also distinct from that of Private Oh in the short story. Whereas the entirety of "The Pagoda" is filtered through the focalization of Private Oh, Yong Kyu is only one of a plethora of perspectives that inhabit the pastiche of *The Shadow of Arms*. The novel narrates not only from the point of view of Yong Kyu but also from that of a female Korean fortune hunter named Hae Jong and from a variety of Vietnamese points of view with diverse ideological, gender, and class perspectives. That all the action of the lengthy novel takes place over a few months and in a relatively contained geography of central Vietnam around Danang reinforces the novel's gesture toward multiple points of view creating a more disrupted, and therefore less generalizing and homogenizing, representation of the history of the conflict during the time immediately following the Tet Offensive, which began at the end of January 1968. Paik expresses skepticism regarding the novel's attempt to represent conflicting alliances inside a typical Vietnamese family, but the move proves critical in using the pastiche technique to create a textual panoply of perspectives. The picture that emerges from this diversity is overwhelmingly one of characters coming to the situation from a variety of historical points of departure only to become conjoined by this later stage of the conflict in a common commitment toward self-interested personal enrichment. The fervently religious Buddhist villagers of "The Pagoda" are absent from this later view of Vietnamese history, and if the author's general sympathies can be said to lie with the Liberation Front, that commitment is even more elusive in this text, in which rampant mass consumerism has infiltrated every relationship and every political or national alliance.[54]

The novel also includes faux transcripts: of investigations into U.S. war crimes, and of a meeting between an American official and local Vietnamese leaders in which the American presents an overview of U.S. rural development initiatives. Both kinds of transcripts present the American point of view as anodyne and hyperrational with an over-reliance on decontextualized "facts" and documents. The presentation by the American official to local Vietnamese leaders in chapter 19 (near the middle of the novel) is particularly telling. Although it presents itself as vaguely defocalized and has almost no relationship to the plots and subplots that run through the entirety of the novel, the critiques of the American discourse offered by the local leaders disrupt the smoothness of his presentation in a manner that goes directly to the American idea that the United States would bring development to the postcolonial world as a more attractive alternative to the Marxist forms of nationalism, which it saw itself contesting in Vietnam, Korea, and other parts of the region. Rhetorically, American development discourse is exposed in the chapter by the pointed questions and commentaries of the locals, but in the novel as a whole, the mercenary attitudes of almost all the other characters reveal the power of the development idea beyond its rhetorical inadequacies.

On the question of what is and is not represented in the novel, Paik remarks in passing that it includes relatively "little criticism of the atrocities committed by South Korean troops"[55] but still imagines that the largest impact of the English translation on American readers will be to "remind . . . them of the variety and pervasiveness of their involvement in the sufferings of other nations."[56] But the question of war crimes committed by the ROK in the Vietnamese theater also returns to historical particularity, the diversity of Asian experience, and the pervasiveness of the idea of development. For example, Hyun Sook Kim's study of the Korea military's history in Vietnam emphasizes the role played by geopolitics and the drive for "growth" in obstructing the writing of an accurate historical record, since both the Vietnamese and ROK governments have a vested interest in maintaining their current symbiotic trade relationship, which includes importing large numbers of Vietnamese working-class immigrants into the rapidly developing ROK.[57] This contemporary history not only reinforces the power of the development idea in the postcolonial world, but it also suggests another explanation for the eventual disappearance of the Vietnamese strategy of *dịch vận*/persuasion in postdevelopment Asia. As a foil to older Chinese and Japanese forms of tributary imperialist expansion or classical French settler colonial practices, *dịch vận* proved formidable, but the seductive pleasures of the consumerist promise in the era of American empire has been a vastly more devastating cultural force.

III. DOMESTICATION AND THE AMERICAN IMAGINARY

The war that Americans commonly call "the Vietnam War" and Vietnamese refer to as "the American War" (or, to be precise, the "war of resistance against the Americans") is routinely understood on the American side of this divide as either a rupture or an aberration. American global power was suddenly challenged and brought low by Vietnamese resilience, leading to a period of soul searching before the one true superpower recovered its global dominance, according to the familiar U.S. domestic narrative. In contrast, my main claim here is that the American experience in Southeast Asia should be read within a genealogy of American imperialism that incorporates the cultural dimension. If nationalist histories of the war by Americans present one obstacle to my reading, the bibliography of postcolonial studies criticism is surprisingly commonly complicit. Edward Said's *Orientalism* concludes with a transitional coda—far more polemical in tone than what preceded it in earlier chapters of the book—that deals with the way the legacy of British and French discourses of the Arabo-Islamic world influences American foreign policy toward the Middle East. In subsequent works, including Said's "sequel" to *Orientalism*, *Culture and Imperialism* (1993), he repeatedly emphasizes the need to analyze the connection between contemporary U.S. foreign policy and the heritage of European colonial dominance. Still, the field of postcolonial studies evolved such that it placed a far greater emphasis on the pre–World War II histories of *European* colonial discourse, parsing this relationship between colonialism and culture in post-Enlightenment Europe ad nauseam. This evolution is one marker of American resistance to a more globalized understanding of the United States in the world.[58]

A key goal of this study is to challenge the immanent separation between the historical emergence of the United States as a global hegemon and the enduring persistence of a provincialized view of American literary culture. The deep structures that evolve over the course of Bowles's several novels will repeat themselves again and again in American literary fiction as it attempts to represent the American experiences in Vietnam, Korea, Central America, Southern Africa, the Caribbean, and the Middle East. As with Bowles, setting becomes an instrument for an internal critique of American values in these later novels. The critical attitude toward America's place in the world and the instability of the creation of meaning in such texts call into question their potential for easily reading American imperialism in them.

At the same time, it must be acknowledged that the settings of the American "Third World" novel *are a pretext*. In functioning as an instrument, they recapitulate the problem of the provinciality of American globality. There are hard limits to the extent to which the American postwar lens is able to cross the transnational epistemic divide between the United States and the Global South. In this sense, the American "Third World" novel reinforces the imperial gaze of the United States' postwar imperium.

Tim O'Brien's *Going After Cacciato* (1978), like much of his writing, demonstrates the typical mechanism by which the American "Third World" novel simultaneously encapsulates a critique of American Cold War normativity even as it leaves intact the cultural conception of America as hegemon. A surprising winner of the National Book Award upon its publication, O'Brien's second novel's reputation has grown as its author has become the preeminent American writer of fiction set in Vietnam. In this sense, O'Brien can also be considered a literary writer with mass appeal. The novel presents a series of events, some imaginary and some "real," that dramatically critique the imperial moment at stake in the text, but it also delimits through its complex focalizing strategy the American-Vietnam War and its traumas to the imagination of the American male subject. This tension—between anti-imperialist content and ethnocentric form—links the novel to the tradition initiated by Bowles.

Going After Cacciato adopts a formal approach reminiscent of high modernist fiction. The novel intertwines three narrative strands that come together in the final pages of the text. The main strand is a road trip from the jungles of Vietnam to the streets of Paris, undertaken by the protagonist, a young midwestern American named Paul Berlin, a handful of his fellow soldiers, and a young half-Chinese woman they pick up along the way. The pretext for the journey, which appears increasingly perfunctory as the novel progresses, is the pursuit of a fellow soldier named Cacciato, the hunted one, who has gone AWOL. Intermixed with this story are two other narrative strands: one a series of ten short, interspersed chapters in which Berlin stays up all night on duty at an observation post and lets his mind wander; another relating Berlin's arrival and integration into his unit, including some of his first experiences of battle and an incident of so-called fragging carried out against the company's commanding officer. The key word in the text is the noun *imagination*, repeated almost incessantly in multiple contexts throughout each narrative strand. The rhythm of this repetition reinforces the mounting evidence that the entire trip to Paris is actually a flight of fancy playing out in Berlin's mind. An initial chapter in the observation post thread establishes the protagonist's mind's eye as the underpinning of the narratives:

> Yes, he thought, a fine idea. Cacciato leading them west through peaceful country, deep country perfumed by lilacs and burning hemp, a boy coaxing them step by step through rich and fertile country toward Paris.
>
> It was a splendid idea.
>
> Paul Berlin, whose only goal was to live long enough to establish goals worth living for still longer, stood high in the tower by the sea, the night soft all around him, and wondered, not for the first time, about the immense powers of his own imagination.[59]

In this passage, firmly focalized through Paul Berlin, the key words *idea*, *thought*, and *imagination* reinforce a Cartesian idealism at the base of the American soldier's experience. It is within his mind that the war becomes most substantive. In this sense, Berlin's reveries at the observation post are prepared for by his father's sagacious comments back home that emphasize the importance of the lens, which fixes point of view: "'You'll see some terrible stuff I guess. . . . But try to look for the good things too. They'll be there if you look. So watch for them.'"[60] This comment by Berlin's father demonstrates—with its repetitive use of looking verbs—the power of words spoken in a middle-class, middle American setting to fix the projective power of the outward gaze of the American soldier in a manner that defers the most disruptive of the non-American realities it confronts.

More generally, the three narrative strands that make up *Going After Cacciato* can be connected via their strongly committed focalization through the main character of Berlin, with his vivid imagination. Thus, the novel's structure reinforces the proposition that both the war and the American experience in Asia can be fit neatly into a middle-class, white male American consciousness. This structure reinforces the theme of imagination in that the protagonist's mind's eye comes to delimit the reader's ability to see and to know. In this sense, the theme of imagination is closely committed to an epistemological probing at the text's core. What can or cannot be known constantly presents itself as a problem, even as the novel scrupulously avoids clarifying its own epistemological dilemmas.

The quintessential example of the unknowable in the novel is the Asian body. The only Asian characters are a North Vietnamese defector who confronts Berlin's chasing troupe inside a network of underground tunnels early in the novel, and the female love interest of Paul Berlin, the half-Chinese woman. Both characters are exceptions that prove the rule, with the rule being an absence of Asianness in the text. Each is seen through the narrow lens of Paul Berlin's mindset—certainly even more impinged by Berlin's cognitive limitations than the rest of the cast of characters. The defector is Li Van Hgoc, a major in the 48th North Vietnamese Battalion, who has sought refuge in an underground tunnel where the Americans find themselves. A main feature of the scene in which he appears is Berlin's fascination with the actual encounter of a human being from the other side: "He had never seen the living enemy. . . . How, he asked Li Van Hgoc, did they hide themselves? How did they maintain such quiet? Where did they sleep, how did they melt into the land? Who were they? What motivated them—ideology, history, tradition, religion, politics, fear, discipline? . . . Was it true they didn't value human life? Did their women really carry razor blades in their vaginas, booby traps for dumb GIs?"[61] The last clause in this quotation manifests the extremely gendered character of the narrative's lens; Sarkin Aung Wan, Berlin's girlfriend, is similarly a creation of a very male American mindset. She is docile, comely, obedient, adoring, and resourceful. Oddly—at least before one thinks of her as a figment of Berlin's imagination—she holds in her head a full panoply of American bourgeois aspirations, without having ever left Southeast Asia. She imagines Paris not as a colonial capital, but as a city of love and romance, and she craves bourgeois domestic bliss—including a pet poodle.

The theme of epistemological unavailability culminates near the end of the novel, in chapter 39, and occupies the third narrative strand—Berlin's initiation into his platoon and the war theater, entitled "The Things They Didn't Know." A central passage reads,

> Not knowing the language, they did not know the people. They did not know what the people loved or respected or feared or hated. They did not recognize hostility unless it was patent, unless it came in a form other than language; the complexities of tone and tongue were beyond them. . . . Not knowing the language, the men did not know whom to trust. Trust was lethal. . . . They did not know if it was a popular war, or, if popular, in what sense. They did not know if the people . . . viewed the war stoically, as it sometimes seemed, or with grief, as it seemed at other times, or with bewilderment or greed or partisan fury. It was impossible to know.[62]

Again, repetition reinforces the thematic center of this homily. The passage represents a culmination of the epistemological leitmotif that runs through the text and is reinforced by its structure. But it is also one of the passages most resonant with the broader American view of the war.

About halfway through the journey, as the travelers await execution in an Iranian prison, the narrator makes direct reference to the trip being a product of Berlin's imagination, and increasingly thereafter, the narrative winks at the reader even as it presents the events in this thread. This Iranian sequence, deserving of more attention from critics of the novel, does much more than reinforce the novel's central question of perspective. As a culmination of a trip across the continent from East Asia to West Asia, it dramatizes the strain placed on the American ability to imagine the world by the burdens of Cold War era hegemony. In other words, it places the Vietnam experience into a longer trajectory of American history, and thus goes beyond much literature by American authors dealing with the war in Vietnam. The Iran presented in the passage is a mythic pastiche constructed through an American lens. It is introduced through a description of a gruesome public execution more reminiscent of Saudi Arabia. The sequence quickly brings the traveling American soldiers into contact with officers from Savak, the notorious secret police of the shah. The first officer they meet is friendly, but he is finally replaced by an evil doppelganger. Both are products of the American imagination. The good officer surprises them by admitting he is "a practicing Christian."[63] He discusses with Doc Peret the concept of the soldier as an instrument of perception, and indulges the Americans' every excuse for their presence in Tehran as deserters. His evil twin, on the other hand, mocks them and randomly breaks their noses before they can object to anything he says. As a caricature of Oriental despotism, he reinforces the mythic and imaginary tone. This imaginary valence proves precisely the dimension of the text that allows Americans to become victims of Savak in spite of the historical American complicity with—even manipulation of—the shah's regime, and in this reversal, the traumatized American so ubiquitous in U.S. narratives of the Vietnam experience is radically complicated. In the Middle East analogy, the traumatized American is both extended and exposed, made the product of geopolitics as partially shaped by American empire, rather than the product of misguided U.S. foreign policy.

William V. Spanos, in his extremely helpful analysis of *Going After Cacciato*, published in the immediate aftermath of the second Bush administration's invasion of Iraq, also emphasizes the epistemological dimension of the novel's representation of the American experience in Vietnam. He summarizes the novel's accomplishments as follows: "O'Brien's threshold novel . . . is on the verge of disclosing that *this* war bore witness to an epistemic break: that the Vietnam War was not only a matter of the self-destruction of the American military machine, but also of the self-destruction of the hegemonic discourses—the relay of the deeply imbedded cultural *narratives*—that 'justified' the United States' intervention and military practice in Vietnam."[64] Spanos's emphasis on the episteme allows us to understand the novel as a representation of epistemological crisis, and one can trace a similar theme—that of American forces' hubristic ignorance of the local Vietnamese context—in various American histories of the Vietnam War. For example, the military historian Spencer Tucker comments that "few Americans lived with the Vietnamese long enough to learn their language and culture and win their allegiance to a government that failed to meet their concerns."[65] Similarly, Mark Atwood Lawrence observes in his more recent history that "U.S. soldiers tended to view all Vietnamese with distrust. Instead of bolstering partnerships with anti-communist Vietnamese and winning over the uncommitted, Americans frequently alienated the local population through demeaning or aggressive behavior."[66] Indeed, one is hard pressed to find any history of the American War in Vietnam without such a passage in it.

Each of these representations—that of the novel, that of the critic, and those of the historians—constitutes a moment in which epistemology is redirected and a knowledge vacuum comes into focus. None of them, however, move forward to an examination of the Vietnam War that is contrapuntal in its method and takes fully into account Asian and transnational representations of the conflict. The relative absence of contrapuntalism in discussions of the history of American involvement in Southeast Asia is striking given the repeated emphasis on "What They Didn't Know" type discourses. Stanley Karnow, one of the first and still most popular historians to write about American intervention in Southeast Asia, boasts in the preface to a recent edition of his classic text, *Vietnam: A History*, that a few years after the book's publication, he went to Vietnam and was surprised to find that many Vietnamese, including General Giap, commander of communist forces in the fights against both French colonialism and American neocolonialism, had read his book. But Karnow makes no mention of Vietnamese sources that he himself—much less an American political or military leader—might have consulted. In fact, it would take more than two decades before an American historian emphasized the use of Vietnamese sources.[67] Ang Cheng Guan has recently undertaken a corrective to this trend in two thin volumes that narrate, in a "history from above" approach, the Vietnamese communist leadership's decision-making processes over the course of the "American War" phase of Vietnamese history. In his introduction, he describes one obstacle to achieving a multifaceted historical narrative. "There are those who are dismissive of 'official histories' (particularly those from the Vietnamese side), as mere communist propaganda and therefore unreliable as source materials for historical research."[68] The author's response is that such material is, in fact, less reliable, but that it is still helpful in producing the fullest picture possible. But another aspect of the tendency Guan observes among American historians must be noted: the way it automatically dismisses any conceivable contribution to the narrative from oppositional knowledge producers. If these U.S. historians are also writing critically of the American war effort, they are virtually an exact equivalent of the producer of the American 'Third World' novel, subversive in their attitude toward American bourgeois normativity, but also dismissive of cultural narratives that live beyond its scope.

The history of Hollywood representations of Vietnam's "American War" follows a similar trajectory. During the late 1970s, critically acclaimed films like *The Deer Hunter* and *Apocalypse Now* broke with the Audie Murphy / John Wayne tradition of representation by showing the senselessness of the war and the trauma it inflicted on the American rank and file. The 1980s were filled with openly critical and critically acclaimed films that followed in the late 1970s tradition. Films by the most respected auteurs in Hollywood, including Francis Ford Coppola, Stanley Kubrick, Brian De Palma, and Oliver Stone, continued to depict the trauma and brutality of America's unknowing campaign in the region. Hollywood's auteur cinema of the war in Vietnam might be read as a critique of propaganda films like Wayne's *The Green Berets* (1968), which makes up historical facts to suit its blatantly polemical ends.

In *The Deer Hunter* (1978), for example, the war is depicted as a betrayal of working-class ethnic American whites. The majority of its scenes take place in a Pennsylvania steel town, where a life that is depicted as both brutal and beautiful at the film's start eventually loses all meaning because of the disruption the war represents to the town's sons and daughters. The first scenes set in Vietnam take place an hour into the film, reinforcing the text's emphasis on American problems. Still, the Vietnamese setting is an ahistorical land of American trauma.[69] The Asian setting is initiated with an image of a National Liberation Front soldier randomly throwing a hand grenade into a storage shelter where innocent civilians are hiding. Within minutes the narrative has shifted to a scene in which the three main characters, Pennsylvanians who have been taken prisoner, are trying to survive a torture session, played out as a game of roulette. Here, as with later films, U.S. policy in Vietnam is depicted with visual verve as damaging to the American consciousness, while Vietnamese history and experience are moved to the margins of the story.

Apocalypse Now famously opens with the main character, Captain Willard, played by Martin Sheen, lying alone in a dimly lit hotel room while a monologue offering his twisted thoughts on the attraction of the horrors of Indochinese war is voiced over. Critic Louis K. Greiff has helpfully connected this to the narrative framing device of the film's source text, Joseph Conrad's *Heart of Darkness*.[70] At the same time, the scene focalizes all of what happens next through the character of Willard. The rest of the film will follow his journey, and no realities of the jungles or the war that fall outside the frame of his vision play an important role in the film. This tight focalization not only connects Willard's journey to the one imagined by Paul Berlin in *Going After Cacciato*, but it also sets a precedent that will be repeated over and over again in the canon of Vietnam War art house cinema. Voice-over narration by the main character in a film is by no means an unheard-of technique. Still, it is rare in films with such artistic pretensions, or at least rare enough that its presence as a pattern should draw our attention in not just *Apocalypse Now* but also *Platoon* and *Full Metal Jacket*, which similarly feature regular voice-over narration by their main characters, all of them, of course, white, middle-class, American men. The strong narrator's voice in each of these films reinforces at the level of form this cinema's investment in the American knowledge-making myth that scrupulously eschews Vietnamese histories, voices, and experiences.

In each of these American discourses of the war, Vietnamese agency operates as a kind of horizon toward which the American discourse aims, but with a high degree of futility. This trajectory reinforces the connection between the American experience in Vietnam and a larger discursive history of American empire, during and after the Cold War. Bowles's career suggests that the literary discourse of America in the world started off at the Cold War's beginning as a discourse of an unreachable epistemological horizon. The reception of the work of Edward Said in American literary criticism also is a product of elite literary culture in the United States. In *Orientalism*, the reader encounters a discourse of a discourse: Said's critique of the colonial discourse of Britain and France during the period of the greatest power of their respective empires. The Arabo-Islamic subject plays no more of a role in this analysis than any Asian does in *Going After Cacciato*. This particular problem in *Orientalism* was its most unsatisfying aspect to the author, who revised his allegiance to a certain Foucauldian lens in the essay "Traveling Theory" five years later, and then proposed his corrective method of contrapuntalism as an antidote to *Orientalism*'s discursive one-sidedness fifteen years later in *Culture and Imperialism*. In the previous chapter I highlighted not only the manner in which contrapuntalism returns to a longer tradition of anti-Orientalism in Arab thought as exemplified by Abdel-Malek, Laroui, Djaït, and al-Jabiri, but also the way Said designated *Culture and Imperialism* as a sequel to *Orientalism*. Here, I would like to suggest that this later work might be read equally as a critique of the way 1970s discourse, including Said's own classic study, packaged the American gaze outward toward the various Asias where its hegemony still held so much sway.

IV. CONCLUSION: AUTOCRITIQUE AND HEGEMONY

The rhetoric of public diplomacy in Cold War America could be very crude and jingoistic. Lyndon Johnson called Vietnam a "damn little pissant country";[71] Robert McNamara less colorfully denominated it "a backward nation";[72] Kissinger was quoted expressing certainty that U.S. bombing could break "a fourth rate power like North Vietnam";[73] and Nixon expressed frustration at having his agenda hijacked by a "little shit ass country."[74] Among opponents of the war, Senator Ernest Gruening of Alaska argued on the senate floor that "all Vietnam is not worth the life of a single American boy."[75] This string of quotations, taken from both the prowar and antiwar sides of the domestic debate, suggests not only the extent to which racist assumptions marred the thinking of the American political elite in their policy making vis-à-vis Vietnam; they also indicate that domestic concerns were the priority of American policy makers, even when they formulated foreign policy. Policy makers' primary—indeed, most of the time, only—concern was the management of the foreign policy issue known as "Vietnam" for domestic political purposes irrespective of the fate of the Vietnamese.

As Nick Turse has recently documented, this policy dynamic resulted in systematic atrocities visited by American forces and their allies upon Vietnamese civilians. For the purposes of my own study, Turse's history is helpful in reading the way U.S. discourses serve to domesticate such global crimes. Before the My Lai massacre entered the American narrative, "the fate of civilians in South Vietnam was rarely reported on," and North Vietnamese claims of multiple massacres resulting in thousands of civilian deaths were dismissed as communist propaganda. "And then, in a stunning reversal, almost immediately after the exposure of the My Lai massacre, war crime allegations became old hat—so commonplace as to be barely worth mentioning or looking into."[76]

My method in this study has emphasized reading discourses contextually, distinguishing, for example, between the rhetorics of policy makers, of popular culture, of the news media, and of the literary novel. My goal in invoking racist utterances of government leaders and the news media's indifference to civilian deaths is not by any means to suggest a discursive equivalence between mainstream cultural discourse and the sophisticated, multivalent language of the American "Third World" novel. In fact, literary fiction, including the work of Tim O'Brien, perhaps especially *Going After Cacciato*, can be read as a sophisticated repudiation of imperial American monologism. I present the dismissive language of politicians here only as a portion of the semantic field in which an American literary text circulates. Plausible deniability, the notion that the American empire is not really an empire, is central to its mainstream discourse; literary fiction challenges this duplicity, but its strategies for doing so usually insist upon American self-referentiality. In retrospect, comparing and contrasting the racist rhetoric of policy makers and the sophisticated reconception of the episteme among literary authors and cinema auteurs provoke questions regarding the possibilities and limits of autocritique in such an "empire as a way of life" environment. How far can American literary culture go in repudiating American normativity as long as the critique maintains that there is no outside to the American idea? Ultimately, the question of knowledge production within this discursive context has remained resolutely domestic.

CHAPTER 4
Gender

Normative Feminism

On Saving Women in the Postdevelopment World

I. INTRODUCTION: THE WOMAN QUESTION AT THE END OF THE COLD WAR

In the introduction to the last edition of Stanley Karnow's expansive history of the Vietnam War, this passage touches on the much remarked upon phenomenon of sex workers in Ho Chi Minh City:

> In 1981, a Communist official had assured me that the "socialist transformation" had abolished the debauchery left from the American era. But fifteen years later, there were an estimated fifty thousand hookers in Ho Chi Minh City—a sharp increase since the war. Dazzling in tight blouses and microskirts, they plied their metier in bars, cafes, massage parlors and hotel lobbies, or boldly accosted clients from motor scooters. They chiefly pursued foreigners but many served party figures.[1]

In general, Karnow is critical of the American war effort in Southeast Asia. For that reason, his emphasis on women's bodies in his representation of Vietnam at the end of the Cold War is particularly telling in that it suggests their centrality in a variety of American discourses, including antiwar discourse. His description of the postwar sex trade interestingly leaves intact the Vietnamese government official's suggestion that the industry resulted from the American occupation of the South, even as it suggests that the government's apparent tolerance of it—or at least inability to do anything to delimit it—constitutes a failure on the part of the regime.[2] The passage also typifies a fascination with the issue of Asian women as a component of American engagement with the region, a fascination that borders on obsession, whether within mainstream, countercultural, popular, or elite academic discourses. This discursive fixation powerfully links gender, sexuality, and nationalism in a way that becomes mind-numbingly common in U.S. discourse of the global as the Cold War bleeds into the War on Terror. The link between Karnow's observation and Bowles's mention of Bangkok's "floozies" in his letter quoted at the beginning of the previous chapter underscores the recurrent presence of the Asian female body in the U.S. discourse of globality during the late Cold War. Both white, American, middle-class, critically inclined male writers imbed deep in their observations an acknowledgment of the U.S. military's role in shaping the modern phenomenon of the Southeast Asian sex worker, even as they direct their comments toward local civilizational decline. The subtle suggestion that Asian women somehow pollute Asia gestures toward a deep ambivalence in the cultural discourse of U.S. imperialism in the later Cold War. Previously, novels like *The Sheltering Sky* and innumerable 1950s and early '60s landmarks—*Invisible Man*; *Catcher in the Rye*; *Rabbit, Run*; *Revolutionary Road*; *One Flew over the Cuckoo's Nest*—critiqued the stifling conformity of America's emerging professional/managerial class culture, using in Bowles's case the "Third World" as an instrument in the execution of this critique. As the Cold War blended into the neoliberal era and the instrumental Third World setting became increasingly widespread, the iconoclasm of an antinormative cultural discourse conflicted with an ideological limit embodied in Third World women. In other words, a highly normative idea of female sexuality insidiously projected itself onto the text of the global, even in the writing of the most nonconformist Americans.

The historic global engagements of the United States during this period evolve in a mutually reinforcing manner alongside cultural texts. While cultures of the American War in Vietnam offer striking examples of the way women's bodies are centered in America's discourse of the global, the female body is also central to the evolution of a U.S. neoliberal image of the world that takes root during military involvement in Vietnam and evolves over the course of the late Cold War and the post–Cold War period. In Vietnam, Iraq, and Afghanistan, the role of the state and the military in rectifying local civilizational decline by force, even corrupting women in order to save them, is front and center. But undergirding these occasional forays into invasion and occupation is an evolving regime of development programs, established after World War II, growing in discursive emphasis over the course of the Cold War and becoming hegemonic in the post–Cold War.

The main claim of this study has been that U.S. global hegemony in the historical periods that followed World War II has had a dramatic effect on all aspects of cultural production, including literature, cinema, philosophy, and other arts both inside the United States, which has tended to domesticate America's ubiquitous foreign entanglements, and in the Global South, whose diverse cultures have responded in numerous ways, almost always involving an element of writing back to U.S. imperial involvement in the local scene. During the final stages of the Cold War and the first decade or so of the post–Cold War years, the approximate time period covered in this chapter, the centrality of women's bodies in U.S. discourse on foreign relations came into sharp focus.

Gayatri Chakravorty Spivak's work, beginning with her classic essay "Can the Subaltern Speak?" (1988), is important for understanding this centrality. In this early piece, Spivak's focus is on British colonialism's representation of Indian women, but the essay raises the resilient notion of colonial rule as a quest to save women in its famous critical aphorism: "White men are saving brown women from brown men."[3] Equally importantly, the essay links the colonial drive to control women through discourse with contemporary debates around knowledge production, a category I have emphasized in earlier chapters. Additionally, Spivak has continued to call attention to the discourse of saving women, even as the Berlin Wall has crumbled, the Washington Consensus has strengthened, and the War on Terror has emerged with its distinctive discourse. Underpinning this history is the increasing reliance among Western neoliberals, liberals, and neocons alike on regimes of "development," which act as a kind of secular missionary project, saving and civilizing by spreading the gospel of mass consumption. So when Spivak revisits and revises this set of issues more than a decade later, in chapter 3 of her *Critique of Postcolonial Reason*, she incorporates the heightened focus in the now *post*–Cold War milieu on relations between the North and South:

> When this book was started, "the Third World" offered an entire privileged discursive *field* within metropolitan radical criticism. In that field, "the Third World *Woman*" was a particularly privileged signifier. As I have already mentioned, today, in the interest of the financialization of the globe, "Women in Development" has changed to "Gender and Development." The result is an altogether speeded up exchange between North and South, where national identities must be preserved intact. (The red herring of nationalist-racist opposition, rather than globalizing imperialist benevolence, to cultural studies makes auto-critique particularly difficult.) Upon the terrain of that exchange, the Woman from the South is a particularly privileged signifier, as object and mediator; as she is, in the market, the favored agent-as-instrument of transnational capital's globalizing reach.[4]

The discourse of development as a frame for understanding and producing meaning about the Global South is a product of a post–World War II series of historical events: the Bretton Woods Conference, Potsdam, the start of the Cold War. But the end of the Cold War brought a new surge in interest in "development" as a tool for understanding the dynamics of the North/South axis, especially through the emergence of the "Washington Consensus," a term coined in 1989, and the rise of "neoliberalism," a reconfiguration for the post–Cold War era of U.S.-centric Cold War theories of economic development.[5] Spivak's analysis is helpful, therefore, through its inclusion of the "development" frame, in understanding the continuity between the figure of woman in British colonial discourse and that same figure during the time of high American imperialism.

The idea of saving women takes on new momentum and finds new vistas as the American War on Terror begins. The continuities and particularities of this new era of missionary zeal in the United States has been studied and critiqued both by Spivak and by a subsequent generation of transnational feminist scholars, including Lila Abu-Lughod, Saba Mahmood, Mohja Kahf, and Elora Shehabuddin. For example, in Spivak's "Globalicities: Terror and Its Consequences," an essay that also examines woman as an object around which meaning is produced, this time in the context of the September 11 attacks, Spivak reads the way continuities in global structures of oppression are hidden by celebratory discussions of globalism, which assert that globalization ushers in a new era. "The keynote I want to strike is that changes in the subject are neither isotemporal nor isomorphic with institutional change" is Spivak's response.[6] In the process of making her argument about globalism (a phenomenon in which the emergence of the Washington Consensus inheres), Spivak makes a powerful connection between the centrality of the figure of woman in the British colonial discourse of South Asia analyzed in her earlier essays and that same centrality in the U.S. campaign to topple the government of Afghanistan in the fall of 2001. The American imperial context is distinct—with its own particularity. Two ostensibly diverging positions were debated in their assessment of the treatment of women by the regime that harbored al-Qaeda. One is the George W. Bush position, summarized in a *U.S. News and World Report* headline, "How Islamic Radicals are Hijacking One of the World's Great Religions." The other is a liberal feminist position that calls for transformation of Middle East / North Africa / West Asia regions through an alliance among European modernizers. This position—designated by Spivak as "single issue feminism"—is exemplified by Polly Toynbee of *The Guardian*, who wrote in late September of 2001, as the United States prepared to invade Afghanistan, "Primitive Middle Eastern religions (and most others) are much the same—Islam, Christianity and Judaism all define themselves through disgust for women's bodies."[7] What ultimately unites these two positions—the one excoriating the "bad Muslim" ruining a venerable faith and the other pillorying Islam itself as bad for women—and connects them back to British colonial discourse is the way in which "women are used as an excuse for violence."[8] In her conclusion that analyses of globalism should "devise ways of attending to the excess, the exclusion, and the remains of globalization, always in the mode of 'to come,'"[9] Spivak suggests the importance of approaching method with a sense of both continuities in structures of global power as well as "changes in the subject." In the United States, the conclusion of the Cold War was designated as the end of everything that had been, but this hyperbole reinforced old schools of knowledge production, which took on a messianic tone.

The Afghanistan invasion of 2001 may not have substantially changed the United States' idea of itself as a global savior, but its discourses did make much clearer for attentive scholars working in the tradition of Spivak that an identitarian and single-issue discourse of feminism could greatly assist the making contemporary of old colonial tropes about saving women. For example, anthropologist and feminist Lila Abu-Lughod writes movingly about the dilemma facing committed feminists in the

United States who also had the bad luck of having expertise in Islam or the North African, Middle East, or West/Central Asian regions. Initially, the post-9/11 moment seemed to present many opportunities to speak about the culture, politics, history, and gender systems of the region. However, it would eventually become clear that U.S. media was only interested in culture understood in a certain manner—that is, as backward and static and in need of revitalization, imposed from outside if necessary. In critiquing this compulsion to save women in the Global South, Abu-Lughod comments:

> I do not know how many feminists who felt good about saving Afghan women from the Taliban are also asking for a global redistribution of wealth or contemplating sacrificing their own consumption radically so that African or Afghan women could have some chance of having what I do believe should be a universal human right—the right to freedom from the structural violence of global inequality and from the ravages of war, the everyday rights of having enough to eat, having homes for their families in which to live and thrive, having ways to make decent livings so their children can grow.[10]

Throughout this book I have discussed the relationship between U.S. imperialism and older forms of hegemony as well as its relationship to literary culture—particularly in its elite form. This chapter traces the way an idea of "saving women" that goes back to British colonial discourse is adapted and reappropriated in U.S. foreign relations after the fall of Saigon.

On the woman question, as elsewhere, U.S. discourse has its own particularity. As I have noted, the rise of U.S. imperialism has at times worked hand in glove with an identitarianism within American culture that domesticates the subject, even as U.S. cultural entanglements are becoming increasingly global. This tension between an identity-focused, single-issue feminism and a globally engaged transnational one brings the exploitation of domestic identity consciousness into focus as a component of imperial culture. Saba Mahmood states the problem directly: "Feminist contributions to the vilification of Islam do no service either to Muslim women or to the cause of gender justice. Instead, they reinscribe the cultural and civilizational divide that has become the bedrock not only of neoconservative politics but of liberal politics as well."[11]

A group of transnational feminists working within the U.S. academy, out of a deep knowledge of history and society in the postcolony, have followed Spivak in her statement that "because there are sex-gender systems in operation everywhere, women are used as an excuse for violence,"[12] and gone on to critique U.S. imperialism's use of the figure of woman. These critics, cited throughout this chapter, have been particularly active in responding to the often mendacious phalange of instant-celebrity native informant Muslim women writers who shoot to superstardom in the U.S. pundit class. But this critical scholarship also points to an equally powerful and subtle phenomenon highlighted by Mahmood, as many transnational feminist critics find themselves also criticizing feminist discourse as expressed by established authors with long-standing, documented commitments to women's equality in First World contexts, as in these critical pairings: Spivak to Toynbee, Mahmood to Ehrenreich, and Shehabuddin to Chesler.

The critical scholarship of transnational feminism demonstrates the extent of the consensus in mainstream U.S. discourses around the need to save women—whether militarily or nongovernmentally, whether in the case of libertine Asian sex workers or captive Muslim harem dwellers. Whether oversexed or undersexed, "Third World" women are represented in the United States as being without agency or history. For most U.S. writers, a notion of a normative woman, liberated, secular, middle-class, and Westernized, increasingly comes into focus and is projected onto the world as the Cold War is ending. This ushers in an instability within the American "Third World" novel, which has grounded itself in the critique of American normativity. This chapter compares the emergence of this tension in America with the global writing against this U.S. lens that has characterized important literary motifs in the post-development world. It does so through four figures. In the Southeast Asian context, Vietnamese nationalism has centered the figure of the woman warrior, a contrastive symbol that challenges the sex worker so ubiquitous in the American imaginary. Meanwhile, in Africa and West Asia, women are captives who need development. This contemporary version of the harem dweller, often the target of development projects, can be contrasted with the postcolonial woman as intellectual, working in the tradition of geohistorically located thought discussed in chapter 2. The thinker has a body, and the body is gendered. Each of these four figures—the warrior, the prostitute, the captive, and the thinker—attaches to a certain myth. Each also, read geohistorically, has the potential to destabilize myths around global women. For the American

"Third World" novel, for example, they expose the pronounced tension between global conformity and domestic iconoclasm that constitutes the genre's unstable foundation.

II. VIETNAM'S FEMALE WARRIORS

The strongest strain in transnational feminist criticism has emphasized the need to understand the "Third World" woman as an agent, with power—a dynamic figure in history. This position contrasts with the representation of women in postcolonial society as victims, oppressed on a daily basis by black and brown men who prop up a regressive patriarchal power structure. Although much of this criticism draws on Spivak, her statements on these questions suggest that her analyses have always embraced the ambivalence inherent in trying to analyze women in postcolonial societies. On the one hand, it is always important to read female agency back into historical situations of oppression. But to write only of this agency necessitates a manner of reading that circumvents cultures of patriarchy—be they global systems of capitalist and imperialist character or local nationalist and comprador ones, which may deploy traditionalist discourse in the service of neoliberal goals.

In the Vietnamese and Southeast Asian contexts, the binary between the nationalist symbol of the woman as fighter/hero and the prostitute as a marker of disorder/corruption operates as a compelling embodiment of the tension between the powerful agent and the victim of patriarchal repression. These two representations of women, as the female warrior (agent) and the sex worker (victim), prove ubiquitous in the transnational discourse on Vietnamese women.[13]

Virtually every attempt to historicize Vietnamese nationalism begins with the Tru'ng sisters, who led a rebellion that overthrew China's first major occupation of Vietnam between 111 B.C.E. and 40 C.E., the year of the Tru'ng sisters' successful uprising. The daughters of a local lord, the sisters' military prowess is seen as crucial in uniting the Vietnamese as a people distinct from their large and powerful northern neighbors, the Chinese. Their three-year reign, which ended with the return of Chinese occupiers, marks the beginning of the Vietnamese nation for many official histories. But the legendary mystique around accounts of their lives and careers infuses the history with a strong air of nationalist mythology. Consequently, this history is put to as various uses as there are ideological types in the historicization of Vietnam's woman warriors. For example, in *Women in Vietnam* by Mai Thi Tu and Le Thi Nham Tuyet, a history produced in 1978 by a government-run Hanoi publisher, the Tru'ng sisters are not only the foundation stone of Vietnamese nationalism but also a bridge between matriarchal, protofeminist gender systems in ancient Vietnam and the tradition of female resistance that would later characterize the fight against occupation by China, France, and the United States. According to this nationalist historiography, patriarchy was imported and imposed on the Vietnamese, first by Confucianism and feudalism, then by imperialism and capitalism. Micheline Lessard's treatment of female participation in Vietnamese resistance during the period of French occupation also references the sisters.[14] In this instance, their example initiates a tradition of active female participation in nationalist resistance, but Lessard focuses specifically on the French colonial period and documents the nationalist dimension of the woman warrior phenomenon as a counterpoint to an Orientalist reading of the history of the period, which interpreted female participation in armed resistance as "based only on a submissive sense of filial piety."[15] Yet another reference to the legendary history of the sisters occurs in the chapter on Vietnamese women in Jayawardena's *Feminism and Nationalism in the Third World*. Here, the historical record of participation in armed resistance by Vietnamese women, traced from ancient times through the American war, evidences the *global* solidarity among women with revolutionary commitments.[16]

An extensive focus on active participation by Vietnamese female combatants during the American war is found in Karen Gottschang Turner's *Even the Women Must Fight* (1998). Turner's method is both ethnographic and historical, incorporating extensive interviews conducted in the late 1990s with female veterans who had fought with the North Vietnamese Army (NVA) against U.S. and South Vietnam government forces. The title is drawn from a proverb quoted repeatedly in Tuyet and Tu's state-sponsored history: "When the enemy comes, women also must fight."[17] The heavy reliance on interviews and voices of NVA female veterans in Turner's study means that by reading it against accounts of the female warrior tradition in Vietnam as presented by Tu and Tuyet in *Women in Vietnam*, the official state account, the reader can construct a version of the Vietnamese native point of view, one that functions effectively as a counterpoint to the focalization of Vietnamese experience through Paul Berlin (the *Cacciato* protagonist), Henry Kissinger, or a Hollywood director like Francis Ford Coppola, but also exposes the impossibility of such an attempt to construct a separate native viewpoint, since any such effort is doomed by its own counteressentialism.

As Turner's work makes clear, the symbol of the woman warrior—always present in Vietnamese history—took on special meaning for the North Vietnamese during the war of American aggression. Iconic images from the period show a small Vietnamese woman carrying a gun and sporting a pith helmet as she takes prisoner a hulking American pilot with bowed head, or a young woman in uniform carrying an enormous backpack that doubles her own weight in support of a celebrated campaign to keep open the bridge at Thanh Hoa in the face of furious American bombing in 1965.[18] Turner cites statistitics indicating that the total number of women who spent time at the front in the NVA, local militias, or professional teams reached 1.5 million.[19] Thus, "in terms of women in combat . . . only the Soviet Union during World War II comes close to the Vietnamese case."[20] Such statistics for women, along with juridical data such as the constitutional stipulation of equal rights—including equal pay for equal work—provided by the Hanoi government form a foundation for critical discourse around the powerful place of women in contemporary Vietnam.[21] According to Turner, anecdotal evidence suggests that sexual harassment within the NVA was surprisingly absent. The exceptionalist tone that fueled the nationalist cohesion around the country's wars of liberation often lingers in this historical narrative. This mythology, however, is counterbalanced in multiple ways by Turner's own evidence as she records complaints of veterans who are celebrated by official nationalist mythology but neglected in basic distribution of resources by policy makers. Turner also places heavy emphasis on the family system, which she interprets as a resilient and still very patriarchal institution in contemporary Vietnam. For many of the veterans she interviewed, the opportunity to marry young, to have children, and to enjoy family life had been permanently sacrificed.

The question of families places the agency and heroism of the female warrior back into a context of patriarchies that limit and oppress. It also invokes a humanist context that highlights the relevance of the novels of Duong Thu Huong (b. 1947) to this discussion. Duong herself fought with the NVA in the American war; like the statements by the veterans interviewed by Turner, her fiction represents an attempt to confront her experience as a mythologized woman warrior in postwar Vietnam. At least six of her novels have been translated from Vietnamese into English. Her themes are the dehumanizing effects of the war and of the nationalist system that promoted the war effort and narrowly benefited from it at the expense of the majority of Vietnamese. Although all of her translated novels directly reference the war and its aftermath, *Novel Without a Name* is the most specifically focused on the final years of the conflict, narrating battlefield experiences as part of its *histoire*.[22]

Like O'Brien, Duong tends in her fiction toward narrative strategies that channel reality through the lens of one particular character—either a first-person account or free indirect discourse. This center of focalization is sometimes a woman in her novels, but often, as in *Novel Without a Name*, her narration focuses on a male point of view. This novel's narration through the main character, the disillusioned soldier Quan, connects directly with the twin themes of humanism and corruption, since it allows her to explore the complexity of a character's consciousness and its evolution against the backdrop of the delimiting milieu that is Vietnam during the war years. The narrator of *Novel Without a Name* begins and ends the book with events that relate to the porous nature of human ontology during wartime. In the first scene, his troop encourages him to eat soup they have made from a wild orangutan, the first meat any of them have had in months. Quan is repulsed by the taste, smell, and look of the dish, reminding him as it does of human flesh. In fact, the description emphasizes the resemblance between the animal and a human, noting the human quality of the hand floating in the broth, for example, and generally suggesting that the distinction between humans and the animals they consume has been deconstructed by the events of the war, reducing soldiers to a kind of cannibalism.

At the end of the novel, another situation pits Quan against his own men, this time raising the issue of nationalist distinction as a marker of difference between humans, as opposed to the species distinction that takes center stage in the soup incident. As the South falls to the NVA, a Westerner—believed to be American—is captured. Finding him surprises everyone, since the presumption is that all Americans had evacuated two years ago. In rejecting his men's plea for permission to conduct an extrajudicial execution, Quan references ideological myth and its role in marking distinctions between humans interpolated into conflicting nationalisms. Between these two incidents—both of which show the degradation of the human component within the oppressive setting—Quan has a series of experiences that raise the issue of wartime gender systems, including the place of the female soldier in Vietnamese nationalism.

Even before the soup episode, the novel begins with an explicit reference to the way the war has challenged the wholeness of its human participants. Quan's troop stumbles upon a group of mutilated bodies; they are only just recognizable enough to be identified as female NVA fighters captured and tortured—their body parts severed—by the enemy. This leads into the orangutan soup episode, which reinforces the theme of bodily wholeness and bodily functions. But the connection between these issues and female fighters soon comes to the fore. Quan is given the assignment of traveling back to his home village to assist the family of a childhood friend who has suffered a mental breakdown at the front. During his trip back, he encounters a living female fighter in an encounter that illustrates the extent to which combat has rearranged the social order.

The female comrade, Vieng, mans a station by herself, where she spends the day taking care of corpses. Quan stumbles upon her and feels lucky that he has found a station where he can rest along his arduous journey. Only slightly later does he recognize that the comrade he has stumbled upon is female, and when he does, his thoughts emphasize his revulsion: "She knelt by the hearth and flames cruelly lit up her face; she was hideous . . . she gave off a nauseating sweaty odor."[23] The species continuum is reintroduced in this context as well in Quan's reference to her "massive, bear-like body." Although Vieng generously feeds him and provides him a warm and comfortable place to sleep for the night, the encounter that he initially sees as lucky turns poignant, when Quan finds himself having to fend off Vieng's aggressive sexual advances in the middle of the night. Only his physical inability to respond convinces her to desist. "She gave me a suspicious look. Suddenly, she plunged her hand between my thighs. The investigation was conclusive; she could feel for herself that I was useless."[24]

This incident inventories a series of important issues connected to the myth of the female warrior. It is one of the few passages in the novel that reference American imperialism, as Vieng explains away Quan's inadequacy with the comment that "it's probably all those chemicals. Those American bastards!"[25] The war is connected to a distortion of the most personal of human relations, and in the aftermath of Quan's failure, he becomes hypnotized, "like an old gibbon."[26] The costs of the myth of the female who sacrifices herself for the national cause are suggested in the dysfunctional encounter between the two characters. Quan then makes explicit reference to the myth:

> This woman was born of the war. She belonged to it, had been forged by it. It wasn't just because she was ugly that I

> had rejected her. I had been afraid to face myself, scared of the truth. I was a coward. Ten years of war had gone by. I had known both glory and humiliation, lived through all its sordid games. I had needed to meet her to finally see myself clearly. I had been defeated from the beginning. The eighteen year old boy who had thrown himself into army life was still just a boy, wandering, lost out there, somewhere just beyond the horizon. I had never really committed myself to war.[27]

In making the example of the "woman . . . born of war" into a piece in the puzzle of himself, Quan connects war, nationalism, gender systems, and the issue of the wholeness of the subject. Thus, the incident frames developments through the rest of the novel. Quan does not really develop as a human, but he does manage to crawl toward a heightened understanding. This trajectory is often plotted through encounters with women.

In fact, the development of Quan and the *histoire* of the novel both pass through this series of encounters with women, beginning with the corpses of the soldiers and the night spent with the hulking and amorous Vieng, who so disgusts him. His encounter with Vieng has established that he is no hero; it has exposed him as passive and devoid of any trace of machismo. (At one point, she even chides him for his affected manner of speaking and presumes he is a city dweller, forcing him to admit that he—like her—is from a village.)[28] Subsequent experiences fill out the novel's theme of the war's rearranging of social relations. After he leaves Vieng, Quan loses his strength before making it back home and is saved by a nurturing child. He thinks to himself, "I imagined she must have looked like a young mother, my second mother." He then revives, and upon getting his first full view of her, realizes "she couldn't have been more than six years old."[29] The idea of a second mother gestures toward the death of Quan's biological mother, referenced through flashbacks, but Quan's search for a replacement in this encounter with a six-year-old implies the acuteness of his need for maternal support in a society where the all-pervasive reach of nationalism has rendered such connections nearly obsolete. This theme of affection as a basic component of complete humanity, eviscerated by the nationalist fervor of the war, returns in a new context once Quan makes it back home. After several days of disillusioning encounters with his father and their old neighbors, he discovers in the middle of an idle conversation that his teenage sweetheart, Hoa, whom he considered his "ideal woman"[30] in his teenage years, had recently become pregnant out of wedlock and been cast out by her family. In the encounter that follows, as he seeks her out in her squat beyond the village grounds, the emphasis is on the corruption of their innocence and the promises that preceded the national commitment to war.

III. SEX WORKERS AND FEMALE AGENCY

To shift from Vietnamese nationalist to U.S. nationalist representations of Asian women is to move from images of heroes to images of victims. In film, the image of the Asian woman's body as contested site of the American struggle in Vietnam is present in the earliest texts, including *The Quiet American*, *The Green Berets*, and *Hearts and Minds*, three very different films all set in Vietnam and featuring a hypersexualized Vietnamese woman as a catalyst. But the trope takes on increasing centrality in the later wave of films about the war. For example, Kubrick's *Full Metal Jacket* (1987) begins with an extended sequence at a stateside army training barracks, where the masculinity of the soldiers in training is repeatedly challenged verbally by their older, white male drill sergeant. As the film moves to Vietnam, the new setting is introduced by the Asian woman's body in a stereotypical scene of street solicitation involving verbal give and take between the main character and a Vietnamese prostitute. In Kubrick's text, the sex worker marks the move from the American setting to the Vietnamese. The film ends with a group of American soldiers discovering that the sniper who has killed their comrades, terrorized their battalion, and left them all cowering is a lone National Liberation Front *female* fighter. This final scene brings the issue of the formation of youthful, white male masculinity to fruition in a subversive manner: the old drill sergeant has faded into the background and the Vietnamese woman unexpectedly emerges as the final challenge.

In De Palma's *Casualties of War* (1989), the main plot line centers on a soldier played by Michael J. Fox attempting to save a young Vietnamese woman who has been kidnapped and gang-raped by his compatriots. The story then follows this protagonist's attempt to see the perpetrators punished and, by the end of the film, his continued haunting. DePalma uses a crude framing device to portray the way the protagonist's post-traumatic stress is centered in the psychosexual/national. Nodding off as he rides a commuter train in the suburban United States, his haunting flashback is triggered by the mere sight of a brown woman noticed at the other end of the car. These opening and closing moments reveal the fetishization of the woman of color's body at the center of the film's action. *Casualties of War* was released in 1989. By the time of Oliver Stone's 1993 *Heaven and Earth*, loosely based on a memoir by Le Ly Haislip, the experience of a Vietnamese woman had become so central to the discourse of the war that the life of one woman is allowed to stand in for all Vietnamese experience.

In the case of American literary fiction, the Asian female body carries a similar status. Katherine Kinney's account of the way the American war in Vietnam has been represented in the United States is particularly cogent on this point, especially in the way it deals with Tim O'Brien's fiction. An important part of her reading of *Going After Cacciato* focuses on the character of Sarkin Aung Wan, who appears as an almost absurd addendum to the group of American soldiers traveling the length of Asia on their way toward Paris. Kinney reads her as an important piece of the fantasy that Paul Berlin so elaborately constructs: "In spite of the scrupulous avoidance of the traditional signs of domination in sex and Sarkin's vocal expression of her dreams of life in Paris, her character always verges on the idealized, transnational, and transhistorical Western fantasy of the Asian woman as supreme servant, the 'geisha.' . . . As refugee, she should represent what the war has done to the Vietnamese, but this crucial point is ultimately displaced by Paul Berlin's need for her to recognize what the war has done to him, to cleanse and heal his symbolically wounded body."[31] Particularly important for my purposes is the way Kinney's reading of the gender dynamic foregrounds its vital connection to the epistemic dimension of American imperial representations. Although O'Brien's handling of point of view in *Going After Cacciato* initiates a sophisticated critique of the epistemological assumptions behind U.S. militarism, as I have argued, all of these American texts reinforce the epistemic privilege of the white American male. At the same time, an exacerbated ambivalence reaching the level of menace inheres in their portrayal of the prototypical figure of the Asian woman, whose transnational status makes her simultaneously unknowing and unknowable. This combination of menace and inscrutability is summed up in the question that Paul Berlin imagines asking: "Did their women really carry razor blades in their vaginas, booby traps for dumb GIs?"[32] As such, Freud's metaphor of the female body as the "dark continent" laps itself in the American imperial imagining of the Asian woman—because the continent and the woman's body are so intertwined, in fact virtually inextricable, in the American Cold War consciousness.

Out of this U.S. emphasis a broad international concern with the compromised or "fallen" sexuality of the Asian woman has emerged, so that even Duong in her novel *No Man's Land* presents a sex worker in a minor role, a "flat character," who offers the protagonist who comes to her in despair nothing more than a reminder of his dissatisfaction, and eventually conspires to rob him. In spite of her limited role in the novel's larger architecture, she constitutes a small reinforcement of a nationalist myth of the prostitute that sits uneasily within the novel's broad dismantling of the myth of the great victory. That is, Duong's novels systematically critique Vietnamese nationalism but leave a space open for that nationalism's conception of the sex worker. Indeed, there is an elusive presence of the Asian prostitute in much of the literature of the female warrior discussed above, nearly always as a fallen woman, who provides a contrast to the national hero that furthers the country's historical destiny. Tu and Tuyet, for example, declare explicitly the origins of the phenomenon in Vietnamese history: "Beggars and prostitutes were vivid images of the benefits of the kind of civilization brought by the colonialists,"[33] and even Turner states in the final pages of her study that by the 1990s, "Vietnamese women [had] become commodities in an international market," adding that feminists with whom she speaks in Hanoi "view this trade as shameful for all Vietnamese women, a betrayal of everything they have fought for."[34] Scholars distinguish between sex work and human trafficking, separate phenomena with distinct ramifications. The only connection here is the way a cross-section of women represent—through either the extent of their exploitation or their lumpen comportment—a direct threat to postwar Vietnamese nationalism in a wide variety of critical discourses, including Karnow's comments with which this chapter began.

However, a recent ethnography focusing on Ho Chi Minh City / Saigon (the putative capital of Vietnam's sex industry) between 2008 and 2013 offers an alternative critical discourse for framing Vietnamese women within the region's post-American-war history. Kimberly Hoang's *Dealing in Desire: Asian Ascendancy, Western Decline, and the Hidden Currencies of Global Sex Work* cites scholarship that connects the rise of the sex industry in Southeast Asia to the U.S. war effort, pointing out that between 1962 and 1975, a "massive injection of U.S. capital into Vietnam triggered the large-scale growth of prostitution, not only in South Vietnam, but also in other parts of Southeast Asia, as outlets for rest and recreation (R&R) were established to entertain foreign soldiers."[35] Thus, Hoang contextualizes Paul Bowles's complaint in his letters from Thailand that American G.I.s and their Thai "floozies" were crowding around his hotel and disrupting the scenery. Generally, both these statements point to a significant cultural reality: the American war in Vietnam offers an obvious example of the way U.S. imperial culture influenced the Global South during and after the Cold War. Its military interventions, financial engagements, cultural infusions, and unavoidable human presence inevitably visited a historical rupture upon the region; still, this historical rupture did not halt the dynamism of local geohistorical change, even though American representations often present U.S. influence as doing so.

The case of the Vietnamese sex worker is a good illustration. It is acknowledged as partially or mostly created by French colonialism but especially by U.S. intervention, and Americans and other Westerners may still understand its character as defined by the upheaval and tragedy of the war years. Hoang's research offers a counterpoint, showing the industry's evolution into a complex marketplace with multiple levels, including—in its more lucrative manifestations—a purely Asian environment catering to rich businessmen visiting from richer Asian nations, to members of the Vietnamese local elite, or to "Viet Kieu," returning Vietnamese who have achieved success in the diaspora. Americans and other Westerners—especially tourists on a budget but also some businessmen—still appear on the scene as clients in the Vietnamese sex industry, but they occupy the less lucrative level of the business culture.[36] Their position in this hierarchy still allows Americans in contemporary Vietnam to nurture and maintain a certain idea of Vietnam's poverty, dependence, and need for American salvation.

The contemporary tradition of the American "Third World" novel that I have traced back to Bowles offers an alternative, clashing engagement with sex work in Southeast Asia after the American war through the work of William T. Vollmann. Vollmann writes as a prolific iconoclast, insisting on technical innovation in his writing that builds on the formal concerns of the postmodern fiction tradition of Burroughs, Pynchon, Gaddis, Acker, and Barth; this attention to technique is combined with a relentless incorporation of the marginalized as characters and subject matter, bringing recurring attention to themes of ethics, epistemology, and U.S. nationalism. Although his appeal has a subcultural element, he has also now garnered a National Book Award, a Whiting Award for fiction, a bevy of important nominations, and several high-profile features in the pages of the *New Yorker*, the *New York Times*, and other prominent periodicals, making it increasingly difficult to study him as a renegade outsider.[37] He has even been grouped with Jonathan Franzen, Richard Powers, Dave Eggers, and David Foster Wallace as the most prominent figures in a literary school designated as "post-postmodernism."[38] This cultural code switching between the countercultural, the elite, and the mainstream is characteristic of the U.S. literary tradition I have been mapping. Vollmann's engagement with U.S. nationalism through its literary canon and its global settings—especially in those of his works that draw on his intrepid new journalism-style travels through the Global South—mark him as a particularly important figure in the recent history of the American "Third World" novel. In several of his works—including an early essay in *Spin* magazine, in which he saves/buys a Cambodian sex worker and confronts the father he accuses of selling her, and a chapter in his ambitious globally scaled *The Atlas*—he draws on experience with Southeast Asian sex workers. In his experimental and autobiographical novel composed of stories, *Butterfly Stories* (1993), this subject matter constitutes the primary focus.

Butterfly Stories begins with a short story about a boy who is bullied at school and eventually is saved by a strong girl. After she vanquishes his older male tormenter, the boy begins to pine for her. This story introduces the main character as an alter ego of the author, presenting him initially as performing and raising the issues of masculinity in the postmodern gender system and of the very quixotic quest (in the case of this "Butterfly Boy" protagonist) for a love whose depth is marked by its transcendence of traditional romantic categories. Unorthodox love continues as a theme in the second story. The boy has grown into a young adult and during a backpacking trip through Europe falls hard for a woman he believes to be a lesbian, until, near the culmination of the story, she hooks up with a pugilistic young German man. The narrative then moves to Thailand and Cambodia in a long story that takes up the majority of the text. The butterfly boy is now "the Journalist," traveling through the region and pursuing prostitutes alongside a photographer, in events that closely parallel Vollmann's personal narrative in his *Spin* essay about a trip through Thailand and Cambodia with photographer Ken Miller. In this section of the narrative, the protagonist develops an intense attachment to a Cambodian sex worker named Vanna, upon whom he projects emotions radically inappropriate for the social context. The photographer's role in this drama is to mock him and provide a more brutal masculinist counterpoint, leading to critical comparisons between this journey and that of the original Quixote with Sancho Panza. The later, shorter stories that conclude the novel follow the protagonist's return to the United States and his disillusionment with American bourgeois normativity, expressed through the breakup of his marriage and his frustration with complacent and comfortable American editors. He seeks solace in Bay Area prostitutes, but ultimately, only reuniting with Vanna will do. He learns that she has disappeared, but he returns to Southeast Asia anyway to look for her and is ultimately reunited with her in a brief and elusive dream sequence.

In several ways, *Butterfly Stories* can be read as an extension of the American "Third World" novel tradition into the discourse of the Southeast Asian sex trade as well as an American "post-postmodern" aesthetic. Vollmann seems persistently to invite comparison with canonical American male writers, as evidenced by the incessant references to Melville, Pynchon, and others on the jacket covers of his books. In fact, rich possibilities for entering his at times proliferating and confusing body of work can be found through reading his texts as writing back to earlier American authors. Hemingway strikes me as a particularly useful counterpoint for his writing set in the lands of the "Other," including his *The Afghanistan Picture Show*. In these works, Vollmann envelops the central narrative consciousness in a masculinity that subverts the Hemingwayesque through its total emptying of any trace of bravado. Examples from *Butterfly Stories* are the protagonist's hiding behind a girl who defends him from the playground bully in the opening story, and later, his repeatedly being passed over by the prettier Thai prostitutes, who always prefer the more handsome and cavalier photographer. At times, he reaches for a Hemingway-type bravado that borders on self-mockery, as when he notices scars on Vanna's body and thinks to himself: "If he could have gotten into his hands the people who'd done that to her, he would have killed them."[39]

But to read Vollmann as writing back to the Bowles novel also proves critically rich. Like Bowles, Vollmann uses travel far outside the commonplace circuits as a way to critique normative bourgeois values back home. Bowles wants to move across to the Other culture but finds his various strategies, including travel, music, sex, and translation, limited in their potential for cultural "penetration." Vollmann's impulse is similar, but his centering of sexuality goes farther. *Butterfly Stories* is set at the nadir of the initial widespread cultural awareness of AIDS and HIV, and its main character is open—seemingly even proud—about flaunting the rules disseminated for avoiding the contagion, as in the following exchange between himself and an American doctor that takes place after his return from Asia:

> How many sexual partners did you say you've had in the last month?
> Seven, the journalist said. No, eight. No, nine.
> Well, now, said the doctor. I think that puts you in our highest risk group, right in this red area at the top of our AIDS thermometer. Did you know the sexual histories of all your partners?
> Oh, I know their histories alright.[40]

This exchange depicts the doctor's deep concern with AIDS as a marker of thinly veiled prudish American values that the journalist wishes to flout. Throughout the Thailand and Cambodia scenes, descriptions of the sex act are ubiquitous, detailed, and appear to be highly insincere and performative at the emotional level.[41] It is as though Bowles's suggestive mentions of sexuality as a culmination of the attempt to go beyond normative American culture are being radically exposed in a manner that makes the complete embrace of the other seem utterly possible but profoundly futile as a means for deep engagement.

The use of point of view and focalization within the text is also telling. For all the celebration in critical writing of Vollmann's technical innovation, his early work has no compunction about funneling everything through one main character—an antiestablishment white male. The experience of the sexuality, geography, and history of Southeast Asia—*setting*, in general terms—comes to the reader unapologetically through this monolithic filter, and the meaning of the text ultimately returns to this individual subject. A very insightful overview of Vollmann's work mentions ethics as one of the central questions raised by his work.[42] Still, the question of ethics, at least in *Butterfly Stories*, returns exclusively, for these critics, to the moral choices faced by the American male without a tether in a new global environment. What is *his* responsibility to the prostitutes that surround him in a bar in Phnom Penh? This question, centered as it is in the subjectivity of the American protagonist, seems to encompass what is called ethics in Vollmann criticism.

In *The Spider's House*, Bowles's novel of the Moroccan independence struggle, Third World nationalism is depicted as fatuous, venal, and decadent. In spite of the novel's subject matter, Moroccan nationalism plays a relatively marginal role, ultimately seeming a threat as much to native Moroccan authenticity as to French occupation. In *Going After Cacciato*, O'Brien moves Vietnamese nationalism even farther to the margins of the action, which focuses directly on the consciousness of the American soldier Paul Berlin and only refers to Ho Chi Minh or the North Vietnamese Army as impenetrable specters that haunt his consciousness from the distant margins. In *Butterfly Stories*, local politics exists only in misty references to the atrocities of Pol Pot in Cambodia, as prostitutes carry scars that trouble the Journalist's imagination and disappear in a manner suggestive of relocation or internment. At times, the political history of the region is fodder for mockery of the renegade Americans, as in an encounter with Cambodian officials who stop the Photographer from taking pictures of Soviet weaponry, provoking him to respond: "What are we doing here when we could be fucking whores?" In the same sequence, they are given a tour, including "waist-high green .107 shells, captured exploded Khmer Rouge trucks with bullet holes in the Chinese starred windshields, golden narrow AK-47 bullets," resulting in a predictable response from the Journalist: "He kept thinking of whores!"[43] In the world of this text, nationalist politics in the Global South is more extreme and menacing, but also more marginal to the actual stage of the action.

These uncertain, fleeting references to national politics through encounters with officials and dream sequences reinforce the central problem of the organizing male consciousness: how to know the Other. This is another point on which the ultra-contemporary post-postmodernist represents continuity rather than innovation. Vollmann virtually plagiarizes Flaubert, whose famous trip through Egypt is thoroughly explicated by Said in chapter 2 of *Orientalism*. Both Vollmann and Flaubert write lyrically and provocatively about the sublime institution that is prostitution. They center their sojourn around prostitutes, and they find themselves disarmed by the inscrutability of their sex partners. The more the prostitute is penetrated physically, the more difficult she is to penetrate cognitively. Thus, she represents an affront to the Western traveler's sense of himself as knowledge producer. In Flaubert's writings about his favorite prostitute in Egypt, Kuchuk Hanem, he responds to his French lover's jealousy, which she expresses after his return to France:

> Set your mind at rest, and at the same time correct your ideas about the Orient. Be convinced that she felt nothing at all: emotionally, I guarantee; and even physically, I strongly

> suspect. . . . You and I are thinking of her, but she is certainly not thinking of us. We are weaving an aesthetic around her, whereas this particular very interesting tourist who was vouchsafed the honors of her couch, has vanished from her memory completely, like many others.[44]

The female other in this passage is mostly a mystery, with the exception that Flaubert is certain of her limited cognitive complexity and emotional depth. In this sense, the Flaubertian radical Romantic strain in the Orientalist discourse Said traces becomes central to the woman-centering discourse of U.S. imperial culture. Here the Journalist thinks about his quest for Vanna, his Cambodian prostitute/wife:

> He knew now that no answering letter from her would ever come, but if he went to Cambodia and found her in the disco or in some anonymous rice field whose corpse-mud and bone fragments oozed between her toes, then she'd smile at him in just the same way, so gently and lovingly and trustingly and sadly; and if he went away or didn't come in the first place she'd never think about him again.[45]

This passage reinforces instances of misunderstanding or partial comprehension between the Journalist, the Photographer, and the local sex workers throughout the text. Their interactions thus prove the most persistent exemplification of the frustrated desire of the renegade American male artist to possess the world cognitively and epistemologically.

Vollmann has explicitly denounced U.S. imperialism in his nonfiction writings and has spoken in interviews of the encounter with and ethical responsibility toward "the Other" as a central concern of his writing. On this point, comparing *Butterfly Stories* to Hoang's *Dealing in Desire* proves useful. In her research, Hoang finds that Vietnamese sex workers in Ho Chi Minh City target the Western male's idea of Vietnam as poor and dependent and of Vietnamese women as in need of salvation, exploiting this attitude in the way they dress and carry themselves and in sometimes exaggerating their financial need.[46] Hoang's study presents a series of representations that show how agency operates within an exploitative global capitalist system that is difficult to capture from inside the consciousness of the American artist, even one who is radical and anti-imperialist. In this sense, such research constitutes a challenge to the claim by Vollmann critics that he represents prostitutes in a way that manifests an "ongoing insistence on agency."[47] The comparison provokes questions around the nature of agency itself that are central to the debates within transnational feminism I have cited here. The potential role of U.S. institutions, artists, and intellectuals in underscoring such subaltern agency is unquestionably challenged by the traces of nationalistic U.S. history that mark them.

IV. WOMEN, DEVELOPMENT, AND THE AMERICAN "THIRD WORLD" NOVEL

The 1990s were a period of transition in global culture. What remained resilient was U.S. global hegemony. Perhaps for that reason, many aspects of postdevelopment global culture, particularly within the United States, continued relatively unmarked by global developments like the collapse of the Soviet Union and the diminishment of global communism. In the United States, an us-against-them binarism still characterized views of the global, and the idea that promoting open markets could be liberating for the peoples of the world endured. So too did the idea that global women needed to be saved. This notion applied particularly to women who were Muslim, nonwhite, or poor, and it was applied to them even more hysterically with the onset of the American "War on Terror."

Indeed, the figure of the Muslim woman became the symbol whose exploitation after September 11, 2001, facilitated wars in Afghanistan and Iraq. As in the Southeast Asian context, growing out of the war in Vietnam, the emphasis on the Muslim woman's sexuality is once again present, although in this case a blatant discursive bouleversement means that the threatening, sexualized female bodies in Indochina are now bodies denied sexual liberation by purdah, burqa, seclusion, honor killing, and so on. The freedom bordering on chaos in East Asia shows its other face as a lack of requisite freedom in Africa and the Middle East.

Scholars have documented the extent to which "stories about oppressed Muslim women" proliferated in U.S. news media before and especially after 9/11/2001.[48] A phalanx of "native informants"—Muslim women based in North America who write and pontificate on television about the deplorable victimization of women in Muslim culture, the urgency with which Islam must be reformed, and the need for Muslim women to be saved—become instant celebrities in popular media because their opinions reinforce stereotypical thinking about "the Other."

These pundits, who have not shied away in some instances from advocating war and invasion as a mechanism to save Muslim women, include Nonie Darwish, Wafa Sultan, Ayaan Hirsi Ali, and Irshad Manji, the latter two monotonously permanent fixtures on U.S. cable news. The polemics of this group of pundits and the neocons who enable them have been answered by many of the scholars cited in this chapter, including Lila Abu-Lughod, Mohja Kahf, Saba Mahmood, and Elora Shehabuddin. In the case of the Muslim world, the fixation on what might be called "the woman question" in U.S. imperial culture has been extreme, even when compared to other regions; still, a substratum of themes undergirds the regional variation in this discourse, with salvation and normativity perhaps the strongest ones. Thus, in the writings of Irshad Manji, development is offered as an alternative to war as a means for saving women. In her carefully documented and argued dissection of the woman-question punditocracy, Shehabuddin shows the direct parallel between Manji's enthusiasm for microcredit and the discourse of George W. Bush, who referenced microlending as a mechanism for global female empowerment in March 2004. Shehabuddin comments, "Just as Manji chooses to ignore the vast critical feminist literature on the Islamic world, as well as on Israel and the West, she—and the White House—seem blissfully oblivious to the scholarship produced over the past two decades on the dangers of seeing microcredit as a panacea."[49] An example of the scholarship to which Shehabuddin refers is the ethnographic research of U.S.-based Bangladeshi scholar Lamia Karim, who has documented the way poor local recipients subvert the woman-centered aspect of microcredit programs. According to Karim, women come forward to collect the loans but then take the money straight to their husbands, who control and spend it. "In my research area, rural men laughed when they were asked whether the money belonged to their wives. They pointedly remarked that 'since their wives belonged to them, the money rightfully belongs to them.' Women also told me that as a Bangladeshi woman, I should know that they would give the money to their husbands who labor outside the home."[50] The picture that emerges from this research shows a performance of women's empowerment in which international NGOs are complicit in maintaining a certain image.

Karim connects the origins of woman-centered development, sometimes referred to as WID (women in development) and most famously embodied in the Grameen Bank founded by Bangladeshi economist and Nobel laureate Muhammad Yunus, with the decline of State power and social movements in Bangladesh during the 1970s after Bangladesh won independence from Pakistan, thus reinforcing its connection to the rise of neoliberalism. In the context of her article broadly criticizing this hysterically popular model for rural development and female empowerment, Karim acknowledges some of the Grameen Bank's achievements, which include proving that the poor are generally credit worthy in spite of their lack of collateral, and performing an educative function regarding personal finance among rural women.[51] Still, the overall effect of its microlending programs is to weaken the State, facilitating NGOs forming "a shadow state in Bangladesh . . . able to exercise tremendous control over the lives of the poor."[52] Corollary to this conclusion are other problems with the bank, such as the effective stifling of all dissent and even harming the social position of some of the poor women it claims to empower, who become caught between an unaltered patriarchal regulation at home and the equally inflexible demands of the microcredit system.[53]

Still, the idea of WID is powerful in its secular mission of saving poor, dark women from patriarchy, and challenges to the model have emerged only recently in corners of the academic scholarship. During the 1990s and early 2000s in particular, the microlending model enjoyed an unchallenged global popularity. According to Karim, by the late 1990s, the bank had been replicated in fifty-four countries, maintaining a rate of borrowing to women that rose to 94 percent.[54] In this context, the model won praise from critic of Islam Manji and global reformer George W. Bush. In more thoughtful corners of American culture, the literary novel as it engaged with the global also absorbed the issue of WID. Specifically, the former Peace Corps worker turned novelist, Norman Rush, who has set most of his fiction in Botswana around the twilight of the Cold War, offers a counterpoint to Vollmann. It would be inaccurate to say the two writers represent poor women in the postcolony in the same way. Indeed, the language, setting, and characters in their fiction are decidedly distinct. What connects them is the consistent tension present in American fiction since at least the early fiction of Bowles: frank critique of American nationalism but inability to make the Other conform to an American mind. In this instance, that tension emerges through a fixation on the postcolonial female body.

At first glance, Rush seems, compared to Vollmann, more interested in sociohistorical subject matter, presented with what appears initially to be little formal or stylistic adventurousness. His major work, *Mating*

(1991), is a nearly five-hundred-page novel narrated exclusively through the first-person voice of the main female character, a white American anthropologist doing fieldwork in Botswana. If Vollmann's appeal is subcultural and (in a fledgling way) academic, Rush's short story collection *Whites* (1986) and *Mating* were both celebrated in major American book reviews, with the novel also receiving the National Book Award and mention in the *New York Times* list of the best American novels written in the quarter century beginning in 1980. Thus, his natural home is in the elite literary fiction branch of mass culture. As with many works written in the American 'Third World' novel tradition, a love relationship is at the center of the story line, but unlike Vollmann's iconoclastic couplings with the subaltern, here the relationship involves two highly educated, heterosexual white Americans surrounded by an African rural setting. Still, the narrative shares with Vollmann's work the manner in which the psychosexual is tied to the geographic from the beginning, as the narrator ends the opening chapter by stating: "I was feeling sexually alert. There's no place like Gaborone for a detached white woman with a few social graces."[55]

Shortly after this opening, the narrator meets Nelson Denoon, a charismatic and mysterious figure whose reputation precedes him. Denoon has founded a utopian commune at the edge of the Kalahari Desert that is run by African women, many of them outcasts from their home village. Female empowerment, solar power, and consultative governance are among the main features driving this enterprise, the success of which promises—at least in Denoon's mind and in many conventional thinkers' fears—to revolutionize traditional ideas about development. Denoon initially resists the narrator's overtures, making it clear that there is no place for another white American in his model community, but she overcomes his suspicions via a daring trek across the desert, at the end of which she arrives at the putative matriarchal utopia called Tsau in dire condition. Once she is nursed to health, the two develop a passionate romance, full of humor as well as emotional, sexual, and intellectual intensity, all played out against the backdrop of a utopian rural African community. But neither the harmonious relationship nor village harmony are fated to endure, and the last third of the novel accordingly chronicles the symbiotic discord in these two parallel spheres of the couple and the community.

Of the very few scholarly studies that treat *Mating*, Agbaw and Kiesinger's comparison between Denoon and Colonel Kurtz from *Heart of Darkness* is quite helpful. Their essay cites Rush's statement that he had abandoned an attempt at a novel in his youth because it was too derivative of Conrad and then goes on to point out a series of parallels between Kurtz and Denoon. Each can be described as "a visionary, with loose family ties in the West," each speaks in a voice that has an almost magical intoxicating effect on listeners, and each establishes a community made entirely of Africans and themselves.[56] Of value here is the way the critics willfully reverse the somewhat understandable emphasis in criticism of the novel on the relationship between the narrator and Denoon, treating it instead as a novel about Africa or, more properly, a novel about whites in Africa and their civilizing impulse, which continues into the age of Reagan and U.S. hegemony. Edward Said's comment that in André Gide's work, Algeria constitutes "an exotic locale for the western subject to work out their spiritual problems" offers an insight that might be broadly applied to an extensive bibliography of colonial discourse fictions, including most of Conrad and Bowles. And this tradition gets directly at one of the most stunning features of *Mating*: its ability to juxtapose an unusually detailed dissection of a relationship between two intelligent but spiritually restless white middle-class Americans with an almost equally detailed description of cultures, geographies, and political atmospheres in southern Africa as apartheid and the Cold War were dying off.

While critical discussion has emphasized continuities between *Mating* and earlier works set in Africa that depict "half a century of [British] fictional and non-fictional attempts to civilize Africa,"[57] the American "Third World" novel tradition is distinct—if related to—this older bibliography, which includes Conrad, Joyce Cary, and Graham Greene, and it is within this newer tradition that Rush's work fits more comfortably. The narrator and Denoon constitute a new type of Port and Kit, who also use the world and its native, darker, and less accessible recesses to reject American bourgeois life—in this case, represented by graduate school, the drudgery of dissertations, and the disengaged comfort of academia. Their commitment to the community of Tsau marks their distinction from a complacent America, drifting toward soft and hard forms of Reaganism. This solidarity—through American individualism that rejects America—draws the two together and cements their relationship for most of the novel. The African community of subaltern, rural, mostly female Africans around them functions as a marker of a singularity shared between Denoon and the narrator. That is, the detailed accounting of the African community does not prevent it from being displaced by the text's own economy.

The broad anticolonialism of the American "Third World" novel, marked most notably in the pivotal scene in *The Sheltering Sky*, in which a French officer interviews Port about the loss of his passport, reemerges with force in *Mating* in an interlude during the couple's happy time in Tsau. Suddenly, two British actors, a man and woman who seem to be a heterosexual couple but turn out to be a gay male / straight female pairing of professional partners, fly into the community as the result of a scheduling mishap by the British Council. They announce their intention to perform a series of scenes from Shakespeare for the benefit of the community. Their appearance provokes in Denoon, who is represented as extraordinarily well read and opinionated regarding every corner of global culture, a demonstration of unadulterated distaste for everything British (except Blake, whom he admires for his anti-British ideas). The obsolescence of British culture and attitudes are on full display in these scenes, but the text also uses them to delineate its neutral position regarding the potential for a new North-South relationship in the postcolonial era of U.S. hegemony. On the one hand, Denoon stages a brittle performance the night before the actors are to depart, in which they are forced to watch an all-African cast perform dramatic monologues describing Anglo-European colonialism's destruction of African culture; on the other, only a short time later, Denoon gets drunk with the visitors and bonds with them over a series of dubious themes, including their shared patriotism toward Ireland, the country of their mutual ancestry. Tellingly, the British man is a misogynist, and the moment of camaraderie between him and Denoon is ended by this irreconcilable ideological clash between the Brit's misogyny and Denoon's feminism. The American engagement with the global is represented here as more liberal and resilient in its woman-centered, heteronormative, development-oriented contemporaneity.

Contemporary though he is, Denoon's generally impressive encyclopedic knowledge of African and global cultures and politics is reminiscent of—but not directly parallel with—proto-ethnographic Orientalists like Edward William Lane. The connection with knowledge-fixated Orientalists like Lane suggests a shift away from the many American characters in the Bowles tradition who show an ignorance—often experienced as an obstacle—that endearingly separates them from the colonialists. Nelson Denoon is a specialist in everything; less an Orientalist than a super-pundit, who recalls Laroui's distinction between the European regionally focused philologist and the relocated U.S. academic generalist-expert. Denoon is fluent in Setswana and conversant in several other African languages and is deeply steeped in cultural habits, folklore, flora, fauna, and dress of the region, but he is also able to offer a highly educated opinion on seemingly any question of geopolitics or global culture that might arise. He is able to pun spontaneously on the name of a South African tribal chief[58] and discourse authoritatively on variations in global socialist movements, the merits of Hegelian philosophy, the damaging effects of Sinhalese being declared the national language of Sri Lanka, and the strengths and weaknesses of the Cuban revolutionary government. "Nelson liked to call Fidel Fidel Catastro,"[59] we are told, and in this joke more is revealed than a highly cerebral and politically aware sense of humor.

As with Castro's Cuba and Vietnam during the American war, Botswana's political cartography includes socialists with some hostility toward "the West." *Mating* consistently depicts the adherents of Boso, the main party representing the Left, as an artless obstacle to African enlightenment and progress. Adherents of the party are present when the narrator and Denoon first meet at a lecture he is giving in Gaborone, the capital; they are there to heckle and naysay but are struck dumb when he breaks into fluent Setswana. They reappear again, much later, in Tsau, which they have somehow infiltrated, and can be found working with the community's least progressive elements. There, they eventually succeed in their scheming to have Denoon exiled, making them the unmistakable villains of the piece. In sum, the Boso in the novel show the constant hostility in the tradition of the American "Third World" novel toward political action initiated from within local nationalisms. This is one of the features in which literary novels by American authors set in the Global South are uncharacteristically in lockstep with the foreign policy discourses of officialdom, including Washington Consensus, NGO, and development organizations.

Upon publication, a reviewer referred to the novel's stylistic tendency toward knowledge proliferation as follows: "Readers receive a palpable sense of having their education sternly tested—and expanded—by Mr. Rush's novel. Geography, history, political science, economics, literature, biology, popular culture and utter trivia—the narrator and her beloved Denoon hash everything out, and in doing so are encyclopedic in the extreme, segueing from bats to Boers to Borges to Botswana."[60] This quotation should be read as a statement of the text's relationship between content and form. The narrator's florid—at times garrulous—verbal style contrasts sharply with the post-Hemingway minimalist voice in Vollmann's *Butterfly Stories*, even though the contrast indicates a similar textual ideology. When the narrator of *Mating* comments that she "once said to Nelson that he should call Tsau Occam's torment instead, because he was always multiplying entities unnecessarily,"[61] her reference to the lack of parsimony seems to apply equally to the novel's prose and to its hero's cherished project.[62] Denoon's ideas and her language together constitute the entirety of the world created by the novel in a way that no proliferation of geographic and geopolitical references can disrupt. The result is a recentering of the seat of knowledge production that undercuts the pretensions surrounding "development" projects, the new mask of Western missionary discourse in the secular and postcolonial era.

O'Brien creates American GIs who openly fear the vaginas of the Vietnamese, while Vollmann attempts to dismantle this hyperrational and militaristic American male consciousness by luxuriating in Third World vaginas. In *Mating*, the African female form is an absent presence that functions as a distant catalyst. The narrator views Dineo, the chairperson of the committee that runs Tsau, as a potential rival. She is as beautiful and powerful as any of the women in the community, and she is a close ally of Denoon in the political struggles that develop in Tsau. Naturally, given the book's structure, she is—like all the African characters—fairly opaque to readers. Her background and personal history, her internal thoughts or feelings are never disclosed. This makes it particularly interesting that her sexuality seems to be such a live issue both within the narrator's head and between the narrator and Denoon. For example, in a confessional moment, Denoon explains that he released sexual tension before meeting the narrator by masturbating and visiting friends with whom he had arrangements in Gaborone, and then adds, "And the real question you want to ask me, and to which the answer is no, is if I slept with any woman in Tsau. So. And the beautiful Dineo is included in that."[63] The contrast between Denoon's attitude toward native sex and that of the journalist/husband in *Butterfly Stories* simply reinforces the political fixation with the postcolonial female body at various levels of U.S. globalist discourse.

A particularly striking scene, even in such a sprawling novel, occurs when Dineo seizes upon a private moment with the narrator to display her naked body. The narrator's first impression is that the goal of the display is to exhibit for her a scar showing a hysterectomy to make it clear that she is not a rival for Denoon's urge to mate. This guess is later partially confirmed, but in the moment, the narrative dwells on the immaculateness of the African female form, with particular attention shifted at one point to Dineo's "escutcheon," a term that is used to describe the female vagina several times. Still, in Dineo's case, the metaphor is interesting, perhaps infusing the descriptive rhetoric with classical connotations, but also suggesting a semblance of protection or impenetrability. Beyond the shield lies the chaotic; it is infinitely imagined and fixated upon with the ultimate aim of restoring order through the creation of knowledge.

V. CONCLUSION: THE MUSLIM WOMAN AS INTELLECTUAL

The move from Southeast Asia to the Muslim world to Africa does not necessarily constitute a smooth transition, but the ways in which the U.S.-centric lens overlaps discourses of women in the regions brings to the fore the special place of the postcolonial figure of woman in cultures of U.S. imperialism. The missionary impulse in both places recalls classical colonialism's commitment to the motto "White men are saving brown women from brown men." The centering of women in development discourse exemplifies this impulse. In fact, it is necessary to foreground "Third World" women as sex objects to facilitate the argument that they must be sexually liberated.[64] But postcolonial women are not only objects for pathos; they are also—to a traditional U.S. mindset—threatening. Their bodies, their psyches, and their anatomies appear to have the potential to disrupt the empire, so their very sexuality must be dissected to prepare for the anomy it prefigures.

This study has attempted to distinguish between popular culture in the United States, which so often embraces without compunction an unreconstructed nationalism, and the more nuanced U.S. cultures of literary fiction, criticism, poetry, art films. On the woman question—perhaps especially on the Muslim woman question—it can be particularly difficult to see any distance between popular and elite cultures in the United States, so comprehensive is the acceptance of the notion that postcolonial women need to be saved. Only a handful who seek out the scholarship of the cadre of intrepid transnational feminists who attempt to present alternative views from within the scholarly community might think of the question distinctively. American literary fiction often operates by either accepting the basic premises behind the woman question, while aiming thoughtful critiques of U.S. globalism at other aspects of American hegemony, or by fashioning representations that critique the premises as empty Americanism without imagining their relationship to the local or to alternative possibilities.

Over the course of the Cold War, as a global American hegemony became entrenched, the global force of U.S. culture increased. In reading cultures of the Global South, this influence presents a dilemma for critics. To overemphasize U.S. imperialism and American influence in readings of literature and other arts means effacing local genealogies of culture that must be accessed to read with a contextualized understanding. Still, ignoring the specter of the United States in post–World War II global cultures creates its own pitfalls. In particular, too narrow a focus on local cultural influence may not only yield an equally skewed reading in a world where even remote villages are affected by developers, NGOs, and commercial trends, but also risks ignoring the extent to which the contemporary world is unevenly developed, marked by powerful elites, and concentrated to a far greater degree in certain areas, with extensive potential for exploitation across regional boundaries.

The Arab intellectual has been emphasized in this study as a particularly repressed figure, at the level of and closely related to the liberated Arab woman. In chapter 2, I attempted to trace a critical discourse about Orientalism and theories of representation whose trajectory was Arab world / North African even though it was regularly and increasingly in conversation with global ideas. In 1998, Jenine Abboushi sparked controversy among scholars of Arab literature with a satisfyingly daring but also reckless argument in the pages of the *Times Literary Supplement* that Arab writers were being "forced" to write for translation.[65] The article provoked interesting responses, notably Michelle Hartman's discussion of the power of translation into English to create its own outcomes. Hartman's focus is literary fiction and classical poetry by Arab women writers/poets, a case in which publishing, translating, and critical writing come into direct engagement with Western idées fixes about Muslim/Arab women. The agency of the Arab author is put to the test in a reception environment that promotes "the sociological rather than literary value of Arab women's writing in the English-speaking world."[66] This dynamic has been studied as well by Mohja Kahf, who has delineated the way a politicized understanding of Arab women shaped the English translation of the pioneering Egyptian feminist Huda Sha'rawi, and Marilyn Booth, who has written from personal experience about the way careful translations can be transformed through redaction and rearranging by publishers whose assumptions about how to package women in the Arab world cannot be shaken by actual Arab women writing.[67] What each of these critical projects—including Abboushi-

Dallal's—calls attention to is the global circulation of texts by Arab women within a polysystem that is neither neutral nor innocuous.

The sexuality of Arab women is very much at issue in these competing discourses, which pit an idea of women as imprisoned and suppressed against more locally sensitive attempts to understand the complexities, contradictions, and contingencies within the social history of gender systems in the Arab world. Moroccan Fatema Mernissi's *The Veil and the Male Elite: A Feminist Interpretation of Women's Rights in Islam* is a helpful text for disrupting the stereotype of the female Muslim captive. Through an analysis that is both historical and textual, Mernissi offers a claim that cannot be fit within the logic of Western views of gender systems in the Arab world, arguing that discussion in Islamic texts around questions of the organization of the sexes in social spaces grows out of a healthy acknowledgment of the power of human sexuality. Mernissi's larger argument is that texts and traditions in Islam contain within themselves feminist values that have been skewed by a history of masculinist traditionalism in local interpretation. Critics who have written about Mernissi have called attention to the way this argument for a lost feminism inhering within Islamic tradition almost directly contradicts her first book, an equally meticulous study of Muslim patriarchy entitled *Beyond the Veil: Male-Female Dynamics in Modern Muslim Society*. Reza Afshari, for example, sides with the earlier text, decrying an absence of modernity in Islamic thought, then goes on to claim, "That book [*Beyond the Veil*] was a positive step toward creating such a modern ideology; Mernissi's new 'feminist interpretation of women's rights in Islam' is, I am afraid, a step backward from that intended goal."[68] More recently, the Morocco-based feminist Raja Rhouni has argued in a book-length study of Mernissi's critical work that what so many commentators saw as the contradictions between Mernissi's earlier secular writing and her later Islamic feminism misunderstands the way the two stages reinforce one another as complementary synchronic and diachronic critiques. Rhouni insightfully points to the way Mernissi's early work exposes the harmful effects of development programs on women's lives when she writes, "One of Mernissi's aims is to shift the gender issue away from rhetoric, that is, its depiction as a religious or cultural issue and to compel decision makers to confront what they try to avoid—its economic nature."[69] Still, in Rhouni's account, all discussions of Mernissi's project must openly acknowledge the distinctiveness of her earlier and later approaches to the problem of women's unequal position in North African society.[70] Rhouni insists that both play a role in Mernissi's construction of a regionally located, antifoundationalist feminist thought. What might be given more emphasis in Rhouni's helpful reading are the global dynamics of reception that every Third World feminist intellectual must navigate.

For example, *Beyond the Veil* and *The Veil and the Male Elite* should both be considered as texts that address an audience. *Beyond the Veil*, written originally in English—a language less familiar than Arabic or French in Morocco and the Arab Maghreb—studies forthrightly the social structures that reinforce male dominance in the Middle East and North Africa. *The Veil and the Male Elite* then steps back from the contemporary era to argue that feminist readings of Islamic tradition are justified, even though they are not given a fair hearing by misogynist male scholars within the Muslim tradition. Rouni mentions the direct influence of Abdelkabir Khatibi on Mernissi's thought, particularly in her adaptation of his method of "double critique."[71] This linkage is fully justified by the personal connection of the two thinkers and reinforced by the fact that Khatibi seems most consistently committed to feminist concerns of all the male Arab intellectuals cited in the intellectual genealogy I traced in chapter 2. Still, Mernissi's initial engagement with questions of development and her later emphasis on historicism connect her work equally to that of Laroui and al-Jabari. Her "secular" and "feminist" studies combined suggest a dialectic between critique and historicism that recalls the methods of Maghreb/Arab intellectuals in the Laroui tradition. But her particular concern with feminism and feminist scholarship in the Arab region exacerbates the Arab intellectual's inside/outside problem, with which the feminist critics cited at the beginning of this section engage. Winning notoriety in Europe and North America as an astute critic of Arab patriarchy provokes the Arab intellectual to rethink her vision, and it is not unusual for such notoriety to lead a writer like Mernissi to develop her analysis in the direction of non-Arab audiences by writing of the untapped potential within Arabo-Islamic writing or by incorporating a critique of *global* patriarchy, including the United States and Europe in their imperial cultures, as a supplement to the more regionally focused analysis. (This type of trajectory might be contrasted with U.S.-based pundits whose reaction to a celebratory reception from U.S. markets is to accelerate their propagation of Islamophobia.)

Generally, Mernissi proves the most telling major feminist example of al-Afghani's philosophical principle that ideas can transcend neither their geopolitical context of origin nor their sites of reception. Another

Muslim feminist example is discussed by Shehabbudin, who contrasts U.S.-based native informant pundits to the Bangladeshi novelist Taslima Nasreen. Shehabbudin's reading exposes the elements of fame and the global reach of a literary or intellectual reputation as highly dependent upon the willingness of the feminist intellectual to take a series of positions that aggrandize the U.S. in its foreign policy aspirations.

The novels of the accomplished Egyptian anglophone novelist and human rights activist Ahdaf Soueif serve as another telling example. Her debut novel, *In the Eye of the Sun*, exposed masculinism in social relationships in Egypt, receiving positive reviews, and was followed by *The Map of Love*, a historical novel also about relationships, this time set against the backdrop of the impacts of Zionism and colonialism on the region. There is an analogy between the early trajectory of the careers of Mernissi and Soueif. Their keener sensitivity to the reception of their work both inside and outside the Arab world, as intellectuals writing in European languages without losing connection to the Arab-speaking milieu, results in a movement away from a critique of regional patriarchy toward a critique of both local and global patriarchies.

Even in critiquing "Islamic feminists," Afshari acknowledges the issues of reception and circulation, noting in the case of the prominent Egyptian feminist Laila Ahmed that "the factor that helped to bring about a shift of emphasis (from critical feminism to Islamic reformism) in Ahmed's writing was, she explained, her realization of the depth of anti-Arab racism in the United States."[72] Fully taking into account such evidence makes suspect attempts to read these writers strictly in terms of one sphere of reception.

But Mernissi remains a uniquely clarifying figure because of her position as a public intellectual, her placement within the Laroui-Khatibi Moroccan intellectual line, and the specific interplay between the dynamics of reception and the evolution of her diverse career. Rhouni calls attention to the importance of the reception of Mernissi's work in shaping her projects: "In 2001, she published another book in the United States, *Scheherazade Goes West*, a book on western constructions of the harem, which is said to be triggered by the western reception of her novel, *Dreams of Trespass*."[73] Part literary criticism, part memoir, *Scheherazade Goes West* is written in English for a general audience and argues that the Western reception of the famous heroine of the *1,001 Nights* has systematically stripped her of her intelligence and artistry, substituting instead a woman who exudes sexuality and is devoid of anything else. Her point of departure is her observation that during a series of interviews in Europe about the book she had written describing growing up in a harem she realized that "my harem was associated with a historical reality. Theirs was associated with artistic images [that] reduced women to odalisques."[74] In other words, the very argument of the book raises the issue of reception across the divide between cultures of the North Atlantic and those of Middle East and North Africa, and its specific concern is the reception of women's bodies. Furthermore, the content of Scheherazade's reception in Europe and America manifests how for Arab women, the figuration of the Arab lands as lands-of-no-ideas has its own stark application. Mernissi's main claim is that odalisques are Arab women imagined by Western men as wearing no clothes and having no intellect. This connects the representation of women directly to the creation of a no-idea-producing-area identified by Laroui. It illustrates the way the view of the captive woman plays a key role in authorizing Europeans and Americans to "believe that Muslim men and women never dream of reform or aspire to be modern."[75] And it demonstrates precisely how the figure of the female intellectual disrupts the stereotyped Arab female captive in a manner highly comparable to the woman warrior's disruption of the East Asian prostitute.

Each of these examples suggests a dialectic between disruptive assertions of agency and the smothering mechanisms of global patriarchy within which such assertions circulate. A central component of U.S. imperial culture is its acumen in denying its own existence, a denial that is fairly distinct within the global history of imperial cultures and presents special problems for global cultures influenced by Americanism. It is possible to read the actions of a female warrior in North Vietnam battling the U.S. military, a sex worker in Ho Chi Minh City asserting her right to control her finances and her sexuality, or a female author in the Arab world attempting to represent human experience with an aesthetic verisimilitude as asserting agency, as scholars cited herein have brilliantly managed to do. Still, these disruptions happen increasingly within a global context that is unequal and not easily disrupted. Indeed, their resilience is recalled in Abu-Lughod's comment that "Islamic movements themselves have arisen in a world shaped by the intense engagements of Western powers in Middle Eastern lives."[76] The transition from the Cold War to the War on Terror has in many ways reinforced this global context.

I have focused in this chapter on representations of female bodies and the way an emphasis on their materiality can assert a space beyond their absorption into a totalizing system of representation that can only etherize women into figures/figments in the American imagination. In turning to the post–Cold War period, I move from the scale of the body to the scale of the nation—again with emphasis on its materiality, its geography, its earth—as a mechanism for reading the contemporary period, which is simultaneously the most chaotic and the most normed.

CHAPTER 5
Space

In Spite of the Land

Partitions, Terror Wars, and the New Idealism

I. INTRODUCTION: THE IDEA OF EMPIRE

As I have discussed, events ending the Cold War also engendered another epochal boost to the U.S. position as a global hegemon. At the end of World War II a series of developments—the Potsdam conference, the Marshall Plan, the crumbling of European colonialism, the onset of the Cold War, and the initiation of "development" programs and institutions—suddenly elevated the United States to a superpower, and this shift influenced the ideas and culture of the United States, including its literary novels, which suddenly started exploring more global settings. The end of the Cold War and the collapse of the Soviet Union, which had been for decades the closest thing to a rival for the United States, further elevated American global power and influence. Suddenly, the United States was the world's only "hyperpower," a development that led—as it did at the beginning of the Cold War—to much reconsideration among American public intellectuals about the future world that the United States would dominate. In general, an American way of dealing with the world through abstraction (enabled by the myth of a grand and global wrestling match between two superpowers during the Cold War) was reinforced in a post–Cold War era of heightened abstraction among U.S. intellectuals.

Outside the metropolitan network of the United States, the new realities engendered substantial, often traumatic realignments in the Global South, where small states that had always felt pressure to align with the United States now found it far more difficult to consider alternatives to cooperation with U.S. global hegemony. Of course, the counterexamples of independent nations in the postcolonial world that continued to pursue anti-American foreign policies—Iran, North Korea, Cuba, Venezuela—do come to mind, but on the whole, this handful of exceptions proves the rule of increasingly limited possibilities for international alignments in the unevenly developed world after 1990, when smaller states could be characterized as more or less pro-American but never part of a large anti-American bloc.

Broad cultural continuity between the Cold War and post–Cold War periods notwithstanding, one distinction between the two eras is a clearer focus on the Global South in American discourse after 1990. Previously, the United States was able to view Korea, Vietnam, Cuba, Angola, Chile, and Lebanon as pieces of a global struggle with the Soviet adversary. But the dissolution of the Soviet Union in late 1991, and the U.S.- and NATO-led Persian Gulf War the same year fashioned a new frame for globalists from various disciplines and observers from multiple perspectives. In the post–Cold War era, the main global rivalry would be a North-South rivalry that in many ways paralleled the old Cold War binarism that organized a complex world for Americans looking outward. At the level of intellectual culture, the moment of a war against a threat from the Global South that reintroduced binary global thinking turned on an abstraction. Oil reserves were very much at stake when Saddam Hussein's forces invaded Kuwait in August of 1989, but most American thinkers viewed the conflict more theoretically, as the introduction of a new historical epoch.

The end of the Cold War also dramatically influenced the diverse cultures of the Global South. Admittedly, the greatest shift in cultures of the postcolonial world had occurred long before the 1990s, during the spread of European colonialism. This process, which evolved over centuries and across continents, instilled in the societies of the Global South forms of capitalist underdevelopment, hybrid cultures marked by colonial languages and institutions, and dramatic discontinuities with older versions of local and regional cultural life. European colonialism created a rupture in postcolonial societies that disarticulated modern life's relationship to local cultural traditions. It is still erroneous, after colonialism, to say that there is one smooth, uninterrupted global culture; but it is at least as wrong to divide postcolonial societies into their cultural or civilizational essences, since everywhere now participates to some extent in a global capitalism that has shaped contemporary society. (The need for this balance between overgeneralizing globalism and overstating the enduring coherence of local "civilization" was completely missed by many U.S. intellectuals in the 1990s, as they argued heatedly about whether a new day of globalism had dawned or old recalcitrant traditions were preparing for counterrevolution.)

Although, generally speaking, the period since the end of the Cold War has not been nearly as dramatic as the era of European colonialism in its rearrangement of culture and society in the Global South, many cultures in the postcolonial world have evolved into weak states with even weaker civil societies. The legacy of European colonialism has gradually become a less urgent cultural issue with each succeeding generation in almost every society of the South, and the influence of Americanization (at the level of culture) and finance capital/neoliberalism (at the level of society and economics) has come more and more to the fore. Part of this change has been a tendency for weaker, unequally developed states to adopt economic policies that fit with a very American conception of how countries develop economically. The Global South makes its own policies with less autonomy and makes its national economies more vulnerable to U.S. and transnational corporation interests. The result is that U.S.-led North Atlantic cultures and Global South cultures are increasingly interrelated, specifically around questions of "development" (economics and finance capitalism) and "liberalism" (democracy, elections, and civil social movements).

I have emphasized throughout this book the way U.S. imperial culture characterizes itself by its own erasure, and notions of a "flat" or "unipolar" world that emerged in the United States after the fall of the wall recapitulated this camouflaging of imperialism. As the Cold War came to an end, far from engaging more deeply with circumstances of the local around the globe, U.S. media, as well as both popular and elite cultures, described the world in terms that were increasingly abstract. This is a generalization, of course, and there are many exceptions; but so often in this period, exceptions that took into account the local component of globalization from a U.S. perspective seem to be fighting against a very abstract dominant discourse. Viewed through the lens of the postcolonial world, there is a particular formal and theoretical response to U.S. hegemony in the Global South that reintroduces a contemporary approach to historical materialism. This response emphasizes disruptions in the notion of a smoothly universalizing new American idealism.

Egyptian political economist Samir Amin, one of the more insightful critics of Washington Consensus discourse around development, has described "the universalist dimension of historical materialism,"[1] and this phrase suggests one way to link the kind of disruptions I have in mind. Resources—like oil reserves, water rights, environmental conditions, and social infrastructures—are as contested today as they were during the era of European colonialism. Intellectuals who think in terms of world systems, critiques of development, or anti-orientalism propose these critiques against a backdrop of U.S.-centric global intellectual culture that effectively keeps such critiques at a remove. Amin's work emphasizes unequal development; in this he is influential for geographers, world-systems theorists, and theorists of globalization. Wallerstein also argued that the world system was deeply rooted in inequality, but the translation of his ideas into literary studies has tended to push these sorts of material concerns to the margins.

Alongside Amin, another helpful frame for thinking about cultural responses to U.S. hegemony during this period is Korean intellectual Paik Nak-chung's concept of the "division system," which is also in conversation with Wallerstein's "world-system" frame and can serve as an appropriate lens through which to read the archival turn in the novels of Hwang Sok-yong and Sonallah Ibrahim (Egypt, b. 1937). In texts by these authors, the struggle against hegemony expresses itself in terms of the contemporary geopolitical phenomenon of partition, a phenomenon much discussed in postcolonial theory, and one that calls attention back to land, space, and control of resources. Scholars working within or influenced by the bibliography of postcolonial studies have examined the British Empire's practice of partitioning states according to sect, as in Ireland, India/Pakistan, Israel/Palestine, and Cyprus. This practice offered both logistical and psychic/cultural advantages for the colonizer, while visiting decades of catastrophic agony on the citizenry of the postcolonies affected by the policy. In the aftermath of World War II, the United States cooperated with its allies and the Soviet Union to revive the practice of partition and engineer a series of "Cold War partitions," which differed from British colonial ones in important ways. The United States maneuvered to bring about partitions behind the scenes or in the context of an international conference that it dominated, rather than openly authoring partition as had the British. Also, it divided nations according to ideological camp, not sect or religious community. Arguably, partition has historically been a highly idealist practice in which land is reconceived as nations. But American-style partitions were more idealistic in several ways. Territory marked secular ideological difference in these cases. Even so, the division itself was made to seem natural or organic. No colonial hand was directly detectable, as in British colonial breakups. In the struggles that ensued, resources took a backseat to abstract ideas of freedom, always defined as openness to American hegemony. Dividing the land according to such ideas set the stage for post–Cold War global claims of the triumph of the liberal idea.

But in general, cultural discourses that were from the Global South and/or antihegemonic never accepted this post–Cold War idea of history having culminated in one transcendent idea. Often, historicism—or more specifically, geohistorically located writing—offered a challenge to the hegemonic American narrative. My own reading of this counter-hegemonic contemporary cultural trend is rooted in the Arab intellectual tradition of radically geohistoricizing knowledge production that I traced in chapter 2. This chapter offers a preliminary description of the new U.S. globalism in its intellectual and novelistic manifestations. At the same time, it emphasizes a response found in the way a clearly discernible strain of postdevelopment culture in the Global South used a literary archivism rooted in the materiality of history and expressed often via the novel. This second collection of texts constitutes an assertion—as all that is solid was melting into air—that there are and were bodies on and earth in other lands that had their own presence in history. Their argument touches on the question of resources, civil society, and self-determination in an era when the global conception of what "development" means has become increasingly narrow.

II. THE INTELLECTUAL UP ABOVE THE WORLD

A central strain of intellectual culture in the United States narrated the end of the Cold War in a manner almost directly opposite to the trend emphasizing the universalist dimension of historical materialism, instead proffering the end of narratives and the final defeat of the materialist method. A highly focused example of this strain is Francis Fukuyama's blockbuster essay "The End of History," which became an immediate sensation when it was published in the U.S.-based conservative foreign policy journal *The National Interest* in the summer of 1989. This essay was celebrated and challenged at the time of its publication, and its author has revised, expanded, and even partially refuted it since its initial publication. In its original version, however, the essay is perhaps the most iconic statement about the global scene after the Cold War from a U.S. elite point of view, and revisiting it shows it to have captured pithily a moment in U.S. intellectual culture, even as it also spoke clearly to the continuities and ruptures that characterized America's relationship with the world as the Berlin Wall crumbled.

In brief, Fukuyama argues that by returning to philosophically idealist principles of thought, the rapid reorganization of the global stage as the Cold War draws to an end can be understood as the end of ideological conflict. His is an argument for the cultural—specifically the philosophical—character of world history. For Fukuyama, the international community was arriving at a consensus that liberal democracy—yoked with a liberal capitalist-consumerist economic model—was the only viable political system in the contemporary world. By the "end of history," he meant that the major events which had characterized the stage-based conception of history would no longer continue to evolve. Nothing comparable to the grand shift from feudalism to petit bourgeois capitalism lay in mankind's future. More immediately, he believed the *ideological contests* between competing political-economic visions, which had mobilized and motivated governments and peoples during the Cold War, would not be replaced by any new ideological challenges to Western-style liberal democracy. Rather, the post–Cold War world would be characterized by the ineluctable spread of the liberal democratic system, the bureaucratic management of it, and the occasional disciplining of the odd rogue state that refused—for whatever epiphenomenal reason—to toe the line.[2]

One aspect of Fukuyama's argument that distinguishes it from other accounts of the American place in the world during globalization (like that of Samuel Huntington or the popular arguments of journalist Thomas Friedman) is his emphasis on the philosophy of history and in particular Hegelian thought. Having studied philosophy under iconic figures from the French Structuralist school, Fukuyama had come to the conclusion before writing "The End of History" that a proper understanding of history required circumventing the polluting influence of Marx to recapture a more purely idealist approach. He attempted to do this by accessing Hegel instead through the work of Alexandre Kojève (1902–1968). Fukuyama's claim is that liberalism as an idea has a social force far greater than any materialist phenomenon like class conflict. In the essay's discussion of recent events, its philosophical idealism presents itself somewhat strangely as being proven by very worldly events, such as the collapse of the Soviet economy or the neoliberal restructuring of Chinese communism, but the argument's oxymoronic logic is less relevant to my discussion of North-South relations than is the use value of Fukuyama's resort to what he understands as a more properly idealist position. For in this move, the author offers philosophical cover for the long-standing notion that ideas are the purview of the advanced industrial societies found in Northern Europe and North America. Indeed, the notion of a "no-idea-producing area" suddenly has much more power at this crucial moment in the peaking of U.S. hegemony, now that ideas are acknowledged as supremely important as a social force and the one true idea is the very Hegelian one of "the West." That there will be more ideas seems unlikely from this point of view, but what is certain is that new ideas will *not* come from the periphery. In Fukuyama's view, "For our purposes, it matters very little what strange thoughts occur to people in Albania or Burkina Faso, for we are interested in what one could in some sense call the common ideological heritage of mankind."[3] Lurking within this comment is a surprisingly dismissive attitude toward the global. The essay's self-justification for this attitude consists of the multiple ways it sees the advanced world—in almost an a priori way—as a model for everywhere else: "Liberal democracy in the political sphere combined with easy access to VCRs and stereos in the economic."[4] "Development" means in this instance a sharp distinction between West and non-West that calls attention to what the latter lacks—specifically in the areas of finance and electoral politics. One little-noted aspect of Fukuyama's argument is its acknowledgment that the liberal concept of "development" was never firmly rooted in economics. It always had a strong narrative dimension, rooted in a story that policy makers and knowledge producers in the United States wished to tell to the rest of the world.

Again the foundation of the distinction persists at the level of ideas, another example being the Western achievement of liberating itself from the backwardness of nationalist thinking. So whereas "since the Second World War, European nationalism has been defanged and shorn of any real relevance to foreign policy, . . . Palestinians and Kurds, Sikhs and Tamils, Irish Catholics and Walloons, Armenians and Azeris, will continue to have their unresolved grievances."[5] As this quotation makes clear, a point of emphasis in reading Fukuyama and his interlocutors should be the way the idea of liberalism can push beyond dismissiveness toward an almost open hostility directed at the Global South, especially toward majority Muslim or Arab regions. For example, in "The End of History," Fukuyama writes that Islam has offered theocracy as the only global alternative to "both liberalism and communism," adding that this alternative is doomed because of its lack of appeal to non-Muslims.[6] When he revisits his argument in 2006, after Islamophobia has become a somewhat sensitive topic in the United States, Fukuyama explains that Germany (a country that did not exist in its present form when his original essay was published) and not the United States is his prime example of the ideal contemporary liberal state and that he does not believe Islam is incompatible with either political or economic liberalism. So, he argues, in the case of democratization of the South, there "is actually not a Muslim exception, but more of an Arab exception; it would appear that there is something in Arab political culture that has been more resistant. What that could be is subject to debate, but it might well be a cultural obstacle that is not related to religion, such as the survival of tribalism."[7] This passage is a portion of a long refutation of the work of Samuel P. Huntington, whom Fukuyama had come to see as his major interlocutor in the debate about globalism as viewed through a U.S. lens. Both agree that a Western liberal idea has achieved a very justified dominance, but they differ on the compatibility of this idea with ideas and cultures in the Global South. In much of this bibliography, Islam or Arab—and often particularly Palestinian—stands in for everything that is not contemporary, Western, and liberal. This is evident in Fukuyama's singling out of Islamic "theocracy," Palestinian grievances, and Arab tribalism, but this type of discourse is more obvious in Huntington, where all of Islam becomes a civilization destined to clash with the West because of core cultural incompatibility. Here is a sample of Huntington's tone:

> This centuries-old military interaction between the West and Islam is likely to decline. It could become more virulent. The Gulf War left some Arabs feeling proud that Saddam Hussein had attacked Israel and stood up to the West. It also left many feeling humiliated and resentful of the West's military presence in the Persian Gulf, and the West's overwhelming military dominance, and their apparent inability to shape their own destiny. . . . Some openings in Arab political systems have already occurred. The principal beneficiaries of these openings have been Islamist movements. In the Arab

> world, in short, Western democracy strengthens anti-Western political forces.[8]

The strategy in this passage of lumping together Saddam Hussein, Islamist movements, and petrodollar states, not to mention unsupported generalizing about the feelings of "some Arabs," is facilitated by the preconceived idea that forms the point of departure for the civilizational argument. Western liberalism is transcendent as an idea here, and Islam, in spite of its long history in and around Europe, is marked as an *Other* civilization. Indeed, the "debate" between Fukuyama and Huntington over whether the liberal idea is pervasive enough to penetrate what they see as backward cultures of the Arabo-Islamic area takes this Western civilizational and cultural ascendance for granted.

This intellectual consensus that post–Cold War globalism can be viewed, through an American lens, as the triumph of liberalism has a particularly accessible manifestation in the highly popular writing of Thomas Friedman. In his runaway best-seller *The Lexus and the Olive Tree*, Friedman not only popularizes many of the ideas found in think tank writing, but he also recapitulates the idea of the Arab Muslim as the embodiment of cultural backwardness in the contemporary world. Friedman hits upon his binary metaphor for a "fast world" and a "slow world" when riding a bullet train from Tokyo to a Japanese Lexus factory. While riding the train, he reads an article in the *International Herald Tribune* about Palestinian resistance to Israeli occupation and meditates on the two worlds of contemporary globalism—one industrialized, consumerist, secular, peaceful, and liberal; the other Arab. These two worlds are embodied in two symbols: the Lexus (high mass consumption, capitalism, liberalism) and the olive tree (Arabs). *The Lexus and the Olive Tree*, "The Clash of Civilizations," and "The End of History" were all published in the period between the breakup of the Soviet Union and the September 11 terrorist attacks. Yet the idea that Islam, Arabs, and in particular Palestinians still embody what Western industrialized societies have transcended is present throughout this bibliography, even though it purports to be about the new global position of the United States. Why dramatize so persistently a perceived Arabo-Islamic threat at the very moment of the dissolution of the Cold War adversary? This representation of the Arab/Muslim world clearly grows out of preconceived ideas that are untroubled by any actual experience with Arab or Muslim life. The deep commitment to fashioning such an Other at the very moment of the collapse of the Soviet Union suggests a desire to maintain an idea of the world as in need of domination by an American version of liberalism. It also belies the claim—made explicitly by Fukuyama—that nationalism has withered away in the post–Cold War culture of the North, for a truly postnationalist intellectual culture should find it less necessary to construct so exceptionalist a discourse, with a persistently Orientalized Other as a component.

U.S. nationalism, in fact, has a great capacity to camouflage itself. The dichotomy between countries that manifest liberalism's highest achievements and the no-idea-producing areas constitutes a powerful tool in this process, which allows for a need for "development" to be promoted throughout the world in a manner that can bring about prosperity, consumerism, and women's rights in countries perceived to be wanting in these areas. Nationalism is actually alive and well in all aspects of U.S. political, popular, intellectual, and literary culture, and this is manifest in discourses of U.S. exceptionalism, the Arab/Muslim Other, liberal idealism, soft/hard power, and so forth. Scholars and writers, including Andrew Bacevich, Donald Pease, Evelyn Alsultany, Amy Kaplan, Melani McAlister, and Christine Klein, have documented as much. Just as with the Cold War evolution of a system of "colonialism without colonies," cultural discourse in the United States has engendered a milieu of nationalist sentiment within postnationalist cultural expression. The power of the postnationalist claim, however, allows for a great deal of generalizing and othering. Under such circumstances, it is ironically novelists who often find themselves insisting on a nonfiction world that exists outside this sacralized realm of imagination and ideas.

III. THE NOVEL AS CRITIQUE OF THE NEW IDEALISM

Fukuyama promotes the hyperemphasis on idealism as a break with earlier scholarly thinking that emphasized an economic or materially based social conception of the historical. The idea of liberal, democratic Western society is what is important, according to his argument. Many of the mainstream American historiographers he critiqued would have little argument with this conclusion. Yet the American "Third World" novel—the generic tradition traced in this book—has often been far more critical of what it sees as the conformity and hyperrationalism that characterizes American life, which might be associated with the intellectual culture that produced a Fukuyama or a Huntington. What

Elghandor and others criticized as Paul Bowles's primitivism was at one level a response to the direction of elite culture in the United States after World War II. As the Cold War drew to a close, the American novel continued its critique of an American conformism that facilitated empire. Elliott Colla, drawing on Lukács, has recently argued for the inherently critical character of the novel form.[9] Although his argument focuses on a very different historical context, the theoretical underpinnings of his claims provide insight into the recent evolution of the American "Third World" novel, which was particularly open to a hypercritical stance toward the United States' global role in the period just after the reunification of Vietnam.

If overemphasis on the rational in U.S. elite culture had been a target of postwar critical American novelists like Paul Bowles, Thomas Pynchon, William Burroughs, and others, Cormac McCarthy's *Blood Meridian, Or the Evening Redness in the West* represents something of an apex of this type of critique. The novel was first published in 1985, ten years after the fall of Saigon and one month after Mikhail Gorbachev became general secretary of the Communist Party of the Soviet Union, initiating the devolution of the Cold War. The fifth of McCarthy's novels, it is the first (and indeed one of the few) to invest directly in the historical placement of events. Whereas his earlier novels are set in a distinctive place—almost always the Appalachian region—but rarely in a specifically rooted time, and include little acknowledgment of any world events taking place outside the novel's milieu, *Blood Meridian* specifies its geohistory, moving within its first few pages from Appalachia to the American West, where its story line participates in a complex network of overlapping mythologies and histories. *Blood Meridian*'s narrative starts in 1849, immediately after the end of the 1848 Mexican-American War, and it borrows from archival documents of the time for its plot premise of a group of marauding Americans who cross into Mexico on a commission from local Mexican officials to headhunt (literally) Apaches, but then end up maniacally scalping all humans in their path. The crossing into Mexico adds the "Third World" element that makes it possible to link this novel by the highly idiosyncratic McCarthy to a tradition initiated by Bowles.

In terms of literary genre, the novel shapes the historical events into an epically framed and stylized version of a "Mexico western," a particular subgenre of cowboy film in which Anglos cross the U.S.-Mexico border in rebellious defiance of geopolitical lines on a mission that cannot be contained within national boundaries or protocols. Examples include the Sam Peckinpah films *Major Dundee* (1965) and *The Wild Bunch* (1969), believed to have influenced McCarthy, and the genre's connection to an imperialist vision in which the twentieth-century United States sees itself as conquering the world the way it once conquered western territory has been documented in the influential work of historian Richard Slotkin.[10] Peckinpah's films, produced during the Vietnam era, push to an unsustainable extreme the celebration of a violence that purports to enact justice. McCarthy is able to move far beyond what seemed the extreme in 1960s film, working in a literary mode near the end of the Cold War. Populating his landscape with trees full of dead babies, decayed corpses, pools of dark blood, and idiots smeared in feces—all rendered in the most elevated of prose—western violence is reduced by the novel's action as far as possible toward an extreme representation as purely destructive.

This innovative genre extremism combines with a critique of Western rationalism in a unique manner. Whereas Bowles uses an essentialist portrait that celebrates *moghrabi* primitivism as a mechanism to critique American fascination with the rational, McCarthy inserts into his narrative a character named Judge Holden, through whom he asserts the justificatory power of American rationalism vis-à-vis its global hegemony, thereby suggesting that philosophical idealism can work hand in glove with crude imperialist violence. The judge pervades the novel as a central organizing presence, and he is pitted against its protagonist—the kid—at the level of both story line and meaning. The simplest characterization of the text would be as a journey narrative following the kid, beginning with its opening imperative, "See the child," his departure from his Tennessee home and his abusive father in the opening pages, the long Mexico trek, multiple clashes with Apaches, his involvement with the marauding "Glanton gang" and the struggles and rivalries that take place within it, and recurring encounters with the judge, until the kid becomes "the man" in the final scenes and meets the judge one last time in a California brothel. If the judge's recurring presence as a character, a symbol, a philosopher, and an aporia is what distinguishes the text from a generic western, it is the internationalization of the questions of violence, nationalism, and normativity that distinguish it from McCarthy's early Appalachian novels. Meanwhile these two features—the character of the philosopher/destroyer (the judge) and the setting in the "Third World" (Mexico)—operate in tandem within the novel to fashion a critique of the intellectual milieu that produced the post–Cold War American turn toward philosophical idealism.

Judge Holden first appears in chapter 1, convincing a crowd to lynch an itinerant preacher by arguing that the preacher has a history of pederasty and confidence tricks. His words stir a mob against the preacher, but only moments later, he is in a bar at repose over whiskey, admitting that he has never seen the preacher before in his life. The incident depicts the way his sophistication and polish allow him to couch as rational rhetoric discourse that is almost always crassly utilitarian. This opening scene conforms with one near the end of the novel that crystallizes the character—and the ultimate ends—of the judge's rhetoric. By chapter 16, the Glanton gang has emerged from a withering series of encounters in Mexico and is working its way back into the western territory of the United States. In an "eating house" in Colorado, they murder the proprietor for trying to place them in a segregated dining area because one of their soldiers is black. (Interestingly, although the scenes that take place in Mexican territory portray a brutal and lawless milieu, there is a fluidity to racial identities that is lost once the gang makes it back into the territory under U.S. legal sovereignty.) In a cantina next door, the murderous gang is confronted by one Couts, who heads the local authority. Glanton responds by denying any knowledge of the murder that the entire settlement knows he was involved in.

This incident enables an understanding of the judge's meaning in the novel through the way he inserts himself as a respondent to protect the Glanton gang from accounting for its violence. After he has "emerged from the darkness," he becomes the face of the gang's unpolished defiance by insisting, "Kindly address your remarks to me, Lieutenant. . . . I represent Captain Glanton in all legal matters."[11] Through rhetorical supremacy, the judge is able to subvert the empirical case against the Glanton gang over a series of exchanges: "The lieutenant came again in the evening. He and the judge sat together and the judge went over points of law with him. The lieutenant nodded, his lips pursed. The judge translated for him latin terms of jurisprudence. He cited cases civil and martial. He quoted Coke and Blackstone, Anaximander and Thales."[12] The reaction of Coats in this passage illustrates the general awe inspired by the sophistication of the judge in characters trying to make their way in the violent, even Hobbesian milieu of the novel.[13] Both his friends and adversaries speak with admiration of his learning, sophistication, and cosmopolitanism, as when Tobin, the "ex-priest" in the group, tells the kid: "He's been all over the world. Him and the governor, they sat up till breakfast and it was Paris this and London that in five languages."[14] Amid the references to his cosmopolitanism, it is easy to miss the strong strain of brutality in the character of the judge, and missing this dimension means missing his real significance. When he sums up his philosophy in a debate near the end of the novel by saying, "Moral law is an invention of mankind for the disenfranchisement of the powerful in favor of the weak [and h]istorical law subverts it at every turn,"[15] he not only expresses an elegant recasting of the phrase "might makes right," but he touches on the significance of history as a rhetorical category, as depicted in the novel. As one pair of critics puts it, "McCarthy's point is that violence is inherently law-making."[16] The turn toward a universalization of history—what Fukuyama might call "the common ideological heritage of mankind"—proves the best justification for the brutality of the historical hegemonic impulse.

A quirky detail that may carry a deeper significance is the judge's baldness. In the extreme desert conditions endured by the novel's Anglo-American marauders, he often appears among them shirtless, and the story picks up a MacGuffin regarding his quest for the right hat in the later chapters, calling attention again to his lack of hair. In the final image of the novel—after much scalping and genocide and one last confrontation with the kid—the judge appears on the stage of a bawdy dance hall: "Towering over them all is the judge and he is naked dancing, his small feet lively and quick and now in doubletime and bowing to the ladies, huge and pale and hairless, like an enormous infant."[17] If the plot drives the American idea of regenerative violence to an extreme, this image of the judge does the same for the mythical trope of American innocence. The judge is an enormous baby with a huge Machiavellian streak and the ability to manipulate masses of less rational countrymen toward rampant genocidal behavior; he is an embodiment of the imperialism/innocence contradiction.

The problem, however, with a reading that focuses too narrowly on the judge is that such approaches, like readings that celebrate the novel's elegant style, have great potential to distract from the novel's thematic focus on imperialism and genocide. Place and time—the geohistory of the novel—must be incorporated into any knowing appreciation of its style and characters, and for this reason, I have also emphasized the way the novel breaks from McCarthy's Appalachian work, initiating a new interest in the western and in Mexico. *Blood Meridian,* published in 1985, has been linked to America's Vietnam experience by critics like Richard Godden and Colin Richmond, and Slotkin also studied the turn toward western films featuring genocidal cowboys during the Vietnam era, including in the subgenre of the "Mexico western." That so much of the rest of the criticism of a novel about genocide perpetrated by white Americans on native peoples and peoples of color has been devoted to McCarthy's purple prose and esoteric monologues says a great deal about the insidiousness of American imperialist culture, and the work of cultural studies critics like Slotkin, Richmond, and Godden is an important antidote to this celebratory bibliography. In this vein, the historical context's link to partition as a motif in discourses of imperialism must be emphasized, as the novel follows events that occurred in the immediate aftermath of the 1848 Treaty of Guadalupe Hidalgo. This pact not only ended the Mexican American War but also formalized and made permanent the partition of Texas and Mexico that was first marked off in 1836 by the short-lived Republic of Texas, after its secession from Mexico.[18] This link between the two partitioned spaces of North/South Vietnam and Texas/Mexico calls attention to something increasingly hidden during the "American century": the connection between the control of space and empire. Also related to these two geographies is the question of partition itself, its relationship to nationalism and colonization—and, most significantly for the purposes of this study, its invisibility in critical discourses of American globality. A key component of U.S. imperialism is its desire to deny its own existence, so the idea that Cold War partitions are negotiated and popular—even natural—reinforces American plausible deniability.

IV. IDEALISM AND THE LITERATURE OF PARTITION

Partition has always been an ideological act, built upon the deeply held belief in metropolitan culture that the postcolonial Other cannot be trusted to behave rationally. This idea of superior rationality is then translated into authority over land and space by the colonizer in the case of British imperial partitions, or by the hegemon (the United States and its cohort) for the Cold War partitions. Joe Cleary's study of Ireland and Palestine and their literatures of partition is enormously helpful as a point of departure for understanding the dynamics of particularity and continuity in American-style partition. Borrowing his preliminary definition from Stanly Waterman, he quotes, "Partition can be said to have occurred when two or more new states are created out of what had been a single [administrative] entity and when at least one of the new units claims a direct link to the prior state."[19] We might add that the prototypical colonial partition was that visited upon the Indian subcontinent, with its disastrous immediate and long-term consequences, and if the idiosyncrasies of the South Asian context are very rarely acknowledged by much of postcolonial studies, which prefers to take British India as a high colonial norm, some similarities with other Anglo-colonial partitions are strong. In Ireland, India, and Palestine, the British projected communal irreconcilability onto a population, favored a minority, and weakened the resultant entity. Cleary comments that "the dilemmas concerning definitions of citizenship and the reconstruction of national identities that emerge in the wake of . . . partitions . . . share important similarities," but he also distinguishes "between imposed partitions that divided relatively homogeneous nations along ideological lines as a direct result of Cold War rivalries (as in Germany, Korea, or Vietnam) and those implemented to resolve communal conflicts within ethnically heterogeneous colonial states at the moment of the transfer of imperial power (as in Ireland, India, and Palestine)."[20]

The American style of partition has gone largely unattended to in the bibliography of postcolonialism, which has generally preferred an elegant dismantling of the colonial discourses of Europe.[21] Borrowing directly from the British colonial practice of partitioning its protectorates, U.S. imperialist practice introduced important variations. As the most powerful of the collective of Cold War powers, the United States, first in Germany then in Korea in 1945, then again in Vietnam in 1954, preferred an idealist approach that sought to divide and conquer along ideological lines, where nationalist, Marxist, and/or anticolonial ideologies were segregated from those that could be packaged as secular and liberal, loving freedom, and unburdened by ideology. In this sense, the Cold War partitions were always, for the United States, about an oxymoronic historical progression toward an "end of history" *avant la lettre*, which is to say they were about dividing ideology as a way of trying to homogenize or erase it. In other words, American-style partition prefigures the idealist strain in Fukuyama's argument; ideas like socialism/justice or democracy/freedom are pitted against each other with the material component—the land—being divided as a consequence. The sense that Cold War partitions are "imposed" (Cleary's term) by outside rivals highlights the deniability contradiction at the heart of U.S. imperial culture. Whereas the British Empire was able to fashion partitions fairly unilaterally in some cases, the United States always affected partition through an international conference that disguised hegemonic manipulation via a distribution of the responsibility among several powerful states. As a result, the partitions imposed by the United States were never attributed to its agency, and so never read as an American style.

Emphasizing the American nature of Cold War partitions is important because doing so helps in understanding global responses to them, which in many ways exemplify responses to the rise of U.S. imperialism in the intellectual, literary, and social cultures of the Global South. In Cleary's discussion of colonial partition, the place of discourses of nationalism, particularly as framed by Benedict Anderson, is prominent in the conceptualization of partition as a cultural and literary phenomenon. But even during the colonial period, partition was primarily about territory for anticolonial intellectuals too. In the era of neocolonialism and the Cold War, this geographic dimension takes on special importance for cultures of decolonization resisting the divide-and-erase approach to ideology because it involves acknowledging what U.S. Cold War culture seeks to cover over: the imperial impulse behind global policy.

In the 1970s, Walter Rodney said of anticolonial intellectuals, "They're coming to grips with the fact that they must have a set of ideas which will enable them to recover their national resources."[22] This statement has many contemporary ramifications of relevance to this study, among them that it constitutes a contemporary stand against dividing territory to cover up ideology. This anticolonial intellectual culture contrasts with that of an idealizing northern elite philosophical discourse in which "space is . . . rendered increasingly irrelevant to social intercourse [because as] the economic, technological, political, and cultural relations expand, the institutional framework for handling these relations also becomes more complex and increasingly loses any intrinsic spatial definition."[23] In this quotation, the geographer Neil Smith describes the marginalization of spatial analysis in late–Cold War discussions of global capitalism. His influential proposed methodological response in his *Uneven Development: Nature, Capital and the Production of Space* is a heightened attentiveness to the scalar levels at which capitalist inequality deploys. Smith sees scales as basic units around which is created "an integrated space economy."[24] In this earlier work, Smith emphasizes the scales of the urban, the global, and the nation-state. In later work, he divides his categories further, down to the scale of the body. U.S. imperialism operates most actively on the scale of the global. Thus, as Smith partially acknowledges, dependency and world-systems theorists, including Rodney, Samir Amin, and Theotonio Dos Santos, can be seen as pioneers in deploying the scalar lens. "Dependency theory, center-periphery theory, and the various theories of underdevelopment all capture something of this process [of the uneven development of capitalism]. But their focus tends to be on the global scale alone."[25] Smith's more expansive critique exposes the pervasive operation of scalar inequality. But the more assertive emphasis on the global elicits more effectively what the culture of American-style imperialism seeks to erase: the intransigence of uneven development at the global scale. Although dependency theorists often emphasized the economic dimension of uneven development, Smith's analysis reveals a direct link to the neoliberal ideas that engender the process. This response has roots in the classical anticolonial thought of the type found in the work of Rodney and Laroui and might be helpful in reframing them to engage with current manifestations of imperial culture through contemporary critical discourses of scale.

In this sense, discourses of scale in global comparative literary studies show great promise for discussions of American-style partition. For example, Nirvana Tanoukhi has deployed geographical scale as a method to critique the globalizing and naturalizing formalism of Franco Moretti's "Conjectures on World Literature." Tanoukhi's argument in her essay "The Scale of World Literature" cogently places this question of who is allowed to imagine space squarely into the context of geography and comparative literature. Whereas Moretti presumes a metropolitan critic with a global lens, culling through the trove of criticism about national literatures from a distance, Tanoukhi sees the centering of African settings before, during, and after decolonization as a disruption of these globalizing conjectures. Against Moretti's trope of compromise as a universal law, Tanoukhi proposes critical attention to geographic scale as a self-consciously localizing rubric that subverts universalizing via the norming of Europe. When it comes to studying literary production, Tanoukhi argues, "we must approach 'spaces' wherever we find them, as the articulation of distance within a particularly spatialized system of social relations. In a landscape like Africa-of-the-Novel, we must reconstruct the process by which the space of the postcolonial novel becomes differentiated, gaining the contours of a place and the fixity of a cultural location. Only by following the dynamics of a landscape will we be able to unearth 'the social determinants of distance.'"[26] Tanoukhi's emphasis on Smith's conception of geographic scale can easily fit a spatiotemporal connection to the work of the decolonizing intellectual described by Rodney.[27] My own emphasis has been on the history of decolonization and the parallel history of an emergent American imperium. The latter's fascination with a Eurocentric version of philosophical idealism performing as globality comes to a head in the writing of Fukuyama, for whom "the relation between world space and national territoriality is viewed as a zero-sum game in which the growing importance of the former is presumed necessarily to entail the decline of the latter," as geographer Neil Brenner has pointed out.[28] In the phase of insidious deterritorializing of a historical moment, the postcolony has produced more complicated sets of scalar responses in which bodies, neighborhoods, cities, regions, and nations disrupt the homogeneity of the end of history.

Smith's various levels of scalar categorization[29]—each with its consequent political valence—and Tanoukhi's emphasis on Smith prove extremely helpful for entering into the topic of the postcolonial novel of partition as a genre. In emphasizing *geographical* scale, both Tanoukhi and Smith offer a rubric for formal features in the anti-neocolonial novel that the trope of "compromise," deployed by Moretti, cannot adequately accommodate. Tanoukhi's citation of Smith appears in this passage dealing with scalar grids that are specifically geographic: "The third, more materialist definition of scale—what Smith properly calls *geographic* scale—sounds more complex and elusive. Though geographic scales are arbitrary, says Smith, they *emerge* (for the geographer) as objectifiable elements in the course of *following* the material processes that shape a landscape. It is this very notion, implied here, of a scale-sensitive procedure—a procedure that 'conceptualizes' by following—which, I think, carries significant consequences for the idea, method, and perhaps the ethics of comparison."[30] In relating scale to world literature, Tanoukhi's critique of Moretti invokes the spatial as a counterweight to the abstraction of world literature discourse.[31] This question of abstraction—edging toward philosophical idealism—plagues world literature discourse and its problematic attempt to translate the work of Immanuel Wallerstein into a strictly literary context. The translation of Wallersteinian historiography into literary space seems to exacerbate the kind of totalizing tendencies that Wallerstein himself almost always circumnavigates, and to which Paik Nak-chung has called attention. Paik's approach—distinct from but potentially complementary to Tanoukhi's—offers a highly localized borrowing of Wallersteinian systems theory as an antidote to the theory's difficulties in dealing with historical difference. Thus, Paik proposes framing via a "division system" as a text "to be read against the larger background text of the world-system."[32] His concept of the "division system" has an explanatory function regarding the enduring partition of the Korean Peninsula as well as general ramifications for critical approaches that seek to travel Wallerstein's ideas. In Korea's resilient division, he finds "a durability worthy of a social system, which calls for an analysis more systematic and holistic than studying each Korea as two discrete components of the world-system."[33] Here, the category of the division system invokes both the synchronic historical legacy of American-style partition and the diachronic scalar issue of a geographical accounting within any systems theory for the place of the body, community, region, and nation.

Throughout this study, I have reiterated the need to emphasize U.S. imperialism and its role in global culture. This task has always faced special challenges. In the midst of contemporary debates, discourses of globalization and worlding present unique challenges in their tendency to hide uneven development and in camouflaging the increasingly subtle instrument of U.S. nationalism. The scalar critique of world literature discourse's globalizing impulse helps with this challenge by emphasizing space's unevenness at the scale of the global. Connecting this disciplinary emphasis with the classical anticolonial argument for self-determination and control over resources and territory becomes crucial as the rhetoric of globalization makes the visible processes of scaling increasingly elusive. This elusiveness can be read as a target of anti-imperialist novels written against American-style partition and interpolating discourses that are documentary, geographical, and archival at the level of form and genre, while simultaneously antagonistic at the level of content to Americanization, liberalism, and the covering over of ideology (substituting in its place idealism in "end of history" discourse). Global novels that assert a geographic counterpoint to idealist discourse do so by deploying archives in a turn that goes beyond McCarthy's American antifoundationalism and, in so doing, calls attention once again to Cold War sites of American imperialism. The specific examples I will examine speak directly to the historical consequences of the post–Cold War world and its division systems.

V. ANTI-IMPERIALISM AND THE ARCHIVAL NOVEL

Bruce Cumings's Modern Library history of the Korean War uses a contemporary Korean novel as an archival source in its discussion of the history of atrocities committed by allied forces in North Korea. The issue in the passage in question is a long-standing allegation that American forces had facilitated a massacre in the northern town of Sinch'ŏn, southwest of Pyongyang and a bit north of the thirty-eighth parallel. According to the official North Korean (DPRK) narrative, Korean women and children were imprisoned in a shed and tortured by Korean and American troops attempting to extract information from them about the whereabouts of their men. The prisoners were subjected to baths of sewage and ultimately burned alive, according to the DPRK allegations. Cumings describes his attempts to verify the official account in 1987 with the aid of a Thames television crew through survivor interviews and the study of archival material. He then marks the publication of the novel *The Guest* in 2000 as a breakthrough in the attempt to document the events, because the text by "the South Korean dissident writer Hwang Sok-yong [is] based on his own investigations and interviews with survivors and witnesses [and] relate[s] that refugee Christians from the South had returned to Sinchon during the occupation and presided over this appalling massacre."[34] Hwang's novel roots a discussion of this massacre in documentable history, but as critic Youngju Ryu has perceptively observed, "*The Guest* forces us to consider scenarios in which truth may be decoupled from reconciliation."[35]

Hwang's novel culminates in a narrating of the incident, and in this climax the documentary material serves as an undergirding for his representation of the psychic results of partition. In other words, the material process of reshaping the land manifests itself in the conceptual clash of conflicting nationalisms, acted upon at the scalar level of the Korean body. To arrive at this point, the novel moves backward, starting with resultant contexts of geographical displacement and fractured identity. In the first chapter, two Korean Christian brothers who have immigrated to the New York / New Jersey area argue over a plan made by the younger brother, a Presbyterian minister, to take a packaged tour of the DPRK set up particularly to facilitate reunion visits for separated Korean families. The younger brother's motivation, however, is not initially to reunite with family members but rather to engage in a kind of reconciliation. When the younger brother suggests that the older join him, they argue, expressing conflicting positions on the legacy of the war, the role of Christian forgiveness, the persistence of trauma, and the mutuality of guilt. At the end of the chapter, as the younger brother is preparing to leave, the older brother suddenly dies, but his ghost continues with the young minister on his journey back to their ancestral land, as an image representing the traces of a historical rupture that is literal and geographical as much as it is psychic and conceptual.

Hwang's introduction to the English translation of his novel comments on the metaphor of the guest, *son-nim* [손님], which Koreans used to refer to smallpox when it first entered the peninsula as a Western import, and which the historical/archival turn in the novel associates with communism and Christianity. But the novel's plotting of temporality suggests a critique of invasion *without* asserting an authentic tradition that the external force has displaced and that must be recaptured. Events in the novel begin with the results of displacement and end with the documented moment of geographic and conceptual rupture. This presentation of a guest that is invasive and insidious operates as a metaphor that contrasts with the notion of "foreign cultures" that are Confucian or Islamic and exhibit an impermeability to Western values. Guests are accepted into a native culture, but invasive guests exploit cultural permeability.

Partition's effects at the scale of the body—specifically Reverend Yosŏp's—and at the scale of the nation (the partitioned postcolonial Korea) are overlaid in the novel's structure. In other words, the novel follows Yosŏp's individual journey but knits back into the narrative his story's inextricability from national and global politics. Yosŏp's older brother, Yohan, dies in the short time between their argument and the younger's departure for Pyongyang, but the elder brother comes along on the trip anyway in the form of a ghost. Much of the account of Yosŏp's trip in the DPRK emphasizes the personal trauma of families victimized by the division system. In Cleary's account of partition's social effects, themes that unite "both Cold War and post-imperial partitions" would be "dilemmas concerning definitions of citizenship and the reconstruction of national identities."[36] Although *The Guest* begins by presenting Yosŏp's trip as a metaphor for national reconciliation in earlier chapters focalized through him, his arrival in Pyongyang marks a shift that introduces the complications inherent in the resolution of a decades-old division that is historical, territorial, ideological, and psychological. Yosŏp alone among his organized group insists (initially) that he has no family remaining, but his North Korean handlers do not accept his insistence, investigating his background, uncovering his brother's first wife and son, and leading him back to an encounter with the massacres that played a role in engendering Korean partition. Before revisiting the massacres, however, he finds his brother's family, who have survived recriminations for the war crimes committed by Yohan. At the end of a first awkward meeting, his nephew tells Yosŏp, "My name is Ryu Tanyŏl, not Daniel! And how dare you show up now, searching for your family! Do you have any idea how hard it's been for us, just to live from day to day!"[37] This retort makes clear that for Tanyŏl the long-lost uncle has been a mere idea, now suddenly become flesh, but for his mother, Yohan's first wife, he is a memory attached to a physical body. For this reason, she has difficulty criticizing his return, but her response is also more complicated, eventually leading from familial division back to national division. For example, she admits to Yosŏp that she often still prays, an admission he has longed to hear, but she then continues with a critique of Korea's military society that undercuts his satisfaction: "I've thought about it all my life. I mean, why is it that men hate each other so much when everything in this world has been created to make us better? Even the Japanese couldn't have had so much hate. I was left here, alone, as a sinner. . . . I lost all my daughters because I could not feed them properly, and trying to go on with that one over there, the only one I have left, well, I couldn't help but think . . . God, too, has sinned."[38]

Although the novel initially follows a journey structure organized around Yosŏp's trip, it becomes more complicated and ambitious as it moves forward. The first complicating element is the presence of ghosts, starting with the spirit of Yohan on the plane and then continuing as spirits from Yosŏp's youth come forward to testify about events surrounding the massacre and the partition.[39] A second element that connects Yosŏp's personal saga to the nation is the introduction of set pieces in which a third-person narrator breaks off the account of the trip to relate the history of the hot war in Hwanghae Province. These narratives interestingly meld into direct testimony from the "ghosts," beginning about halfway through the novel. Finally, there are the direct descriptions of the physical setting as Yosŏp arrives in the DPRK after decades of exile. In his first trip outside his hotel, he reads street signs—a habit he has picked up in visits to European cities as a "way of reconciling himself to alien surroundings."[40] As his tour bus continues, he finds himself mentally cataloging the clothes worn by the various types walking through the streets: "Every now and then a man in a suit would come into view. High school and junior high school students' uniforms were the color of persimmons, complete with hats that resembled Lenin caps. . . . The women all wore fairly similar two piece outfits."[41] This initial trip culminates in Yosŏp expressing his alienation through a rendering of the urban space: "The city was like a cinema screen; a flat square of life lay out there. Watching it made Yosŏp himself feel as if he were no longer quite three-dimensional. The multitude of people who had created this movie for themselves had singled out Ryu Yosŏp, and they had no intention of letting him in, no matter how desperately he tried to climb into the screen."[42] In this passage, the multiple valences of the physical setting shape Yosŏp's alienation. His inner motivation seems to be to recapture the land as a home rooted in the material realm. His experience of it, however, is ethereal, and he blames this inability to recapture the materialist component of space on the North Koreans surrounding him.

The somewhat controversial presence of ghosts in the story operates similarly. As I have noted, *The Guest* is important not merely as an early twenty-first-century work of global fiction but also as an archival novel that helps correct the historical record around incidents that precipitated the partition of the Korean Peninsula. Hwang's interviews with survivors have been incorporated into the fictionalized narrative. This research revealed that Christian fundamentalist Koreans, with the support (but crucially not the participation) of the ROK regime and the American military, carried out the reign of terror in Sinch'ŏn, working as proxies for American forces who had been accused earlier of war crimes. The novel's approach of having these events narrated by ghosts of the participants on both sides of the conflict engenders a complex grouping of textual consequences. Ryu frames the tension inhering in the novel's form as follows: "A paradox unfolds when we stop to consider that the novel establishes cognitive superiority over official accounts of the event only by admitting the supernatural into the court of empirical evidence."[43]

Each ghost/witness is a departure from third-person narration that creates a pastiche-like structure similar to Hwang's longer and more structurally dispersed earlier novel *The Shadow of Arms*. In this case, the formal disruption parallels the traumatic redirecting of history. Ghosts who narrate history might also be read here as markers of the ambivalent nature of scale's impulse toward materiality, since on the one hand the characters themselves have become pure spirit, but on the other, earth is the only material realm that remains. That *ghosts* narrate historical *facts*, particularly ones that have been effaced by dueling nationalist narratives, also raises questions around the nature of the historical, which emerges here as elusive but geographically differentiated. The irony of the immaterial ghosts uncovering the concrete realities camouflaged by the nationalist professional historian or historiographer constitutes a gesture parallel to that of the North African historiographer who saw the example of the Orientalist as the ur-text illustrating the limits of traditional historicism. The critique proposed by the novel is the end of a certain type of history, rather than of history itself.

In his 2002 State of the Union address, George W. Bush attempted to inaugurate a new post–Cold War binarism in American foreign relations by denominating an "axis of evil" in the world that represented a challenge to U.S. global standing, and therefore had to be countered with the force of the U.S. military. The idea of an axis of evil was, from the start, highly idealistic. It drew on both Cold War memories and contemporary domestic fears of a nebulous foreign threat to imagine the United States at war with an agglomeration of small states (Iraq, Iran, and North Korea—then, in later statements, other Third World countries) that had in no way participated in the still freshly remembered and felt attacks of September 11, 2001. Even at that time and even among supporters of the Bush administration, the inclusion of North Korea on the short list was perplexing. Hwang Sok-yong has directly linked the publication of his *The Guest* with Bush's idiosyncratic targeting of the Korean Peninsula. In his introduction to the English translation of the novel, he writes, "I began work on *The Guest* in 2000, the fiftieth anniversary of the Korean War. The September 11 attacks a year later came directly after *The Guest* was first published, and the onset of this new 'Age of Terror,' along with the inclusion of North Korea in the so-called Axis of Evil, and the beginning of a whole new war, made the fragility of our position clearer than ever. It was a chilling experience to be so reminded that despite the collapse of the Cold War infrastructure, our small peninsula is still bound by the delicate chains of war."[44] Here the *systemic* character of American empire emphasized by Paik Nak-chung comes into focus. It is rooted in an idealistic binarism—one that allows Germany to be partitioned as a consequence of its policy of invasion and killing in Europe, but Korea to be partitioned as a consequence of being invaded and occupied by Japan. These sorts of contradictions grow out of a system that is simultaneously a "world system," an imperialist system, and a division system. When analyzed from within the confines of end-of-history discourse, the system can be understood as highly abstract, greatly facilitating the sort of contradictions on the ground embodied by Korea. If these systemic contradictions seem most acute on the "forgotten" (by many Americans) peninsula of Korea, their highest profile during the post–Cold War is on the Arabian Peninsula, where terror attacks by rogue Saudis result in the visiting of American wrath on Saudi neighbors—Iraq, Yemen, Bahrain, Iran, and Syria.

Sonallah Ibrahim's *Warda* was published in Arabic in Egypt in 2000, making it not only a product of post–Cold War global culture but also almost exactly contemporaneous with *The Guest*. The novel artfully uses a split narrative to document a history of ideological commitment imperceptible through the American globalizing lens, as well as show the contemporary invisibility of that history in a profoundly Americanized Arabian Peninsula. The frame story of the novel is narrated by an autobiographically resonant Egyptian writer visiting the Sultanate of Oman to work on story ideas and visit family. The glitziness of this petrodollar milieu shakes loose antithetical submerged memories of the writer's association with Marxist students from the southern Arabian Peninsula in Cairo in the 1950s. Within this frame narrative are the diaries of the title character, one of the writer's former leftist associates.

Warda moves from Cairo to the American University in Beirut in the 1960s, where her dedication to the cause of global socialist change through armed Marxist revolution coalesces, culminating in her commitment to move to the Dhofar region of southern Oman, live in camps with tribal guerrillas, and fight alongside them with the support of the People's Democratic Republic of Yemen (aka South Yemen) for the Marxist overthrow of the sultanate.[45] Sonallah Ibrahim has mentioned two points of origin for this novel. One was his desire to compose an antidote to his early 1990s tour de force, *Zhaat*, which follows the life of a middle-class Egyptian wife and mother in the bourgeois Cairo suburb of Heliopolis, whose life revolves around one-upmanship at work, gossip in her apartment building at home, and futile, mock-heroic attempts to bring to justice local supermarkets selling packaged food with forged expiration dates. Ibrahim had set out to create a heroine who was Arab but wound up with a novel that critiqued Egyptian consumerism via the body of a bourgeois woman. *Warda* was a second attempt to envision Arab female strength in the era of WID. In this discursive context, women are central not only to the contemporary politics of representation but also to the American idea of refashioning the post–Cold War world by spreading its conception of global economic development. The passages in *Warda* that emphasize women's education, family planning, and reform of patriarchal legal structures during the revolutionary fight against the sultanate must be read, therefore, against this historical context.

The author's second inspiration was discovering documents at a Beirut archive relating the experience of Arab women who fought in the Dhofari uprising in the 1960s and '70s, a history that parallels the engaged female combatant in the North Vietnamese Army. This second inspiration represents the archival/documentary turn in this particular novel, a strategy that appears in most of his novels, perhaps most famously in *Zhaat*'s use of copious strings of newspaper clippings to fill the even-numbered chapters, alternating with the heroine's story in the odd-numbered ones.[46] Whereas Cormac McCarthy's archive aspires to deconstruct an American mythology from the inside via a *reductio ad nauseum*, Hwang and Ibrahim both use the archival to assert ruptures in the homogenizing, liberal, global American narrative. The end of history as the triumph of an abstracted liberal idea expressed in a nationalist polemic disguised as detached epistemology by American thinkers is directly opposed by the use of the historical archive to document the globality of distinct ideologies expressed in a novel.[47]

In Ibrahim's novel, Warda may have started as a figure who radically complicates the American myth of the incarcerated and passive Arab woman—the proverbial brown woman waiting to be saved by white men from brown men—but the character evolves into a figure far beyond the grasp of American cognitive mapping and even challenges Arab nationalist versions of an epitomized Arab woman. Such conceptions of the Arab woman held hostage would become crucial in the years after *Warda*'s publication, as a cultural justification for the Bush campaign against Arab civil society. As I suggested in the previous chapter, this discourse has been relentlessly countered by a group of transnational feminist scholars who sought to respond to the tropes that fueled the link between an idea of women held hostage and militarism. *Warda*, then, is one of many important texts that evoke the diversity of female experience in the Arab world, which was systematically ignored in order for the myth of the captive Arab woman to be propagated.

At the time of the book's publication, Ibrahim may have already had in mind a long-standing Orientalist idea—which has driven both military and economic policies—of the passive, supine Arab female, but surely the novel also comments on woman's place in the Egyptian novel, which has always found it difficult to lift its heroines above an immaterial symbol for the nation, uniting its various classes and sects through romantic attraction. *Warda* is one of the few examples of an Arabic novel that manages not only to transcend, but even systematically to deconstruct, this idealized female form. In this sense, Ibrahim's strategy in *Warda* might be compared to the celebrated Algerian Arabophone novelist Ahlam Mosteghanemi, whose first novel, *Memory in the Flesh*, published to unprecedented success in Arabic in 1985 and in English translation in 2000, uses the story of a veteran from the Algerian war of independence describing his obsession with the daughter of a former hero of the resistance to dismantle the idea of the strong woman as national allegory, which no longer resonates in the postcolonial context. In her excellent discussion of the novel and the television series based on it, Olivia Harrison describes Mosteghanemi's writing as "interrogating the limits and dangers of national allegory, particularly the feminine national allegories that have been the hallmark of modern and anticolonial nationalism."[48] A specifically Egyptian version of this problem grows out of the tendency of early Egyptian novelists like Tawfik al-Hakim and Muhammad Hussain Haykal to employ such feminine allegories unproblematically. Ibrahim's *Warda*, like Mosteghanemi's works, harkens back to the specifically Arab version of the allegorized woman only to critique it. As an internationalist and communist, Warda has no resonance with the old Arab nationalisms. Far from being an object to be loved and adored, she seizes opportunities to defend herself using hand-to-hand combat or light weaponry, and the many male admirers she attracts are represented as at best a nuisance and at worst hypocritical obstacles to global justice and liberation of the masses. Thus, the character has much in common with the Vietnamese woman warrior but constitutes an affront to the myth of the Orientalized odalisque,[49] as well as the Arab woman as national allegory.

As a student in Beirut, Warda (or Shahla, the given name by which she is then called) begins to learn the requirements of navigating between her femininity and her ideological and personal-political commitments. For example, she describes in her diary an incident near the end of her time in college, when she is invited to a committee meeting by one Comrade Samer, only to find out that the committee is made up of only the two of them. Warda responds to his boastful assertions of prowess as a lover with an equally bold defiance:

> But once I processed what was happening, I felt insulted. He remarked with this twisted smile that he knew how to make me happy, that I would experience total pleasure, and that women always had a good time with him. He was going to show me things that my Jordanian boyfriend could not. I thought about leaving, but then I changed my mind. I took off all my clothes and stripped away my stockings and panties. I lay across the couch and quietly said, "help yourself." He looked confused for a second, but then took off his

> clothes and came to me. I held my frozen look on him while he tried to do it. Of course, he couldn't do anything since I was so dry. All of sudden, he came onto my bare thighs. I said while I was putting my clothes on, "I didn't enjoy it. Did you?" He didn't answer, so I said, "Wouldn't it have been better to just bring home a prostitute from Place El Burj? You might have had a better time."[50]

Weeks later, Warda kicks Samer in the groin while role-playing in front of a group of guerrilla trainees. These interactions highlight the main character's emerging sense of her own agency in the midst of a complicated social system that presents what she perceives as multilayered challenges of capitalism, imperialism, nationalism, and patriarchy, each of which has the potential to operate on the scale of the globe, the region, the nation, and the body. In Arab nationalist literature, male attraction to Warda might represent the bourgeois Arab male's love of the nation; in Orientalist representations, Samer's pass would be yet another Arab male attempt at subjugation. Here, however, as a consequence of the overlapping scalar grid set up in scenes featuring Warda, the power relations in an attempted seduction by a playboy become difficult to extricate from the power relations that systematize geopolitics. These challenges with patriarchy operating at multiple levels endure and even become more pronounced later in the novel, when she leaves the cosmopolitan milieu of Beirut for a guerrilla camp in Dhofar.

The novel's structure channels geohistory on two distinct levels. As I have said, the novel turns to the archival to disrupt clichés about the region—not just the passivity of women, but also the political complacency of the Arabian Peninsula as an area filled with rich sheikhs, happy to follow the lead of Western regimes, while clinging to reactionary personal beliefs. Warda, her brother, and her comrades undercut such notions. Still, the novel itself enacts the historical erasing of radical social movements through its dual narrative. The "present moment" of the novel is the placid Sultanate of Oman of the 1990s as seen through the eyes of an aging Egyptian writer once active in leftist politics. This character, Rushdy, experiences contemporary Oman as a land almost completely devoid of the radicalism that undergirds Warda's story. Through a concerted effort, he finds the diaries, but retelling parts of her story only reinforces the yawning gap between the present and the recent past in the southern peninsular region. The present is full of filthy-rich petrodollar magnates, consumerism, and a distinctly hypocritical but pervasive soft Islamism. Although surrounded throughout the trip by air-conditioned comfort (in sharp contrast to the circumstances experienced by Warda in hilltop guerrilla camps more than twenty years earlier), Rushdy's physical health begins to deteriorate, and he decides to return to Cairo. A plot twist brings the two narrative strands together when Rushdy runs into Warda's brother at the airport. Now far from being a leftist, he has become a comfortable apologist for the sultanate, even assisting in intelligence, surveillance, and security. But the novel does not end at this point.

After this moment at the Muscat airport comes a final archival note. A short epilogue steps outside the two narrative strands and narrates, in a few brief sentences, the way the Marxist Left of the Arabian Peninsula was eviscerated in the 1990s by a civil war in "united" Yemen that (the last sentence of this 2000 novel tells us) featured the participation of one Osama Bin Laden, who claimed to have overseen the assassination of 158 Marxist leaders in southern Yemen between 1990 and 1994.[51] Recall that South and North Yemen were unified in 1990, ending a twenty-four-year experiment with an Arab Marxist republic in the southernmost of the two. The theme of religious fundamentalists, supported by Americans, "ethnically" cleansing Marxists reappears here in a peninsular context parallel to, but distinct from, the Korean one dramatized in *The Guest*.

The Yemen example reintroduces the American style of partition in imperial practice. Although it seems at times that the United States rediscovered sectarianism (in the Balkans, for example) as an excuse for partition after the Cold War, this is probably just a new stage in the dividing of ideologies so as to conquer and erase. After all, then-senator Joseph R. Biden's suggestion in a *New York Times* editorial of May 2006 that Iraq be partitioned along communal lines was never formally implemented. Furthermore, the ability of the Obama administration, the *New York Times*, and National Public Radio to think of southern Yemen as a flashpoint in the global campaign against Islamic terrorism has been a highly effective rhetorical mechanism for erasing the distinctive ideological position of communities in southern Yemen on issues of global justice. Indeed, Yemen might now be viewed as being punished by recent American administrations for being poor, just as earlier American presidents punished Korea for being occupied (by Japan). Again the point is made by Paik Nak-chung, who noted that the 1990 unification of the two Yemens happened by agreement between two sets of leaders, with almost no participation of civil society on either side of the North/South divide.[52] While the two Koreas remain divided, Paik finds no model for their unification in the other Cold War examples of Germany (where the West swallowed the East whole), Vietnam (where the North swallowed the South), or Yemen, a country that has been brutalized by first a drone campaign and then a U.S.-supported Saudi campaign of indiscriminate bombing, ever since a group made up mostly of rogue Saudis carried out the Bin Laden–inspired September 11 attacks. In both cases, the place in the global capitalist order of the local hegemon—Japan and Saudi Arabia, respectively—causes the U.S. response to a global provocation to ricochet onto a weaker neighbor.

The division of Yemen into a northern pro-Saudi, U.S.-dependent, capitalist military dictatorship and a southern leftist Marxist state that aligned itself with peasants, workers, Palestinians, and the USSR has origins distinct from those of Korea, Vietnam, China/Taiwan, and Germany. Indeed, the origins of the division go back to the nineteenth-century British occupation of the Port of Aden and subsequent deal brokering between the Ottomans and the British begun in 1904 and reinforced by a 1934 border agreement.[53] Still, the division took on a Cold War valence by the 1960s, when former colonial masters retreated and the impoverished and crowded regions at the bottom of the Arabian Peninsula became of strategic interest to the United States and its main regional ally, Saudi Arabia—as well as its much less influential rivals, Nasserist Egypt and the USSR.[54] That the Yemens were subjected to a Cold War partition illustrates the power of American Cold War hegemony to shape cultural formations in the Global South. Paik's interest in the Yemen example connects it to his concept of the division system as a Korean marker of historical difference. The Korean parallel suggests the roots of contemporary geopoliticals in historical conflicts that are ideological and scaled, and rooted in regionally inflected historical specificity.

Laroui has critiqued an American historiography that portrays large swaths of the Global South as "no-idea-producing" areas. This phrase, coined by an American Orientalist writing in the 1960s, has its contemporary equivalent in Fukuyama's rough dismissal of the "strange thoughts [that] occur to people in Albania or Burkina Faso," since he considers these outside the sphere of "the common ideological heritage of mankind." Along these lines, consider the representation of the Korean Peninsula as a tech-savvy and rich emerging market with a hermit kingdom run by a comically insane dynasty appended to it, or of the Arabian Peninsula as filled with reassuringly rich and pro-American oil sheikhs, helping the United States to keep in line a cesspool of terrorists, tribals, drone-strike candidates, and fanatics. Both these pictures reinforce the idea that historical difference on a global scale has become inconsequential. As a disruption of this smoothening account of the global, the archival novel can be aligned with social movements—democratization in the Arab world, reunification in the Koreas, social justice in both—which find themselves facing an existential threat from finance capital and the power of an idea of post-history.

VI. THE AMERICAN "THIRD WORLD" NOVEL IN THE AGE OF TERROR

Paul Bowles died in November of 1999 at his home in Tangier, Morocco. The Cold War had come to an end by then, and the subsequent "War on Terror" had, in some senses, already begun. Middle Eastern "terror," Islam, Saddam, and Iran had replaced global communism as major foci for discussions in foreign policy circles, and domestically "secret evidence laws" that laid the groundwork for the post 9/11 "Patriot Act" were enacted in the United States after a failed attempt to blow up the World Trade Center on February 26, 1993. Fukuyama and Huntington (with the help of their interlocutors and commentators) had provided a frame in which to fit the new binarism pitting United States against the Arab/Muslim/developing world, which replaced the old Cold War binarism in the American mind.

The engagement with the Global South as setting that Bowles spurred on after World War II, and then eventually found himself futilely attempting to refashion, continued to accrue significance for literary authors in the United States. Certainly, literary novelists often felt less tortured than Bowles had been about appropriating global settings. An illustrative anecdote I cannot forget features one of the most famous and celebrated American novelists of our time, who, after being asked about the recurring reference to science and medicine in his work at a question and answer session, responded that he had returned regularly to science because of a special interest and expertise that had made him come to think of it the way other novelists of his generation might think of a particular foreign country they knew well. In the context, I understood him to be saying deep knowledge of a particular foreign landscape or culture had become a kind of reliable source material for the ambitious American fiction writer. The East is a career, in Disraeli's famous maxim about an earlier imperial epoch.

It is difficult to generalize about the goals of such a large body of fictional works. The Bowles tradition of American "Third World" novel writing had become too diffuse by the time of his death to sum up with a few bullet points. Individual novels continue to have value as active documents within this discourse, having their own capacity for disruption or diversion. Still, the War on Terror has special significance for this tradition after September 11, 2001. Not only have critics and readers been particularly interested in anything that might be called "post-9/11 fiction," or that promises in some way to foster understanding of the inscrutable events of that day; as a defining historical event of the new century, 9/11 has turned into something like interpretive quicksand into which all influential texts dealing with the globe sink when placed beneath the scrutiny of American critics.

Don DeLillo's *Falling Man*, Jonathan Safran Foer's *Extremely Loud and Incredibly Close*, and John Updike's *Terrorist* are among the most cited examples of the American literary novel's response to 9/11, although what is striking about these works is how thoroughly domesticated the global question becomes.[55] I have emphasized questions of scale in this chapter and attempted to connect them to setting. That critics have found novels about the American experience of living around New York to be telling regarding the new U.S. position in the world speaks volumes about the continuing power of processes of domestication during an era when citizens are more globally connected than ever. The New York / New Jersey setting has a scalar power in this grouping of novels and in the criticism they inspired, which seems therapeutic inside the U.S. context.

A more complicating view of globalization's effects on literary fiction, however, emerges if we think of the more technical aspects of the Bowles-tradition novel in their post-9/11 trajectory, for the "Third World" setting favored in the Bowles novel continues to be much in evidence in more contemporary fiction. In fact, examples are many, but for these purposes, two significant, notable novels that converse tellingly with Ibrahim's *Warda* and Hwang's *The Guest* must suffice as illustrations. The two peninsulas of Arabia and Korea serve as settings in Dave Egger's *A Hologram for the King* (2012) and Adam Johnson's *The Orphan Master's Son* (2012). Both novels were nominated for prominent awards, and *The Orphan Master's Son* won the Pulitzer Prize. Both authors are critically acclaimed, but they represent distinct branches of America's literary elite, with Eggers engendering a large popular following through a variety of activities, work with diverse media, and engagement with community work, while Johnson holds a position at one of the most renowned creative writing programs in the country.

A Hologram for the King follows the traditional Bowles structure but evolves the narrative of the restless American in the desert to reflect contemporary realities. In the novel, Adam Clay, an American salesman who has transitioned from the manufacturing sector to IT, finds himself recently divorced at the peak of middle age, and at the beginning of the story has set off for Saudi Arabia to get his middle-class consumerist groove back. He hopes to return to the United States at the end of the sales trip with a substantial commission that will pay for his daughter's college tuition and liberate him from the financial concerns that plague downwardly mobile middle-class white men in twenty-first-century America. The specific project is to set up a demonstration of a holographic communication system that will seduce the Saudis into naming his home company a preferred service provider. The novel then follows Clay's solitary, sterile sojourn in the mundane world of contemporary petrodollar culture. He spends most of his mornings missing appointed arrival times, only to find that there is nothing for him to do at the arrival point but wait. He and his young American assistants work to achieve mundane goals like obtaining a better internet connection or a stronger air-conditioning unit as they wait for the elusive title character, who seems destined never to arrive. Meanwhile Clay's movements outside the work environment become increasingly haphazard, underscoring that he is adrift in life. The culmination of the novel feels ambiguous: on the one hand, the king suddenly appears across the compound in another tent and signs a contract with a Chinese team without looking at the presentation of Clay's group; on the other, the protagonist decides to stay in Saudi and pursue a new life by trying his luck with a new network of friends and contacts engendered by his bumbling adventures outside of work.

The best-known Bowles narratives feature a frustrated white middle-class man abandoning American soil to seek spiritual renewal in Arab deserts. With noteworthy variations, this plot describes "A Distant Episode," *The Sheltering Sky*, *Let It Come Down*, and *The Spider's House*. Of these texts, *A Hologram for the King* most closely tracks *Let It Come Down*. The main characters are comparable in their situations and their attitudes and respond to the Arab/Muslim setting in remarkably similar ways. The two are similarly motivated to escape America at the start of their respective novels. Both pursue flirtations with expat women and relations with local/Arab ones. Both make friends with younger Arab men, who eventually lead them toward Arab hinterlands. Nelson Dyar, the main character in *Let It Come Down*, experiments with drugs as part of his escape; Clay passes out from drinking too much of a homemade cocktail that an expatriate source has slipped to him. Both claim to be in pursuit of increasingly tenuous-looking professional opportunities that serve as a fig leaf to cover a raw spiritual vacuum ("He could assume a new name. He could abandon all debts . . . leave the crushing vice of his life in America behind. He had done fifty four years of it. Wasn't that enough?").[56]

In its invocation of the early American "Third World" novel structure, *A Hologram for the King* represents a return to a particular strain in that tradition, one that sees the individual as adrift and unknowing in a sea of global challenges that have been thrust upon America in all its innocence by the geopolitics of the Cold War. In this narrative, the Western male subject—particularly the white American—symbolizes a bedraggled United States venturing forth to fill the vacuum left by a decadent and collapsed European colonialism. *A Hologram for the King*, however, redeploys this master narrative in distinctive contemporary circumstances. Literary critics have described this context as, for example, "capital's move toward the financial-insubstantial, and the corresponding decline, at least in America, of a manufacturing-based economy,"[57] an era of "the new precariousness of work [in which] work has lost its long-time predominant form and meaning as stable, paid employment and has tumultuously turned into a new, much more fragmented, multidimensional and globalized form."[58] A third critic, writing specifically of a post-9/11 turn away from irony in the writing of contemporary American novelists, sees the novel as "deflating claims to US economic, ideological, and moral dominance by showing the ways the rest of the world, the space the United States seeks to dominate, is infiltrating and remaking US economic, ideological, and moral spaces."[59] These critics suggest that within Clay's specific dilemma there lies a synecdoche for a civilizational dilemma facing the United States, and indeed, this reading is very much encouraged by the regular gestures toward U.S. nationalism whenever topics related to corporatization, finance, work, or the global are mentioned in the text. Examples include when a passenger in Clay's row on the airplane to Saudi Arabia drinks too much and holds forth about America's decline into "a nation of doubters, worriers, overthinkers,"[60] when Clay muses that "Banana Republic was killing the ability of entrepreneurs like himself to move this country forward,"[61] or when an architect at an expat cocktail party in Saudi tells Clay in reference to grand building projects, "In the U.S. now there's not that kind of dreaming happening . . . the dreaming's being done elsewhere for now."[62] Petrodollar Arabs and—in the concluding *Rex ex machina*—the Chinese constitute global forces before which Americans look hapless and fumbling. The critique of America in the classical American "Third World" novel is revisited, but in the post-9/11 era, a dosage of victimhood has been infused into it. Herein, the United States has jumped from a land of callow innocents to the "country for old men" that finds itself cornered by the globe's irrationalities and unwillingness to accept history's ends.

The comparison with Bowles might be enhanced via a contrast to Ibrahim's *Warda*. Of the few critical notes published so far on Egger's very recent novel, none has made specific reference to the Saudi/U.S. relationship as a context—even when invoking the 9/11 attacks or corporate globalization in the twenty-first century. Meinig does include a helpful discussion of "space" in the novel,[63] but this discussion only calls our attention to the manner in which the novel's narrative emphases direct us away from the geopolitical underpinnings of an American business trip to Saudi Arabia at the present moment. In many ways, Adam Clay is highly comparable to Rushdy in *Warda*. Both are past their prime and arrive on the Arabian Peninsula with hopes of regaining part of the spirit of their youth. Clay is an ambivalent partial antihero; for many readers, his situation might critique a new Western decadence—or at the very least suggest Western decline. But Rushdy must share his novel with the heroine whose presence insists on the geohistorically constructed realities of this same peninsula that is easily read in *A Hologram for the King* as posthistorical and postscalar. Clay exposes the pretention behind the Western narrative of liberal triumph but does so curiously while still accepting history's end.

Process serves as a connector between Hwang Sok-yong of *The Guest* and Adam Johnson of *The Orphan Master's Son*, for both authors speak of the use of interviews with live subjects as an aid in their attempts to construct a differently understood North Korea. For the most part, however, the two novels strike a series of contrastive notes at both formal and other levels. In the case of *The Orphan Master's Son*, the text can be read as an innovative leap forward in the tradition of the American "Third World" novel. Johnson states that his motivation for narrating a North Korean story was that "the notion that there is an official narrative for a nation—a script written by one person, essentially—that conscripts every citizen into being an unwilling character of someone else's story was really compelling to me."[64] This statement presents North Korea as the least knowable of spaces. In this sense, another motivation behind the novel is a Bowlesian desire to cross the wall to the Other. The post-Bowlesian innovation, however, comes in the structuring of the novel's point of view through North Korean lenses. Such a move, we have seen, is not completely absent from Bowles's oeuvre, but no Bowles work, nor any prominent examples from the American "Third World" novel tradition, attempt so thoroughgoing a focalization through the Other. When Americans appear in the novel, they do so fleetingly, in brief—albeit very significant—scenes, and the narrator never presents their thoughts and feelings in a free indirect manner. They are always viewed from what is presented as the North Korean side. If McGurl is correct in stating that point of view constitutes the central fixation of North American literary discourse since modernism, *The Orphan Master's Son* can be viewed as an audacious writerly experiment in which the construction of a novel's point of view strives toward the fashioning of the least imaginable human mindset: a North Korean citizen's inner world. This sets the novel's form within a version of "program era" discourse, but as I have tried to show, literary point of view has a particularly geopolitical valence in the Bowles tradition. Therefore, it is important to contextualize it also within this genealogy, where the presence of North Korea in the "Axis of Evil" undergirds its reception as the least knowable of spaces.

Compared to *A Hologram for the King*, *The Orphan Master's Son* is a long novel with a complex structure. The main through line for the novel is the story of Jun Do—the name is later revealed to be a Koreanization of "John Doe"—whose life is traced in part 1 from a bleak childhood in an orphanage, through an upwardly mobile career as a kidnapper of Japanese citizens, a radio transmission operator, and eventually a translator for an official entourage. It is in this final capacity that he becomes one of the few North Koreans ever to travel to the United States, but luck in this instance proves double edged, and he finds it impossible to avoid behavior that will be translated as disloyal back home, so he disappears into a North Korean political prison at the end of part 1.

Part 2 evolves away from the confines of Jun Do's point of view by adopting a tripartite structure of focalizations. A narrative strand is focalized through an officer in Pyongyang's secret police whose job is to construct the biographies of the citizens he tortures and interrogates. A second strand is represented by fictionalized official communiqués that alternate between dark and comical as they present the national story that so intrigued Johnson, which he felt motivated to write against. The third strand continues the narrative thread from part 1. A third-person limited narrator presents Jun Do's story predominantly from his point of view, but at this point his identity has shifted. He has appropriated the name, the family, the house, and the lifestyle of one Commander Ga, having killed him in prison and escaped, with the goal of taking his place next to his movie star wife, Sun Moon, whom Jun Do / Commander Ga has idolized since youth. The story suggests that the Dear Leader, Kim Jong-il, who had lost patience with the original Commander Ga, is complicit in the audacious identity theft, but identities and facts increasingly lose their fixity to the extent that it becomes difficult to know exactly how the new Commander Ga's performance is being accomplished.

The complexity of the narrative structure in part 2 is one of the novel's many strengths. The three distinct narrative discourses force vocal diversity onto the monological official story. Curiously, Jun Do / Commander Ga's thought world evolves in a direction that turns him into something very like a liberal American, and thus he almost becomes the equivalent of the bourgeois male American adrift in the world, which one finds in other novels of this tradition. He is obsessed with the film *Casablanca*, and he values the domesticity of his life with Commander Ga's family and the pet dog they have imported from Texas. In one scene, he explains to the investigator the pleasures of intimate sharing that the police state has subverted. The explanation evolves toward an expression of an inner liberal man inside Ga, struggling to be born: "I may not know who I am. But the actress is free. I'm not sure I understand freedom, but I've felt it and she now has it too."[65] The novel is meticulous in its attempt to construct a North Korean world out of the imaginative consciousness of an American mind. Yet increasingly as the novel nears its climax, the liberal consciousness advances within the novel's world. The story becomes about a kind of societal captivity, highly comparable—at least in the end—to the other genres of captivity upon which the myth of U.S. globalism in general, and divisional conceptions of the Korean Peninsula in particular, are constructed.

An interview conducted with the author by David Ebershoff, a writer and editor at Random House, the novel's publisher, appears in the 2012 paperback edition. Ebershoff begins with a statement that implies a liberal and postscalar end to all literary fiction: "It's one thing to think about North Korea as a subject for a novel, but of course countries and political structures are never really the subjects of good fiction—people are."[66] The author's responses propose the idea of fiction as a medium that can go beyond the wonkish representations of politicians and academics to get at the human heart still beating in the individual North Korean subject. The narrative is one of American author liberating the captive human hearts of the North Korean Other. Putting it this way crudely reduces the accomplishments of *The Orphan Master's Son*, a literary work that is indeed innovative and subtle. The discussion that has emerged around the text to date is less complex, however, and in fact suggests that the American script of the global has its own limitations. Therefore, it is commonplace to read interviews with Johnson devoted largely to discussions of North Korean society or the "North Korean problem." In the face of such questioning, the author is reduced to restating banalities: "The people there are just as human as we are, driven by the same needs and motivations."[67]

I have taken as axiomatic in this study the notion that a complex cultural text—a literary novel, a poem, an art film, a work of cultural criticism—can have the power to complicate the mythologized notions that make American empire's enduring force a foundation for the U.S. understanding of the global. There is no comparison, in other words, between *The Orphan Master's Son* and a Hollywood blockbuster that demonizes North Korea, like *Olympus Has Fallen*, or between a literary novel of the Africa/Middle East regions and a jingoistic picture like *The Delta Force*. The complex text in this sense is more helpful in understanding the extent to which—to borrow a phrase from William Appleman Williams—empire has become a way of life within U.S. culture. This is because while *Olympus Has Fallen* has little or no potential to reorient the nationalism and mythologization that shape the U.S. attitude toward the globe, a critical cultural text may have such potential. This potential, however, could only be realized in a different environment of reception, discussion, and circulation of such texts, and this new environment could never be built without a more precise and honest acknowledgment of the strange global/imperial position of the United States in the twenty-first century. More specifically, the way knowledge about the world is produced in the United States must be critically examined with a view toward understanding the divisions before history's end that allowed for the construction of these new Others.

CONCLUSION

The End of "Foreign"

In her 2015 novel *The Diver's Clothes Lie Empty*, the author Vendela Vida—a public intellectual who has won many awards for her writing, been featured on NPR and in the *New York Times*, founded the influential cultural magazine *The Believer*, and received numerous high-profile awards for her fiction—proves that the American "Third World" novel continues to develop dynamically. The story, set almost entirely in Morocco, invokes the Bowles tradition of novel writing in its setting, language, and structure. To prove the self-consciousness of these strategies, it interweaves an early reference to the father figure of American cultural producers in Morocco:

> "You know Paul Bowles?" the driver says, out of nowhere. Because you're staring at the old leather shoes, you think for a brief moment he's going to tell you that they belonged to Paul Bowles.
>
> "Yes," you say. You know who Paul Bowles is. You devoted a paragraph or maybe even a page to him in a college essay you wrote about post–World War II bohemians. You had no prior interest in the subject, nor any sustaining interest for that matter; you signed up for the class because the professor was intriguing to you.[1]

The narrative's use of the rare second-person voice illustrates how the novel innovates at the same time as it maintains a sense of the tradition in which it is operating. The second-person voice concentrates the narrator's perspectival monopoly on her surroundings, leaving the Moroccans around her further removed from the at times disconcerting inside joke between the reader, the narrator, and the protagonist. While Moroccans are again excluded from the novel's discourse, the second-person voice suggests a heightened self-awareness regarding the textual politics of this exclusion.

The Diver's Clothes Lie Empty is set in Morocco and features an American traveler. In this sense, the reference to Bowles reinforces an intertextual dynamic that is out of its setting and context. Still, Bowles is hardly treated with adoration in this passage. Rather, his name appears arbitrarily out of the mouth of a Moroccan driver, and the reference obviously has no special resonance for the main character, who is distracted by just having lost her wallet and passport. The dismissiveness with which the main character recognizes the name Paul Bowles suggests the author's ambition to move beyond the Bowles tradition, which she also winkingly admits to be working within. In the work of writers like Vida, a writer of prestige literary fiction, or Kathy Acker (1947–1997), a significant producer of countercultural works, the female American traveler exposes the masculinity deeply imbedded in the stories found in novels by Bowles, Kerouac, Bellow, O'Brien, McCarthy, Vollmann, Rush, and Eggers (Vida's husband), in which white American men attempt to cognitively possess the new and complex Global South through experiences of travel.

In the process, however, novels like Vida's *The Diver's Clothes Lie Empty* or Acker's *Kathy Goes to Haiti* demonstrate that it is possible to expose the masculinity of such texts without dismantling the patriarchy in which they are imbricated. In both novels, the threat to a markedly white masculinity by the darker "Third World" male Other survives the narrative's withering satirical tone. The Arab men in *The Diver's Clothes Lie Empty* are taciturn and duplicitous, while the Haitian male represented by Acker is dogged and sex crazed. U.S. culture tries to solve problems of imperialist patriarchy by invoking a domesticated discourse of identity. Melani McAlister has documented the way this process has worked in American cultural representations of the Middle East—particularly after the U.S. withdrawal from Vietnam.[2] My reading of the American "Third World" novel tradition has similarly called for a focus on the imperial American lens, one that demonstrates its power to appropriate discourses of liberty or gender equity or diversity in a manner that etiolates their critical edge.

In this vein, the whiteness of the American "Third World" novel also engenders complications. Generations of critics have progressively broadened the canon of American letters to account for a more diverse understanding of U.S. domestic culture, and this evolution invites the critical scrutiny of the scholar who studies the American "Third World" novel. How, for example, does the presence of Africa in the novels of black American writers like Alice Walker or Reginald McKnight complicate the Bowles tradition?[3] In general, can it not be said that these high-profile writers of color in the circles of the American literary elite offer an alternative view of American whiteness with great potential for dismantling American imperialism? My answer here is that the recent history of multicultural movements within the United States has actually not proven to be a helpful antidote to structures of imperialism. In fact, the rise of multiculturalism in studies of American literature and culture has paralleled the acceleration of U.S. imperial culture via increasingly insidious means since the end of the Cold War.

My emphasis has been on processes of domestication in American arts and letters—those mechanisms by which the pervasiveness of the United States' global implication is replaced by a cultural rhetoric of the national. Referencing texts by writers of color trained in an American milieu and working within American institutions does not in and of itself solve the problem of domestication, and in reality, there is a history of questions of the multicultural, the ethnic, and civil rights reinforcing the domesticating impulse.[4]

The impact of any given literary text depends heavily on the many individuals involved in that text's distribution, circulation, and reception—editors, advertisers, reviewers, readers, teachers, and critics. Each of these agents in the process constitutes a lens, or filter, that plays a role in determining the multifarious impacts of the text. Therefore, the power of the individual writer or artist—as an Asian or Arab or Latina body—to disrupt the cultural discourse of domestication has limits. I would argue that more recent generations of U.S.-based writers of color show a greater degree of engagement with geohistories, geopolitics, and geographies beyond the borders of the United States than have earlier generations. Susan Abulhawa, Chimananda Adichie, Julia Alvarez, Edwidge Danticat, Kirin Desai, Junot Díaz, Randa Jarrar, Chang Rae Lee, and Viet Thanh Nguyen are a few examples among a great many. Poets like Fady Joudah and Khaled Mattawa have incorporated the translation of poetry coming out of traditions quite distinct from and even disruptive of contemporary American poetics into their practice as poets. And the poet Hayan Charara—not a translator but an Arab American from Detroit working very much in the vein of new writing from diverse U.S. authors—has recently published the brilliant poem "The Prize," in which he juxtaposes the topics of top prize–winning American poems with historical acts of U.S. military aggression inside Iraq occurring in the same year. Thereby, Charara brilliantly sums up in a mere 128 extremely short lines the U.S. problem of domestication and the literary.

One of the strengths of these new authors is the way their work resists more provincialized readings of "multiethnic" American writing. Still, the real issue for this study is what ultimate effect these and other new presences in the American public sphere will have on the cultural preference for domestication of global realities, and this question involves more than a very gradual evolution of contemporary American letters toward a somewhat more ethnically diverse literary scene. In addition, it requires a more direct focus on the filters through which a literary text moves and the lenses that participate in its construction.

Even "world literature" cannot by itself subvert the American impulse toward domestication, because cultural domestication grows out of U.S. institutions with a direct interest in perpetuating global hegemony, and it is within these institutions that so much of the "world literature debate" plays out, acting as yet another filter through which ideas of the global circulate within the domestic sphere. Only an openly dissident critical lens that calls attention to America's globality wherever it finds it hidden in domesticating discourse can initiate a sustainable challenge to cultural domestication. I have found it helpful to emphasize for these purposes critical approaches that invoke geohistory, that incorporate both translated texts and processes of literary and cultural translation, and that center the work of global intellectuals. These three strategies share a potential for disruption of processes of U.S. cultural domestication at the present moment.

A few concluding points might be made regarding the last of these three strategies: an emphasis on global intellectuals. First, while critical discussions of literary globality in the United States have increasingly included prominent thinkers with roots in the Global South—influential, transformative scholars like Edward Said, Gayatri Chakravorty Spivak, Rey Chow, and the generations that have followed them—global cultural studies has remained broadly indifferent to intellectuals working in Global South institutions and writing in languages other than English or French. This problem is not merely a theoretical challenge. To simply produce an English translation of a text by a thinker working in a non-European language from the Global South and have the translation distributed in the United States faces immense obstacles, as I have learned from personal experience.[5] How exactly a greater emphasis on such bibliographies might change cultural studies in the United States cannot be guessed until more work of this type can be done, but it is already clear that there are many old chestnuts in American discourse of the global that would not survive such a shift of emphasis in reading practices.

For example, to find a serious cultural producer outside the United States who would argue that the United States enjoys an exceptionalism among nations of the world and therefore has a global responsibility to use its power for good would be almost impossible. Of course, the intellectual culture of any complex modern society will have diversity; still, global intellectuals who would accept the idea of American exceptionalism are extremely rare. The case of intellectual thinking about American exceptionalism is only one example, albeit a particularly resonant one, of how the intellectual culture of the most powerful country in the world might prove idiosyncratic in ways that are insidious. The point is not to simply debunk the notion of American exceptionalism, as helpful as doing so may be in and of itself. A sustainable critique will require more. The critical lens that produces notions filled with invisible nationalism must be revisited and reconsidered. That U.S. culture can be characterized by so many idiosyncratic conceptualizations of the global calls attention to the challenge presented by an anglophone, U.S.-based critical lens. Within this challenge inheres the irony of a most nationalistic cultural discourse in a most globalized historical era.

Notes

INTRODUCTION

1. Martin Woollacott, "Europe Losing Faith in American Leadership," *Manchester Guardian Weekly*, June 18, 1995, 10.

2. Ibid, 10. In his turning a public statement about an international incident into a film pitch, President Clinton here evidenced the way Ronald Reagan's blatant embrace of the confluence between fictional narrations and historical ones had become commonplace by the end of the Cold War.

3. Ibid, 10.

4. Franco Moretti, "Conjectures on World Literature" *New Left Review* 1 (2000): 54–68; Pascale Casanova, *The World Republic of Letters*, trans. M. B. DeBevoise (Cambridge, Mass.: Harvard University Press, 2007); David Damrosch, *What Is World Literature?* (Princeton, N.J.: Princeton University Press, 2003).

5. Of the many studies that have taken up the world literature question more recently, it will be clear to those familiar with the bibliography that I have drawn on the work of Emily Apter, Pheng Cheah, Paul Jay, Neil Lazarus, Aamir Mufti, Shaden Tageldin, and the Warwick Research Collective, to name a few. My particular interest is in critical paradigms that not only move beyond the old nationalist prejudices of literary studies but also offer an awareness of the inequalities produced by global capitalism and model the rich potential of literary analysis that fully acknowledges the complexity of cultural historiographies *outside* Europe. Three studies therefore particularly influence my thinking about the world literature question: Gayatri Chakravorty Spivak, *The Death of a Discipline* (New York: Columbia University Press, 2003); S. Shankar's *Flesh and Fish Blood: Postcolonialism, Translation, and the Vernacular* (Berkeley: University of California Press, 2012); and *Immanuel Wallerstein and the Prob-*

lem of the World: System, Scale, and Culture, ed. David Palumbo-Liu, Bruce Robbins, and Nirvana Tanoukhi (Durham, N.C.: Duke University Press, 2011).

6. On the dependency theorists, see chapter 1 of Hosam Aboul-Ela, *Other South: Faulkner, Coloniality, and the Mariátegui Tradition* (Pittsburgh: University of Pittsburgh Press, 2007); as well as Jorgé Larain, *Theories of Development: Capitalism, Colonialism, and Dependency* (Cambridge: Polity, 1989); and Theotonio Dos Santos, *A teoria da dependência: Balanço e perspectivas* (Rio de Janeiro: Editora Civilização Brasileira, 2000).

7. For example, the renewed focus upon Goethe, the Marx of *The Communist Manifesto*, and Auerbach may be salutary, but it also carries ironies as a foundation for a more fully globalized discussion, given that the three were born within a 230-mile radius of one another. A study that considered what aspect of German cultural heritage produced such a keen interest in notions of the global could be most welcome, on the one hand. On the other, an unwillingness to at least point to these ironies constitutes a tacit acceptance of the Eurocentric idea that the new thinking in comparative literatures should be exerting an effort to move beyond.

8. The Warwick Research Collective in its study *Combined and Uneven Development* (Liverpool: Liverpool University Press, 2015) models some helpful practices in navigating the difficult overlap of the cultural and the material. See especially chapter 2.

9. Pheng Cheah has demonstrated this latent quietism in the sociological approaches represented by both Moretti and Damrosch: "Although Moretti posits a direct causal link between literature and the world of social forces, as in Casanova's account, world literature also has no transformative agency in the world. A work of world literature merely acts by reflecting and refracting the stronger primary social forces operative within it and to which its form corresponds via a natural symbolic relation" (Pheng Cheah, *What Is a World? On Postcolonial Literature as World Literature* [Durham, N.C.: Duke University Press, 2016], 36).

10. As, for example, in the work done by Hayden White, Fredric Jameson, and others in the 1980s.

11. Cheah begins mildly self-critically in his recent study of postcolonial literature as world literature: "The organization of this book can give the wrong impression of a division of labor between European philosophy and literature from the postcolonial South, where postcolonial texts have the subordinate function of illustrating the ontological and normative problems concerning worldliness that European philosophy elaborates" (*What Is a World?* 14). Cheah is fairly singular among authors publishing with U.S.-based academic presses in having an awareness of this extremely common issue, and he is right to answer himself with the explanation that "the impact of the history of colonialism on literary and intellectual production has made it impossible to clearly separate Europe from the postcolonial world and to say dogmatically that texts produced in different places do not share thematic and stylistic continuities and enter into debate with each other" (15). Still, if it is true that Europe and non-Europe are so inseparable, it should also follow that the repetition of this formula, which "subordinates" postcolonial literature as illustration for European philosophy, is not inevitable. In this sense, the present study is consistent with the rest of my

work in searching for alternatives to the more common framing that elevates the position of the philosopher within the Global North.

12. In the late 1990s, a branch of scholarship in the fields of American Studies and American literature began to emphasize a "transnational turn" in the field that has taken as its point of departure the anachronistic way older versions of the discipline sacralized the borders of the nation-state in spite of the new postnationalism. Particularly valuable within this bibliography are these studies: Wai Chee Dimock, *Through Other Continents: American Literature across Deep Time* (Princeton, N.J.: Princeton University Press, 2006); Brian T. Edwards, *After the American Century: The Ends of U.S. Culture in the Middle East* (New York: Columbia University Press, 2016); and George Handley, *Postslavery Literatures in the Americas: Family Portraits in Black and White* (Charlottesville: University of Virginia Press, 2000); as well as the following essay collections: Jon Smith and Deborah Cohn, eds., *Look Away! The U.S. South in New World Studies* (Durham, N.C.: Duke University Press, 2004); Russ Castronovo and Susan Gilman, eds., *States of Emergency: The Object of American Studies* (Chapel Hill: University of North Carolina Press, 2009); and Lawrence Buell and Wai-Chee Dimock, eds., *Shades of the Planet: American Literature as World Literature* (Princeton, N.J.: Princeton University Press, 2007), to cite just a few more recent works. In a sense, this disciplinary turn contributes as much or more than world literature discourse to my own scholarly foci in this study. Still, this bibliography also can at times be surprisingly hesitant to cite the U.S. role in the world as an imperialistic one. There are clear exceptions: particularly influential for me in the way they foreground imperialism are Amy Kaplan, *The Anarchy of Empire in the Making of U.S. Culture* (Cambridge, Mass.: Harvard University Press, 2002); Donald Pease, "U.S. Imperialism: Global Dominance without Colonies," in *A Companion to Postcolonial Studies*, ed. Sangeeta Ray and Henry Schwarz (Malden, Mass.: Blackwell, 2000), 203–220; and Amy Kaplan and Donald Pease, eds., *Cultures of United States Imperialism* (Durham, N.C.: Duke University Press, 1993).

13. Hardt and Negri, for example, argue that "the U.S. notion of sovereignty . . . poses an idea of the immanence of power in opposition to the transcendent character of modern European sovereignty" (Michael Hardt and Antonio Negri, *Empire* [Cambridge, Mass.: Harvard University Press, 2000], 167) and criticize Said for what they view as his notion that U.S. imperialism is merely a "weak echo" of the classical European empires.

14. The critics of the Warwick school, drawing on the work of Jameson, have called attention to this critical effacing of the U.S. imperial role: "Fredric Jameson has urged us to take on board the implications of the fact that 'the United States is not just one country, or one culture, among others, any more than English is just one language among others. There is a fundamental dissymmetry in the relationship between the United States and every other country in the world, not only Third World countries, but even Japan and those of Western Europe' (1998: 58)" (Warwick Research Collective, *Combined and Uneven Development*, 41).

15. Amy Kaplan, in a study that analyzes the history leading up to World War II, vividly demonstrates the cultural roots of the current moment in the

United States: "Domestic metaphors of national identity are intimately intertwined with renderings of the foreign and the alien, and . . . the notions of the domestic and the foreign mutually constitute one another in an imperial context" (Kaplan, *The Anarchy of Empire*, 4).

16. With respect to soccer/football, consider a reference to Zineddine Zidane, the former French superstar of Algerian descent, who led the French national team to a World Cup title in 1998 and a European Cup in 2000, a man who is surely among the most famous individuals in Europe, Africa, and Latin America. A notorious incident in which he was given a red card during the final of the 2006 World Cup in Germany during overtime, thus ending his participation in the last game of his career, was described by the U.S.-based *Time* magazine six months later in its end of year issue as his "fifteen minutes of fame" (Rebecca Winters Keegan, "15 Who Had their 15 Minutes of Fame," *Time*, December 25, 2006, http://content.time.com/time/magazine/article/0,9171,1570785,00.html).

17. I have learned a great deal from excellent recent scholarship in American studies. In particular, I have in mind Evelyn Alsultany, *Arabs and Muslims in the Media: Race and Representation after 9/11* (New York: New York University Press, 2012); Christine Klein, *Cold War Orientalism: Asia in the Middlebrow Imagination, 1945–1961* (Berkeley: University of California Press, 2003); Melani McAlister, *Epic Encounters: Culture, Media, and U.S. Interests in the Middle East since 1945* (Berkeley: University of California Press, 2005); Mary Renda, *Taking Haiti: Military Occupation and the Culture of U.S. Imperialism, 1915–1940* (Chapel Hill: University of North Carolina Press, 2001), and others. These studies have exposed the cultural workings of imperialism from a U.S. point of departure, and I draw on this body of criticism explicitly in this study. Where I distinguish my own research from this bibliography, however, is on this particular point of contrapuntal method. Just as Orientalism in nineteenth-century Europe should not be studied as a hermetically enclosed discourse with disregard for the anticolonial responses it provoked, U.S. imperialism has another side, and it is particularly incumbent on scholars to discuss these two sides together in light of the strong tendency for the American empire to domesticate.

18. Edward Said, *Orientalism* (New York: Vintage, 1994).

19. In the first of his books to be translated into English, Laroui starts a history of Morocco by critiquing the statement made in a recent volume covering the same topic from an Orientalist point of view to the effect that Morocco could be considered "a no-idea-producing area" (cited in Abdallah Laroui, *The History of the Maghreb: An Interpretive Essay*, trans. Ralph Manheim [Princeton, N.J.: Princeton University Press, 1977], 23n18). This characterization of the Global South as seen through an American lens continues to have force in later American conceptualizations of Africa, Asia, Latin America, and the Middle East. Indeed, its force is central to the American gaze outward.

CHAPTER 1

1. Odd Arne Westad, *The Global Cold War* (New York: Cambridge University Press, 2007), 110. Westad speaks here in primarily economic terms, noting that "in 1950, the US gross domestic product (GDP) was higher than all of Eu-

rope's put together, and possibly equal to that of Europe plus the Soviet Union" (110).

2. Of course, American interventionism dates back much earlier than the end of World War II, as Amy Kaplan, Stephen Kinzer, Ussama Makdisi, William Appleman Williams, and others have documented. It is the nature and the central position of interventionism in American foreign relations that takes a new direction as the United States' post–World War II international role evolves.

3. Brian T. Edwards, *Morocco Bound: Disorienting America's Maghreb, from Casablanca to the Marrakech Express* (Durham NC: Duke University Press, 2005), 36–56.

4. McAlister, *Epic Encounters*, 43–83.

5. Klein, *Cold War Orientalism*, 2.

6. Andrew Hoberek, *The Twilight of the Middle Class: Post–World War II American Fiction and White Collar Work* (Princeton, N.J.: Princeton University Press, 2005), 7.

7. Paul Bowles, *The Sheltering Sky* (New York: HarperCollins, 1999), 161.

8. Henry Luce, "The American Century," http://www.informationclearinghouse.info/article6139.htm.

9. Klein, *Cold War Orientalism*, 9.

10. See Thomas H. Schaub, *American Fiction in the Cold War* (Madison: University of Wisconsin Press, 1991), especially chapter 1, "The Liberal Narrative," for the way the omnipresence of the vituperative charge of communist sympathy shaped an emphatically anticommunist American liberalism in the 1940s and '50s.

11. Evan Brier, "Constructing the Post-War Art Novel: Paul Bowles, James Laughlin, and the Making of *The Sheltering Sky*," *PMLA* 121, no. 1 (2006): 186–99.

12. Edwards, *Morocco Bound*, 109–14.

13. Greg Bevan, "Beyond the Father and Son: The Rise of Modern Morocco in Bowles's *The Spider's House*," *Journal of the American Literature Society of Japan* 5 (2007): 21–33. It is fairly common in very recent Bowles criticism that the work of Edward Said is mentioned at some point without any sustained engagement. Brian T. Edwards and Rob Wilson (in his comparative study of the lyrical engagement with peasant solidarity in both Bowles and Jack Kerouac) display a broad general command of the field of postcolonial studies unusual for critics writing about Bowles. See Rob Wilson, "Masters of Adaptation: Paul Bowles, the Beats, and 'Fellaheen Orientalism,'" *Cultural Politics* 8, no. 2 (2012): 193–206. Of the criticism I have seen, only Edwards makes a direct link, however, between American global hegemony and the Bowles output. In his *Morocco Bound* (2005), he connects the U.S. Army's occupation of Morocco during World War II with a spike in interest in North Africa within the U.S. domestic cultural sphere, exemplified in films like *Casablanca* (1943) and, a few years later, the early fiction of Bowles.

14. Bowles, *The Sheltering Sky*, 6.

15. Mona El-Sherif quotes Michelle Green's description of the contrast felt by Bowles and his friends when they went from the United States to Tangiers at the time: "Since foreigners were virtually immune to criminal prosecution,

American intellectuals had a sense of invulnerability that was particularly exhilarating during the McCarthy era when their colleagues were under siege. It was a heady setting, and it provided expatriate artists like Paul with a perspective that would influence the next generation of the avant-garde." See Mona El-Sherif, "Reclaiming Tangier: Mohamed Choukri's *Al-Khubz Al-Hafi* and Subaltern Citizenship in Urban Literature," *Research in African Literatures* 44, no. 3 (2013): 105.

16. Norman Mailer, *Advertisements for Myself* (Cambridge, Mass.: Harvard University Press, 1992 [1959]), 468. For an excellent discussion of "Pages from Cold Point" as a variation of the prototypical Bowles narrative that depicts travel as escape from American normativity, see Stephen Levin, *The Contemporary Anglophone Travel Novel: The Aesthetics of Self-Fashioning in the Era of Globalization* (New York: Routledge, 2008), 94–97.

17. In this sense, Port is comparable to the linguistics professor in Bowles's most widely cited short story from the 1940s, "A Distant Episode." The short story subtly mocks the ill-fated professor's klutzy overreliance on an academic rationality that reveals itself as totally incongruous with the more natural and improvisational lives in Morocco. While Port is comparable to the professor, his status as what Mailer calls a "square" is not immediately evident but rather revealed more gradually over the course of a couple hundred pages.

18. Bowles, *The Sheltering Sky*, 6.

19. Joseph Allen Boone, *The Homoerotics of Orientalism* (New York: Columbia University Press, 2014), 16.

20. Bowles, *The Sheltering Sky*, 152.

21. Ibid., 179.

22. Schaub, *American Fiction in the Cold War*, 17.

23. Bowles, *The Sheltering Sky*, 278.

24. Mahmoud Mamdani, *Good Muslim, Bad Muslim: America, the Cold War, and the Roots of Terror* (New York: Pantheon, 2004), 234.

25. Allen Hibbard, "Expatriation and Narration in Two Works by Paul Bowles," *West Virginia Philological Papers* 32 (1986): 61.

26. Ibid., 61.

27. Paul Bowles, *Let It Come Down* (Santa Barbara, Calif.: Black Sparrow, 1980), 133.

28. Mohamed Choukri, *Bul Bulz wa 'Uzla Tanja* (Tangier: Altopress, 1996), 12.

29. Hibbard, "Expatriation and Narration in Two Works by Paul Bowles," 65.

30. Ibid., 69.

31. Paul Bowles, *The Spider's House* (Santa Barbara, Calif.: Black Sparrow, 1982), 105.

32. Hibbard, "Expatriation and Narration in Two Works by Paul Bowles,"; Bevan, "Beyond the Father and Son: The Rise of Modern Morocco in Bowles's *The Spider's House*"; and Francine Prose, "The Coldest Eye: Acting Badly among the Arabs," *Harper's*, March 2002, 60–65.

33. Mary Martin Rountree, "Paul Bowles: Translations from the Moghrebi," *Twentieth Century Literature* 32, nos. 3–4 (1986): 388.

34. Edwards, *Morocco Bound*, 233; Nirvana Tanoukhi, "Rewriting Political Commitment for an International Canon: Paul Bowles's *For Bread Alone* as Translation of Mohamed Choukri's *Al-Khubz Al-Hafi*," *Research in African Literatures* 34, no. 2 (2003): 128.

35. Rountree, "Paul Bowles: Translations from the Moghrebi," 400.

36. Edwards, *Morocco Bound*, 234.

37. Rountree, "Paul Bowles: Translations from the Moghrebi," 389.

38. Although Stenham seems to share more in common with his author, one could also parallel the almost maniacal drive of Port, in *The Sheltering Sky*, to find a place untouched by the ruinous influence of Europe and to connect with the least Europeanized locals over dinner, through music, and by having sex with them.

39. A far more appropriate concept out of Spivak's oeuvre is her recent writing on "counter-essentialisms," which applies directly to the way Bowles emphasizes the purity of an ancient "Berber" civilization in Morocco that is untouched by Christian/modern Europe or the Islamic Arab world. On subalternity, see Gayatri Chakravorty Spivak, "Can the Subaltern Speak?" in *Marxism and the Interpretation of Culture*, ed. Carey Nelson (Urbana: University of Illinois Press, 1988), 271–315 . For "counter-essentialism," see Spivak, "Introduction," in Marilena Chaúi, *Between Conformity and Resistance: Essays on Politics, Culture, and the State* (New York: Palgrave, 2011), vii–xi.

40. Rountree, "Paul Bowles: Translations from the Moghrebi," 389.

41. Ibid., 392.

42. While Bassnett and Trivedi, Venuti and others have found translation across the postcolonial divide inherently harmful to the source culture, Shankar, Apter, and Spivak have suggested a complicated politics of transaction at play in translation from and to the postcolonial South. See Susan Bassnett and Harish Trivedi, eds., *Post-Colonial Translation: Theory and Practice* (New York: Routledge, 1999); Lawrence Venuti, *The Scandals of Translation: Toward an Ethics of Difference* (New York: Routledge, 1998); Shankar, *Flesh and Fishblood*; and Apter, *Against World Literature*.

43. Tanoukhi, "Rewriting Political Commitment for an International Canon," 127. See also Mustafa Ettobi, "Cultural Representation in Literary Translation: Translators as Mediators/Creators," *Journal of Arabic Literature* 37, no. 2 (2006): 206–29.

44. Kathleen Fitzpatrick, *The Anxiety of Obsolescence: The American Novel in the Age of Television* (Nashville: Vanderbilt University Press, 2006); Lawrence Hogue, *Postmodern American Literature and Its Other* (Champaign: University of Illinois Press, 2008); Mark McGurl, *The Program Era: Postwar Fiction and the Rise of Creative Writing* (Cambridge, Mass.: Harvard University Press, 2011); Rachel Smith, *Affect and American Literature in the Age of Neoliberalism* (Cambridge: Cambridge University Press, 2015).

CHAPTER 2

1. Abdelhak Elghandor, "Atavism and Civilization: An Interview with Paul Bowles," *Ariel: A Review of International English Literature* 25, no. 2 (1994): 8.

2. Ibid., 11, 21.

3. Ibid., 25.

4. In the early stages of thinking about this project, I was walking down a street in Cairo when I met a friend who also happens to be a prominent scholar of Arabic literature and who published and taught in the United States for several decades. When asked what I was working on, I answered that I was starting a project about Paul Bowles and was shocked by the response: "I hope you kill him!"

5. Choukri, *Bul Bulz wa 'Uzla Tanja*; and Ibrahim Khatib, *Bul Bulz fi al Maghreb: Aqn'at al Kitaba* (Rabat: Firdaws [Kitab al-Mojat], 1996). For overviews of Moroccan responses to Bowles's work, see Edwards, *Morocco Bound*, 84–87, and Ralph Coury, "The Twain Met: Paul Bowles's Western and Arab Critics," in *Writing Tangier*, ed. Ralph Coury and Robert Lacey (New York: Peter Lang, 2009), 129–50.

6. Elghandour, "Atavism and Civilization," 10.

7. See Introduction, note 19 above.

8. Elghandour, "Atavism and Civilization," 12.

9. Laroui mentions Bowles in passing in at least two of his works: *L'ideologie arabe contemporaine* (Paris: Maspero, 1982 [1967]) and *Al-'Arab wa al fikr al tarikhi* (Dar al-Beidha: Al-Markaz al-Thaqafi al-'Arabi, 1973). These references do not constitute a reading of Bowles's place in Moroccan society or in world literature but prove interesting and telling with respect to the relationship of the discursive contexts of the two writers. See section 3 of this chapter. It is unlikely that Bowles was aware of Laroui's existence. Elghandor mentions him (along with Edward Said and Anouar Abdel-Malek) at the end of his interview with Bowles in the course of listing intellectuals who have critiqued Orientalist thinking. Bowles answers the question in vague terms without acknowledging any specific knowledge of the writers mentioned.

10. I consider in more detail the comparison between Said and Laroui in a specifically Arab context later in this chapter.

11. Bart Moore-Gilbert, *Postcolonial Theory: Contexts, Practices, Politics* (New York: Verso, 1997), 51.

12. Tarek El-Ariss's current scholarship takes the tradition of Arab anti-Orientalism farther back, extracting a critique of Eurocentrism from the work of Ahmad Faris al-Shidyaq (1805–1887) and connecting al-Shidyaq's perspective to classical Islamic thought. See, for example, his "Recasting Tradition: Al-Shidyāq and the Orientalists in England and France (1840s–1850s)," in *A Life in Praise of Words: Aḥmad Fāris al-Shidyāq and the Nineteenth Century*, ed. Nadia Al-Bagdadi, Fawwaz Traboulsi, and Barbara Winckler (Wiesbaden, Germany: Reichert, 2016). Having learned a great deal from El-Ariss's groundbreaking work, I have chosen to begin my own genealogy with al-Afghani because of the greater prominence of colonial politics in the latter's particular style of challenging Europe.

13. Nikki Keddie, *Sayyid Jamal ad-Din al-Afghani: A Political Biography* (Berkeley: University of California Press, 1972), 25–26.

14. Ibid., 4n1.

15. Pankaj Mishra, *From the Ruins of Empire: The Revolt against the West and the Making of Asia* (New York: Picador, 2012).

16. Both essays are available in English translation in Nikki R. Keddie, *An Islamic Response to Imperialism* (Berkeley: University of California Press, 1968). The scholarly literature records that al-Afghani wrote the response to Renan in Arabic, which was then translated for him into French, but no Arabic original is extant. Keddie argues here and elsewhere that the French translation must be reliable because even though al-Afghani's French was not polished enough for him to author an article, he eventually became very fluent, and thus would have stepped forward to correct the record if major problems with the French translation were found. Still, Keddie's defensiveness regarding the missing original belies what might be learned from attention to the author's own terminology and rhetoric, and it might be more productive to think of the original text as occupying a place in Emily Apter's concept of the untranslatable.

17. Albert Hourani, *Arabic Thought in the Liberal Age, 1789–1939* (New York: Oxford University Press, 1970), 122–23.

18. Keddie, *An Islamic Response*, 39.

19. Keddie, *Sayyid Jamal ad-Din al-Afghani: A Political Biography*, 194.

20. Keddie, *An Islamic Response*, 182.

21. Ibid., 182.

22. Charles Smith, *Islam and the Search for Social Order in Egypt: A Biography of Muhammad Husayn Haykal* (Albany: State University of New York Press, 1983), 26.

23. Ibid., 99.

24. Muhammad Husayn Haykal, *Tarajim misriya wa gharbiya* (Cairo: Dar al-Ma'arif, 1985 [1929]), 62.

25. Muhammad Husayn Haykal, *Thawrat al-Adab* (Cairo: Dar al-Ma'arif, 1986), 81.

26. Hourani, *Arabic Thought in the Liberal Age*, 324.

27. A note under the title says "translated by J.W.C.," perhaps from French, in which Abdel-Malek frequently wrote.

28. Anouar Abdel-Malek, "Orientalism in Crisis," *Diogenes* 44 (1963), 104.

29. Ibid., 107.

30. Said himself was overly modest when he wrote in 1985, "At bottom, what I said in *Orientalism* had been said before me by A. L. Tibawi, by Abdallah Laroui, by Anouar Abdel Malek, by Talal Asad, by S. H. Alatas, by Frantz Fanon and Aimé Césaire, by Sardar K. M. Panikar and Romila Thapar, all of whom had suffered the ravages of imperialism and colonialism, and who, in challenging the authority, provenance, and institutions of the science that represented them to Europe, were also understanding themselves as something more than what this science said they were" ("Orientalism Reconsidered," in *Reflections on Exile and Other Essays* [Cambridge Mass.: Harvard University Press, 2002], 202). The main thrust of this passage is to place Said's work in the context of other anti-imperialist thinkers, but it gives some indication of Said's awareness of the genealogy of Arab critiques of Orientalist discourse that I am tracing here.

31. The term "tricontinental" was coined by Abdel-Malek to describe a cultural and political solidarity based on some shared history across Latin American, Africa, and Asia in the period of decolonization and in decolonization's aftermath. Recently, the influential scholar of postcolonial studies Robert J. C. Young has argued for a return to this terminology, arguing that it is more precise in marking the political commitments growing from the shared history compared to more familiar terms like "postcolonial" or "south."

32. I make the argument for a "Mariátegui tradition," growing out of the work of the influential Peruvian José Carlos Mariátegui, in the first chapter of my *Other South: Faulkner, Coloniality, and the Mariátegui Tradition.*

33. Laroui, *The History of the Maghreb*, 20.

34. Ibid., 3.

35. Laroui, *The Crisis of the Arab Intellectual: Traditionalism or Historicism?* trans. Diarmid Cammell (Berkeley: University of California Press, 1976), 46.

36. Laroui, *The History of the Maghreb*, 23.

37. Said, *Orientalism*, 5.

38. Ussama Makdisi, whose historical work represents the most exemplary product of what Said's critique made possible for the study of the Arab Middle East in the U.S. academy, has provided a helpful overview of the text's influence (and resistance to same) in the disciplines of history, American studies, and diplomatic studies. Among his conclusions: "*Orientalism* inspired two parallel genres of scholarship: those in American literature and studies who explored how Americans represented the Orient but overlooked the cultures and nations of the Middle East, and historians who sought to convey richer, and presumably non-orientalist understandings of Ottoman, Arab, and Iranian history, but who had very little to say about American or European history itself" ("After Said: The Limits and Possibilities of a Critical Scholarship of U.S.-Arab Relations," *Diplomatic History* 38, no. 3 [2014] : 670–71). See also Zachary Lockman's overview of responses to Said's work from within Middle Eastern studies, especially in chapter 6 of his *Contending Visions of the Middle East: The History and Politics of Orientalism* (New York: Cambridge University Press, 2004).

39. Said, *Orientalism*, 96, italics added.

40. Ibid., 271.

41. Ibid., 116.

42. Ibid., 42.

43. Ibid., 166.

44. "Renan derives from Orientalism's second generation: it was his task to solidify the official discourse of Orientalism, to systematize its insights, and to establish its intellectual and worldly institutions" (ibid., 130). On Renan's role in shaping the critiques of Orientalism that would emerge from a group of intellectuals including al-Afghani, see David Fieni, "French Decadence, Arab Awakenings: Figures of Decay in the Arab *Nahda*," *Boundary* 2 39, no. 2 (2012): 143–60.

45. Said, *Orientalism*, 140.

46. Ibid., 23.

47. Sabry Hafez, "Edward Said in Contemporary Arabic Culture," in *Edward Said: A Legacy of Emancipation and Representation*, ed. Adel Iskander and Hakem Rustom (Berkeley: University of California Press, 2010), 178.

48. Ibid., 179. Said refers to the regional, pro-Islamist misreading of his book in his 1994 afterword. See Said, *Orientalism*, 333 and 338–39. For a more recent example of the Arab critique of Orientalism that ignores most of the intellectual detail of the historical critique of the institution and chooses to view the problem of Orientalist scholarship as a binary conflict resulting in a clash of civilizations, see Hassan Hanafi, "From Orientalism to Occidentalism" *Hermes* 1, no. 2 (2012), 7–16.

49. Hafez, "Edward Said in Contemporary Arabic Culture," 189n39.

50. Sadiq al-'Azm, "Orientalism and Orientalism in Reverse," in Alexander Lyon Macfie, ed., *Orientalism: A Reader* (New York: New York University Press, 2000), 219 .

51. Hichem Djaït, *Europe and Islam*, trans. Peter Heinegg (Berkeley: University of California Press, 1985), 3.

52. Ibid., 19.

53. Ibid., 62.

54. Ibid., 163.

55. "When we criticize attempts like that of Laroui, it is not mere polemic, but rather because it is possible for us to demonstrate fairly easily that this truth he calls 'historicism' is nothing more than a theological artifice taking the form of an ideological stance" (Abdelkebir Khatibi, *Oeuvres de Abdelkébir Khatibi III: Essais* [Paris: Éditions de la Différence, 2008], 19).

56. "This unity is then, for us, an old fashioned idea, to be analysed for its insistence on the imagined. Moreover, this supposed unity that is so sought after must include not only the specifically marginalized (Berbers, Copts, Kurds . . . and those marginalized by the margins: women), but it must cover as well divisions inside the Arab World among countries, peoples, sects, classes, and divisions of divisions all the way to the individual, deserted to wait for his God to make all visible" (ibid., 11).

57. Hisham Sharabi, *Neopatriarchy: A Theory of Distorted Change in Arab Society* (New York: Oxford University Press, 1988), 113.

58. Hassan explicates the distinction between Khatibi and Kilito as follows: "If the emphasis on love [found in Khatibi's work] seems utopian at a time when the crusader language of the 'clash of civilizations' and the 'war on terror' has polarized public discourse in many parts of the world, Kilito's intervention challenges us in the U.S. context to interrogate the production of knowledge in Middle East and area studies, the pedagogy of world literature, and the role of comparative literature and the multicultural curriculum in disseminating cultural literacy" (Wail Hassan, "Translator's Introduction," in Abdelfattah Kilito, *Thou Shalt Not Speak My Language* [Syracuse, N.Y.: Syracuse University Press, 2008], xxiii).

59. Olivia Harrison, *Transcolonial Maghreb: Imagining Palestine in the Era of Decolonization* (Stanford, Calif.: Stanford University Press, 2016), 6.

60. Hosam Aboul-Ela, "The Specificities of Arab Thought: Morocco since the Liberal Age," forthcoming in Jens Hanssen and Max Weiss, eds. *Arabic Thought against the Authoritarian Age: Towards an Intellectual History of the Present.* (Cambridge: Cambridge University Press, 2018).

61. Laroui, *Mafhum al-tarikh*, 4th ed. (Dar al-Beidha: Al-Markaz al-Thaqafi al-'Arabi, 2005), 28.

62. Ibid., 136.

63. Ben Salem Himmich, *Al-Istishrāq fī ufq insidādihu* (Rabat: Manshūrāt al-Majlis al-Qawmī lil-Thaqāfah, 1991), 9.

64. Said, *Orientalism*, 339.

65. Edward Said, *Culture and Imperialism* (New York: Vintage, 1993), 1–14, 239–61.

66. Said, *Orientalism*, 272.

67. W. J. T. Mitchell, "Representation," in *Critical Terms for Literary Study*, ed. Frank Lentricchia and Thomas McLaughlin (Chicago: University of Chicago Press, 1995), 21.

68. Anna Gibbs, "After Affect: Sympathy, Synchrony, and Mimetic Communication," in *The Affect Theory Reader*, ed. Melissa Gregg and Gregory Seigworth (Durham, N.C.: Duke University Press, 2010), 187.

69. Spivak, "Can the Subaltern Speak?" 280.

CHAPTER 3

1. Christopher Sawyer-Lauçanno, *The Invisible Spectator: A Biography of Paul Bowles* (New York: Grove, 1989), 388.

2. Similarly banal is a note comparing the Arab invasion of Morocco with the conquest of Siam by Thais. The analogy and the quotation appear in the Bowles notebook of his trip, in the Delaware University Library's Paul Bowles collection.

3. Paul Bowles, *In Touch: The Letters of Paul Bowles*, ed. Jeffrey Miller (New York: Farrar, Strauss & Giroux, 1994), 385.

4. Unpublished letter quoted at Sawyer-Lauçanno, *The Invisible Spectator*, 390.

5. This absence of the brutality that often shocks the reader in so much of Bowles's earlier short fiction draws attention to "You Have Left Your Lotus Pods on the Bus" as a noteworthy later story, set aside for praise by Gore Vidal, but for Allen Hibbard less satisfying and a marker of fading talent. See Gore Vidal, "Introduction," in Paul Bowles, *Collected Stories* (Santa Rosa, Calif.: Black Sparrow, 1997); and Allen Hibbard, *Paul Bowles: A Study of the Short Fiction* (Boston: MacMillan, 1993).

6. Bowles, *Collected Stories*, 398.

7. Ibid., 399.

8. McGurl, *The Program Era*, x.

9. Bowles, *In Touch*, 385.

10. Ibid., 386.

11. Ibid., 389.

12. The presence of the (Asian) "floozies" in gaudy outfits has its own significance in reinforcing a heterosexist and hypermasculine U.S. nationalism that would be both repulsive to Bowles and indicative of a telescoped generalizing of Asianness that Bowles in the end participates in. This Americanized view of women in the Global South is the topic of chapter 4.

13. Abdallah Saaf, *Savoir et politique au Maroc* (Rabat: Société Marocaine des Editeurs Réunis, 1991), 32–56.

14. Under King Hassan II, Morocco aligned itself with other regional dictatorships in severely limiting the activities of civil society and brutally repressing all dissent. A limited political liberalization began in Hassan II's later years and continued under his son/successor, Mohammed VI. See Susan Slyomovics, *The Performance of Human Rights in Morocco* (Philadelphia: University of Pennsylvania Press, 2005) for an overview, and for one excellent example among the many possible primary sources, see Youssef Fadel, *A Rare Blue Bird Flies with Me*, trans. Jonathan Smolin (New York: American University of Cairo Press, 2016).

15. Abdallah Saaf, *Histoire d'Ahn Ma* (Paris: Harmattan, 1996), 26, 29.

16. Ibid., 42.

17. Ibid., 23.

18. Ibid., 9. It is difficult for me to believe that such a figure might be barely noticed until now by the national press.

19. Ibid., 83–90.

20. Ibid., 77ff.

21. Ibid., 81.

22. Citing several examples, Laroui's overview of historical thinking includes a section on the American overreliance on statistics, footnotes, and "evidence." Whatever the validity of the critique as a general statement, the distinction between Fall and Saaf is clear. For the former, documentation proliferates and creates an ethos of authority; for the latter, the holes in the documentary record are foregrounded as part of the historical account. See Laroui, *Mafhum al-tarikh*, 136–39.

23. Bernard Fall, *Hell in a Very Small Place: The Siege of Dien Bien Phu* (Cambridge, Mass.: Da Capo, 2002 [1966]), 414.

24. Ibid., 455.

25. Ibid., 417.

26. Saaf, *Histoire d'Anh Ma*, 119–20.

27. Fall, *Hell in a Very Small Place*, 79.

28. Ibid., 80.

29. Ibid., 438–39.

30. Saaf, *Histoire d'Anh Ma*, 16–17.

31. Ibid., 14–15.

32. Marc Jason Gilbert, "Persuading the Enemy: Vietnamese Appeals to Non-White Forces of Occupation, 1945–1975," in *Vietnam and the West: New Approaches*, ed. Wynn Wilcox (Ithaca, N.Y.: Cornell Southeast Asia Program, 2010), 132n98.

33. Fall, *Hell in a Very Small Place*, 423.

34. One historian lists the "peak strength" of the Republic of Korea force in South Vietnam as 48,000 (Spencer Tucker, *Vietnam* [Lexington: University Press of Kentucky, 1999], 125). Hyung-Sook Kim says that the total number of Republic of Korea troops that fought in Vietnam between 1964 and 1973 was 300,000 (Hyung-Sook Kim, "Korea's 'Vietnam Question': War Atrocities, National Identity, and Reconciliation in Asia," *Positions: East Asia Cultures Critique* 9, no. 3 [2001]: 621).

35. Kim, "Korea's 'Vietnam Question,'" lists the number of "unarmed Vietnamese civilians" killed by Koreans during the American war in Vietnam in

the thousands. Nick Turse mentions the discovery of war crimes committed by ROK forces as a byproduct of a U.S. military strategy that showed an indifference to the lives of Vietnamese civilians (Nick Turse, *Kill Anything That Moves: The Real American War in Vietnam* [New York: Picador, 2013], 126–27).

36. John Updike, *Rabbit, Run* (New York: Fawcett, 1996), 120.

37. Tim O'Brien, *If I Die in a Combat Zone* (New York: Broadway Books, 1999), 107–8.

38. There are, of course, exceptions, less well known and less studied than the volumes of fiction, memoir, and film that deal with the American experience in Vietnam. They include the relatively obscure popular novel that inspired the film and television show called *M*A*S*H*.

39. See Jinim Park, "The Colonized Colonizers: Korean Experiences of the Vietnam War," *Journal of American-East Asian Relations* 7, nos. 3/4 (1998): 217–40, for an overview of some Korean writing on the war in Vietnam in the 1960s and '70s. Youngju Ryu has recently reviewed the way representations of the ROK experience of the war in Vietnam have evolved in Korean popular culture in "Korea's Vietnam: Popular Culture, Patriarchy, Intertextuality," *Review of Korean Studies* 12, no. 3 (2008): 101–23.

40. Paik Nak-chung's concept of the division system both borrows from and includes a subtle critique of Wallerstein's world-systems theory, which has become increasingly influential in the field of comparative literature. In my reading of Paik's approach, the key distinction goes directly to the issue of historical particularity. This reading is my focus in chapter 5.

41. Paik makes this point while interviewing Fredric Jameson. See "Fredric Jameson Interviewed: South Korea as Social Space," in *Global/Local: Cultural Production and the Transnational Imaginary*, ed. Rob Wilson and Wimal Dissanayake (Durham, N.C.: Duke University Press, 1996), 348–71.

42. Paik Nak-chung, "Preface," in Hwang Sok-yong, *The Shadow of Arms*, trans. Chun Kyung-Ja (New York: Seven Stories, 2014 [1988]), 7.

43. Park, "The Colonized Colonizers," 218; compare Youngju Ryu's study of the figure of the traveler in Hwang's early writing as a mechanism to critique the effects of dictatorship and globalization on the Korean working class during the 1960s and '70s (Youngju Ryu, *Writers of the Winter Republic: Literature and Resistance in Park Chung Hee's Korea* [Honolulu: University of Hawai'i Press, 2016]).

44. Hwang Sok-yong, "The Pagoda," in *The Voice of the Governor-General and Other Stories of Modern Korea*, trans. Chun Kyung-Ja (Norwalk, Conn.: EastBridge, 2002), 33.

45. Ibid., 39.

46. Ibid., 34.

47. Ibid., 60.

48. Ibid., 61.

49. Ibid., 61.

50. Ibid., 61.

51. Paik, "Preface," 8.

52. Hwang, *The Shadow of Arms*, 41.

53. Ibid., 399. "Hanguk" transliterates [한국] one of the most common Hangul terms for Korea.

54. See the excellent analysis of the novel by Duy Lap Nguyen in "Allegories of Developmental Dictatorship in Hwang Sok-Yong's *The Shadow of War*" (paper presented to the Association of Asian American Studies, San Francisco, April 2015) for an interpretation that emphasizes its depiction of American-style capitalism's infiltration of the Vietnamese economy during the war. For Nguyen, the PX, where American products are traded, sold, and pilfered, is the driving force of the novel. Also compare historian Charles Armstrong's argument that the economic benefits of the war in Vietnam to industry in the ROK played a key role in fueling the country's "Asian Tiger" economy as it evolved out of the dictatorship of the 1970s and '80s. Armstrong's research suggests another resonance to the novel's story for its Korean readers beyond the question of partition. See Charles K. Armstrong, "America's Korea, Korea's Vietnam," *Critical Asian Studies* 33, no. 4 (2001): 527–39.

55. Paik, "Preface," 6. In Ryu's study of the way Korean popular culture represented the Korean experience of the Vietnam War through various eras and historical evolutions mentioned above, she says of the earlier period, when Hwang's fiction set in Vietnam appears: "The dismantling of the ideological apparatus formed by the triple alliance of anti-communism, developmentalism, and patriarchy first necessitates a critique of asymmetrical U.S-Korea relations" ("Korea's Vietnam," 119). Although her study does not deal with literary fiction, the historical context she provides for cultural production in the era of the first texts representing Koreans in Vietnam suggests that even a large novel like *Shadow* may have had very complicated representational challenges within the ROK market before ever dreaming of treating the important issue of atrocities committed by ROK troops.

56. Paik, "Preface," 8.

57. Kim, "Korea's 'Vietnam Question,'" 631.

58. See the previously cited analysis of Donald Pease for a cogent polemic against excluding U.S. imperialism from the main emphases of postcolonial studies. Pease connects the field's emphasis on Europe to American exceptionalism in "U.S. Imperialism," 219.

59. Tim O'Brien, *Going After Cacciato* (New York: Broadway Books, 1999 [1978]), 26.

60. Ibid., 63.

61. Ibid., 85.

62. Ibid., 261–62.

63. Ibid., 203.

64. William V. Spanos, *American Exceptionalism in the Age of Globalization: The Specter of Vietnam* (Albany: State University of New York Press, 2008), 171 (emphasis in original). Here, Spanos makes the very salient point that the epistemic dimension drives O'Brien's narrative. Still, I would diverge from Spanos's analysis in the extent to which he seems to see that the text is "a threshold novel," since I read it as a continuation of the tradition started by Bowles.

65. Tucker, *Vietnam*, 127.

66. Mark Atwood Lawrence, *The Vietnam War: A Concise International History* (New York: Oxford University Press, 2008), 108.

67. There are now several such histories that take advantage of Vietnamese sources, although in aggregate, they are still completely overwhelmed by U.S.-centric histories. As counterexamples to the general trend, see histories by William J. Duiker and Sophie Quinn-Judge.

68. Ang Cheng Guan, *The Vietnam War from the Other Side: The Vietnamese Communist's Perspective* (New York: RoutledgeCurzon, 2002), 6.

69. Stewart O'Nan's discussion of the film summarizes a revealing critical debate over whether the film is prowar or antiwar. He begins by referencing the charge that the film "seems to blame Vietnam for what it's done to America rather than vice versa." See Stewart O'Nan, "First Wave of Major Films," in *The Vietnam Reader*, ed. Stewart O'Nan (New York: Anchor, 1998), 264. In a partial defense of the film's politics, he astutely points out the way the Pennsylvania portion of the narrative thread seems to undercut the American institutions of church, family, and hard work that the war purports to be defending. O'Nan's reading places the film in line with the domesticating impulse of the American "Third World" novel's approach to geopolitics in that it sees America's global entanglements as an occasion for critiquing the domestic space. At the same time, this defense of the film is only partial because it leaves intact the critique that Vietnam and the Vietnamese are mere instruments in the film's larger purpose.

70. Louis K Greiff, "Soldier, Sailor, Surfer, Chef: Conrad's Ethics and the Margins of *Apocalypse Now*," *Literature/Film Quarterly* 20 (1992): 188–98.

71. Lawrence, *The Vietnam War*, 99.

72. Turse, *Kill Anything That Moves*, 49.

73. Lawrence, *The Vietnam War*, 145.

74. Ibid., 154.

75. Stanley Karnow, *Vietnam: A History* (New York: Penguin: 1997), 391.

76. Turse, *Kill Anything That Moves*, 5.

CHAPTER 4

1. Karnow, *Vietnam*, 47.

2. Scholars studying the sex trade in Vietnam have linked the resurgence in Ho Chi Minh City's sex industry in the 1990s to the government's shift in policy toward a perestroika-style market economy, known in Vietnamese as *Đổi Mới*. Karnow tellingly elides this policy shift in his account, instead reinforcing a reading that dichotomizes Vietnamese nationalism against American debauchery, ignoring regional historical change.

3. Spivak, "Can the Subaltern Speak?" 296.

4. Gayatri Chakravorty Spivak, *Critique of Postcolonial Reason: Toward a History of the Vanishing Present* (Cambridge, Mass.: Harvard University Press, 1999), 200–201.

5. See David Harvey, *A Brief History of Neoliberalism* (New York: Oxford University Press, 2007), for a review of the rise of neoliberalism, beginning in the Reagan/Thatcher 1980s and transitioning into the post–Cold War period.

6. Gayatri Chakravorty Spivak, "Globalicities: Terror and Its Consequences," *CR: The New Centennial Review* 4, no. 1 (2004): 73.

7. Polly Toynbee, "Behind the Burka" *Guardian*, September 28, 2001, http://www.theguardian.com/world/2001/sep/28/religion.afghanistan.

8. Spivak, "Globalicities," 87.

9. Ibid., 92.

10. Lila Abu-Lughod, "Do Muslim Women Really Need Saving? Anthropological Reflections on Cultural Relativism and Its Others," *American Anthropologist* 104, no. 3 (2002): 787. Elora Shehabbudin and Evelyn Alsultany, to name a few, have also discussed the exploitation of the concept of oppressed Muslim women in U.S. media. See the concluding section of this chapter.

11. Saba Mahmood, "Feminism, Democracy, and Empire: Islam and the War of Terror," in *Women's Studies on the Edge*, ed. Joan Wallach Scott (Durham, N.C.: Duke University Press, 2008), 97.

12. Spivak, "Globalicities," 87.

13. As David Marr has shown, the older history of the figure of the courtesan in Vietnamese culture is far more complicated than the dichotomy between warrior-nationalism and prostitute-corruption would suggest. My discussion is built on the way this dichotomy becomes entrenched during the period of the Vietnam/U.S. conflict. For a historical perspective, see David G. Marr, *Vietnamese Tradition on Trial, 1920–1945* (Berkeley: University of California Press, 1984), 191–220.

14. Mai Thi Tu and Le Thi Nham Tuyet, *Women in Vietnam* (Hanoi: Foreign Languages Publishing House, 1978); and Micheline Lessard, "More than Half the Sky: Vietnamese Women and Anti-French Political Activism, 1858–1945," in Wilcox, *Vietnam and the West*, 91–105.

15. Lessard, "More than Half the Sky," 92.

16. Kumari Jayawardena, *Feminism and Nationalism in the Third World* (London: Zed, 1986).

17. Tu and Tuyet, *Women in Vietnam*, 81.

18. The latter heroine is identified by Turner as Ngo Thi Tuyen, living in the mid-1990s as a somewhat disgruntled veteran in Thanh Hoa village (Karen Gottschang Turner, *Even the Women Must Fight: Memories of War from North Vietnam* [New York: Wiley, 1998], 51–69).

19. Ibid., 20.

20. Ibid., 23.

21. Tu and Tuyet, *Women in Vietnam*, 149.

22. Scholarship in English about Duong's writing is not yet extensive and naturally focuses on the first novels that were translated. Liparulo delineates techniques in *Novel without a Name* that parallel American postmodern fiction. Both he and Searle—not to mention several reviewers—write about *Novel without a Name* together with another Vietnamese novel translated into English at the same time: Bao Ninh's *The Sorrow of War*, which also focuses on a disillusioned North Vietnamese Army soldier. Given the recent work being done in comparative literary studies on world systems and their relationship to the literary, the phenomenon of literature by Hanoi dissident writers being translated into English and celebrated in the United States immediately after *Đổi*

Mới and the end of the Cold War deserves further attention. Blodgett's "The Feminist Artistry of *Paradise of the Blind*" focuses on that earlier novel, drawing thematic connections between it and novels by other women writers from Senegal, Egypt, Nigeria, India, and Mexico. While the essay does help to illuminate the presence of feminist themes in the work of an author who claims not to be concerned with them, the effortless global connection between women writers from the Global South suggests a woman-as-a-universal-category approach that—among other problems—removes Duong from any locally geohistoricized context. In contrast, Healy discusses film and screenplays by Duong and several other Vietnamese writers in her precise, contextualized study, the only one in English from this first group of essays on Duong that effectively incorporates Vietnamese language sources. See, respectively, Steven P. Liparulo, "'Incense and Ashes': The Postmodern Work of Refutation in Three Vietnam War Novels," *War, Literature & the Arts: An International Journal of the Humanities* 15, nos. 1–2 (2003): 71–94; William J. Searle, "Dissident Voices: The NVA Experience in Novels by Vietnamese," *War, Literature & the Arts: An International Journal of the Humanities* 10, no. 2 (1998): 224–38; Harriet Blodgett, "The Feminist Artistry of *Paradise of the Blind*," *World Literature Today* 75, nos. 3–4 (2001): 31–39; and Dana Healy, "From Triumph to Tragedy: Visualizing War in Vietnamese Film and Fiction," *South East Asia Research* 18, no. 2 (2010): 325–27.

23. Duong Thu Huong, *Novel without a Name*, trans. Nina McPherson and Phan Huy Duong (New York: Penguin, 1995), 40.

24. Ibid., 48.

25. Ibid.

26. Ibid.

27. Ibid., 49.

28. Ibid., 44.

29. Ibid., 61.

30. Ibid., 140.

31. Katherine Kinney, *Friendly Fire: American Images of the Vietnam War* (New York: Oxford University Press, 2000), 58. Technically, Arkin Saung Wan is "part Chinese, part unknown" (O'Brien, *Going After Cacciato*, 53), so it may or may not be accurate to refer to her as Vietnamese, although many critics do. Still, the imprecise reference to her national origin only reinforces Kinney's larger point regarding the character's status as a projected white male fantasy of Asian womanhood, because the ambiguity of O'Brien's "part Chinese, part unknown" displaces her from a specific geographic identity and constitutes her as the generically Asian female.

32. O'Brien, *Going After Cacciato*, 85.

33. Tu and Tuyet, *Women in Vietnam*, 106.

34. Turner, *Even the Women Must Fight*, 188.

35. Kimberley Hoang, *Dealing in Desire: Asian Ascendency, Western Decline, and the Hidden Currencies of Global Sex Work* (Oakland: University of California Press, 2015), 29.

36. Ibid., 5.

37. In the words of the critic Daniel Lukes, "There has always been something cultish about Vollmann's readership" ("'Strange Hungers': William T. Vollmann's Literary Performances of Abject Masculinity," in Christopher K.

Coffman and Daniel Lukes, eds., *William T. Vollmann: A Critical Companion* [Lanham, Md.: Rowman and Littlefield, 2015], 255).

38. Coffman and Lukes, *William T. Vollmann*, 5.

39. William T. Vollmann, *Butterfly Stories* (New York: Grove, 1993), 128.

40. Vollmann, *Butterfly Stories*, 169.

41. Kathy Acker, the American writer sometimes associated with postmodern punk, who preceded Vollmann by not quite a generation, can also be read as using graphic sex as a way of critiquing a Bowles-style metaphysical valence surrounding sexuality with the Other in novels like *Kathy Goes to Haiti*, *Blood and Guts in High School*, and *Algeria*. Acker also used provocative pencil sketches, autobiographical reference, and an emotionally distant narrative voice in her work, as does Vollmann in much of his "Third Word" fiction. However, the absence of any reference to Acker as either a direct influence on Vollmann or an important point of comparison with him in criticism produced so far around Vollmann's work is striking and highly suggestive of this critical discourse's masculinism.

42. Coffman and Lukes, *William T. Vollmann*, 13.

43. Vollmann, *Butterfly Stories*, 106.

44. Gustave Flaubert, *Flaubert in Egypt: A Sensibility on Tour*, ed. Frances Steegmuller (New York: Penguin, 1996), 220.

45. Vollmann, *Butterfly Stories*, 220–21.

46. Hoang, *Dealing in Desire*, 13, 62.

47. Lukes, "'Strange Hungers,'" 251.

48. Evelyn Alsultany, "Arabs and Muslims in the Media after 9/11: Representational Strategies for a 'Postrace' Era," *American Quarterly* 65, no.1 (2013): 165. In addition to Alsultany, see Moustafa Bayoumi's "The God That Failed: The Neo-Orientalism of Today's Muslim Scholars," in *Islamophobia/Islamophilia: Beyond the Politics of Enemy and Friend*, ed. Andrew Shryock (Bloomington: Indiana University Press, 2010), 79–93.

49. Elora Shehabuddin, "Gender and the Figure of the 'Moderate Muslim': Feminism in the Twenty-First Century," in *The Question of Gender: Joan W. Scott's Critical Feminism*, ed. Judith Butler and Elizabeth Weed (Bloomington: Indiana University Press, 2011), 132.

50. Lamia Karim, "Demystifying Micro-Credit: The Grameen Bank, NGOs, and Neoliberalism in Bangladesh," *Cultural Dynamics* 20, no.1 (2008): 15.

51. Ibid., 13.

52. Ibid., 7.

53. Ibid., 13, 19.

54. Ibid., 13.

55. Norman Rush, *Mating* (New York: Vintage, 1992), 6.

56. See S. Ekema Agbaw and Karson L. Kiesinger, "The Reincarnation of Kurtz in Norman Rush's *Mating*," *Conradiana* 32, no.1 (2000): 47–58. The essay focuses on the Kurtz/Denoon connection, but once the comparison to Conrad's *Heart of Darkness* has been made, a reader might find other—seemingly planted—parallels, including the narrator's several statements denouncing lying (315, 384, 477), which recall Marlow's profession of disgust for lies in chapter 1 of *Heart of Darkness*, undercut, of course, in that novel's final scene.

57. Agbaw and Kiesinger, "The Reincarnation of Kurtz," 50.

58. Rush, *Mating*, 312.

59. Ibid., 325.

60. Jim Shepard, "The Perfect Man, the Perfect Place, and Yet . . . ," *New York Times*, September 22, 1991, http://www.nytimes.com/1991/09/22/books/the-perfect-man-the-perfect-place-and-yet.html?pagewanted=1.

61. Rush, *Mating*, 188.

62. In analytical philosophy, Occam's (or Ockham's) razor is also known as the parsimony principle and is associated with William of Ockham (1285–1347). The principle posits that the simplest solution is always the most philosophically sound.

63. Rush, *Mating*, 303.

64. This, in fact, is the realization that surprises prominent Arab intellectual (and protégé of Abdel Kebir Khatibi) Fatema Mernissi when she conducts an informal survey of attitudes in Europe and the United States toward "harem culture" after 9/11. See Fatema Mernissi, *Scheherazade Goes West* (New York: Pocket Books, 2001).

65. Jenine Abboushi-Dallal, "The Perils of Occidentalism: How Arab Novelists Are Driven to Write for Western Readers," *Times Literary Supplement*, April 24, 1998, 8–9.

66. Michelle Hartman, "Gender, Genre, and the (Missing) Gazelle: Arab Women Writers and the Politics of Translation," *Feminist Studies* 38, no. 1 (2012): 37.

67. Mohja Kahf, "Packaging 'Huda': Sha'rawi's Memoirs in the United States Reception Environment," in *Going Global: The Transnational Reception of Third World Women Writers*, ed. Amal Amireh and Lisa Suhair Majaj (New York: Garland, 2000), 148–72; and Marilyn Booth, "'The Muslim Woman' as Celebrity Author and the Politics of Translating Arabic: Girls of Riyadh Go on the Road," *Journal of Middle East Women's Studies* 6, no. 3 (2010): 149–82.

68. Reza Afshari, "Egalitarian Islam and Misogynist Islamic Tradition: A Critique of the Feminist Reinterpretation of Islamic History and Heritage," *Critique: Journal of Critical Studies of Iran and the Middle East* 3, no. 4 (1994): 29–30.

69. Raja Rhouni, *Secular and Islamic Feminist Critiques in the Works of Fatima Mernissi* (Boston: Brill, 2010), 44.

70. Ibid., 6.

71. Ibid., 46.

72. Afshari, "Egalitarian Islam," 20.

73. Rhouni, *Secular and Islamic Feminist Critiques*, 9.

74. Fatema Mernissi, *Scheherazade*, 14.

75. Ibid., 111.

76. Abu-Lughod, "Do Muslim Women Really Need Saving?" 789.

CHAPTER 5

1. Samir Amin, *Eurocentrism*, trans. Russell Moore (New York: Monthly Review Press, 1989), xiii.

2. Fukuyama wrote in a 2006 revisiting of his famous essay that "many criticisms [of it] were based on simple misunderstandings of what I was arguing, for

example on the part of those who believed that I thought events would simply stop happening" (Francis Fukuyama, *The End of History and the Last Man* [New York: Free Press, 2006], 346). Clearly, from the author's point of view the question of "history" is rooted in a viable ideological or systemic challenge to Western-style capitalist liberal democracy—i.e., liberalism—of the type that some considered Soviet-style communism to be.

3. Francis Fukuyama, "The End of History?" *National Interest* 16, no. 16 (1989): 9.

4. Ibid., 8. W. W. Rostow's *The Stages of Economic Growth: A Non-Communist Manifesto* (Cambridge: Cambridge University Press, 1960) had earlier proposed as an American vision for global progress the movement of underdeveloped societies toward the most advanced stage of economic growth, defined as the stage of "high mass-consumption." In that Fukuyama would much later advocate mass consumption as a marker for the ultimate civilizational achievement, the foundations of his argument that history had ended were present in much older and more utilitarian American geopolitical thinking.

5. Fukiyama, "The End of History?" 16, 18.

6. Ibid., 14.

7. Fukuyama, *The End of History and the Last Man*, 348. Fukuyama's comments about Islam—very dismissive, but still more sympathetic than those of Huntington or Thomas Friedman—might be read as a contemporary version of Renan's argument about Arabo-Islamic culture's backwardness in the area of philosophical thinking, which al-Afghani challenged in the debate described in chapter 2.

8. Samuel Huntington, "The Clash of Civilizations?" *Foreign Affairs* 72, no. 3 (1993): 32.

9. See Elliott Colla, "Revolution on Ice," *Jadaliyya*, January 6, 2014, http://www.jadaliyya.com/pages/index/15874/revolution-on-ice. Colla's essay focuses on Global South social movements as represented in Egyptian fiction. His main example is recent fiction by Sonallah Ibrahim that appeared at the time of the January 25, 2011, revolution in Egypt. Ibrahim's earlier novelistic treatments of regional revolutions are my focus in the next section of this chapter.

10. See especially Richard Slotkin, *Gunfighter Nation: The Myth of the Frontier in Twentieth Century America* (Norman: University of Oklahoma Press, 1992).

11. Cormac McCarthy, *Blood Meridian, or That Evening Redness in the West* (New York: Vintage, 1985), 237.

12. Ibid., 239.

13. It is possible to argue that most criticism of the novel holds the judge's rhetoric in a similar kind of awe. An exception is the very helpful essay about the judge's role by Dana Phillips, who correctly notes that earlier critics focus upon "oppositions" in the novel, which "evoke rather than interpret it" ("History and the Ugly Facts of Cormac McCarthy's *Blood Meridian*," *American Literature* 68, no. 2 [1996]: 434). Regarding the judge, he argues that McCarthy is "rewriting character as something else—character not as self, but as language, as a suggestive artifact or trace of the human" (440).

14. McCarthy, *Blood Meridian*, 122.

15. Ibid., 250.

16. Richard Godden and Colin Richmond, "'Blood Meridian,' or the Evening Redness in the East: 'Itinerant Degenerates Bleeding Westwards,'" *Comparative American Studies: An International Journal* 2, no. 4 (2004): 456.

17. McCarthy, *Blood Meridian*, 335.

18. Godden and Richmond's essay discusses the historical context in an opening section that extends the Vietnam analogy over several of its first few pages: "The Treaty of Guadeloupe [*sic*] of 1848, which ended the war, redefined the border between Mexico and the USA, the USA gaining a huge area of the South West and, at a stroke, transforming native Mexicans into native Americans. Glanton's band kills indiscriminately on either side of the new border; consequently their victims are both native Mexicans and native Americans" ("'Blood Meridian,'" 448).

19. Joe Cleary, *Literature, Partition and the Nation State: Culture and Conflict in Ireland, Israel and Palestine* (New York: Cambridge University Press, 2002), 19.

20. Ibid., 20.

21. Aamir Mufti's brief, helpful, and generally positive review of Cleary's book, for example, comments that "India, another instance of partition linked to the end of British rule, is missing almost entirely from the book" ("Comparative Partitions," *Journal of Palestine Studies* 33, no. 1 [2003]: 105), but never mentions the book's unwillingness to incorporate fully "Cold War partitions" into its vision of the place of partition in the connection between poetics and politics.

22. Walter Rodney, *Walter Rodney Speaks: The Making of an African Intellectual* (Trenton, N.J.: Africa World Press, 1990), 66.

23. Neil Smith, *Uneven Development: Nature, Capital, and the Production of Space* (Athens: University of Georgia Press, 2008), 111.

24. Ibid., 181.

25. Ibid., 6.

26. Nirvana Tanoukhi, "The Scale of World Literature," in Palumbo-Liu, Robbins, and Tanoukhi, *Immanuel Wallerstein*, 85.

27. Such a connection causes Tanoukhi's critique to expose the way the world literature debate in the United States in the 2000s functioned as an effective distancing from the anticolonial foundations of the postcolonial criticism that was emerging in the 1980s and '90s and was often openly in solidarity with anti-imperialist culture.

28. Neil Brenner, "The Space of the World: Beyond State Centrism?" in Palumbo-Liu , Robbins, and Tanoukhi, *Immanuel Wallerstein*, 122.

29. Neil Smith, "Contours of a Spatialized Politics," *Social Text* 33 (1992): 69ff.

30. Tanoukhi, "The Scale of World Literature," 84.

31. Peter Hitchcock has recently taken up this element of Tanoukhi's reading of Moretti and extended it to the etiolating of global politics in "world literature" discourse's rhetoric of the global, which he finds "symptomatic of a more general spatial crisis in the cultural forms of globalization to which comparative literature has valiantly responded. A deployment of scale is salutary in this re-

gard, and literary criticism has been attentive to it" ("The Function of Agon at the Present Time," *Comparatist* 37 [2013]: 10). See also his quotation of Smith's early 1990s description of his work as a critique of Fukuyamaism (15).

32. Paik Nak-chung, *The Division System in Crisis: Essays on Contemporary Korea*, trans. Kim Myung-hwan et al. (Berkeley: University of California Press, 2011), xvii.

33. Paik, *The Division System*, xvi.

34. Bruce Cumings, *The Korean War: A History* (New York: Random House, 2010), 198.

35. Youngju Ryu, "Truth or Reconciliation? *The Guest* and the Massacre that Never Ends," *Positions: East Asia Cultures Critique* 23, no. 4 (2015): 637.

36. Cleary, *Literature, Partition and the Nation State*, 20. Cleary's larger point is compelling, although clearly I would not agree with describing this context as "post-imperial."

37. Hwang Sok-yong, *The Guest*, trans. Kyung-Ja Chun and Maya West (New York: Seven Stories, 2001), 87.

38. Ibid., 142.

39. Consider the Koreanist scholar Bruce Fulton's telling observation that North American students who were polled enjoyed reading the English translation of *The Guest* less than other Korean novels in translation because "the presence of ghosts was problematic for some students" ("The Modern Korean Novel in English Translation," *Journal of Asian Studies* 70, no. 3 [2011]: 782), whereas another review of the novel by a North American may be slightly over-exoticizing with the opening: "Perhaps more than most Asian peoples, Koreans live with ghosts" (Ronald Suleski, "Review: *The Guest*," *Azalea: Journal of Korean Literature and Culture* 1 [2007]: 289).

40. Hwang, *The Guest*, 69.

41. Ibid., 70.

42. Ibid., 71.

43. Ryu, "Truth or Reconciliation?" 648–49.

44. Hwang, *The Guest*, 8.

45. The People's Democratic Republic of Yemen (aka South Yemen)—which came into existence in 1967, upon the expulsion of British occupying forces, and ceased to exist in 1990, when a unification agreement was signed with the Yemen Arab Republic—was the only Marxist member of the Arab League and the staunchest supporter of Soviet and anti-imperialist foreign policy in the Arab region. The Dhofar region shared a border with South Yemen and was the site of a radical, armed separatist movement that opposed the central authority of the Sultanate of Oman beginning in the mid-1960s and lasting for about a decade. Historian Abdel Razzaq Takriti has authored an authoritative history of the Dhofar revolt—one partially inspired by Sonallah Ibrahim's novel. (And the phenomenon of an award-winning work of academic history published by Oxford University Press and inspired by a novel written in Arabic speaks to my argument for a global archival novel genre.) Takriti writes of the connection between the People's Democratic Republic of Yemen and the Dhofari rebels: "The South Yemeni connection to Dhufar was immensely strong. The two regions were tied by geography, history, culture and political organization. Dhufar

immediately bordered the easternmost Mahra province of Yemen. Fostered by this propinquity, trade, tribal, and cultural relations flourished for centuries" (*Monsoon Revolution: Republicans, Sultans, and Empires in Oman, 1965–1976* [Oxford: Oxford University Press, 2013], 98). This passage goes on to describe the cooperation and collaboration among political organizations on the two sides of the border during the Dhofar revolt. The connection between the PDRY and the Dhofari revolt manifests itself in sporadic but significant allusions scattered through Ibrahim's novel.

46. See discussions of Ibrahim's provocative use of newspaper quotes as found objects in *Zaat* in Samia Mehrez, *Egyptian Writers between History and Fiction* (Cairo: American University in Cairo Press, 2005); and Hosam Aboul-Ela, "Review of Sonallah Ibrahim's *Zaat*," *Edebiyat: Journal of Middle Eastern Literatures* 13, no. 2 (2003): 251–68.

47. Compare in this context historian Omnia El Shakry's use of Sonallah Ibrahim's 1981 novel *The Committee* to illustrate challenges facing attempts to construct historical narratives in postcolonial, postdevelopment contexts. Writing for an audience of academic historians, El Shakry calls attention to the way "historians have become increasingly accustomed to openly discussing the very material difficulties of accessing archives, which are so intensified in postcolonial contexts" ("'History without Documents': The Vexed Archives of Decolonization in the Middle East," *American Historical Review* 120, no. 3 [2015]: 921. It is precisely such challenges that engender the response of the archival fiction penned by Hwang and Ibrahim.

48. Olivia Harrison, *Transcolonial Maghreb*, 65.

49. My personal experience has reinforced the point that the character Warda effectively turns on its head Western expectations discussed by Mernissi regarding the representation of the Arab woman. Initial attempts to interest a New York trade press in an English translation of the novel elicited expressions of disbelief that such a character could actually exist, despite her archival foundations.

50. Sonallah Ibrahim, *Warda* (Cairo: Dar al-mustaqbal, 2000), 91, translation mine.

51. The note cites as a source a French police novel that does not corroborate the Bin Laden connection, and the French and Swedish translations of the novel therefore leave off the last sentence. Even if the connection is fictional, it manages—in the Arabic text—to draw a line between an alternative, materialist way of conceiving "development" in the Global South and the emergence of the post–Cold War terror wars.

52. Paik, *The Division System in Crisis*, 149–50.

53. Noel Brehony, *Yemen Divided: The Story of a Failed State in South Arabia* (New York: I. B. Tauris, 2011), 3.

54. Compare Yemen expert Fred Halliday's statement: "The intersection of the unification issue with the east-west conflict in the post-1945 period, one also evident in the cases of Germany, Korea, and Vietnam, became part of the Yemeni unity question as well" (*Revolution and Foreign Policy: The Case of South Yemen 1967–1987* [New York: Cambridge University Press, 1990], 139).

55. See Bruce Robbins, "The Worlding of the American Novel," in *The Cambridge History of the American Novel*, ed. Leonard Cassuto, Clare Virginia Eby,

and Benjamin Reiss (New York: Cambridge University Press, 2011), 1096–1106; and Robert McLaughlin, "After the Revolution: U.S. Postmodernism in the Twenty First Century," *Narrative* 21, no. 3 (2013): 284–95, for helpful overviews of the U.S. literary scene during this period that prominently feature the role of 9/11's shadow. *Terrorist* is a particularly interesting example. Updike is unquestionably one of the most accomplished American novelists of his time. *Terrorist* may be his worst novel in a long and very prolific career. As a literary critic, one tries to be subtle in discussions around the issue of verisimilitude, but in this case, it must be said that the main character in the novel is a veritably preposterous invention. Although there should be no shame in a master who has produced many important works of fiction having an off day, the celebratory positive reviews of the novel are disturbing, especially when one considers that they may certainly have less to do with Updike's stature than with the desire for any type of text in America during the years most immediately following September 11, 2001, that might offer some probing of a Muslim Arab consciousness, no matter how fatuous the result. Note that not all of the initial reviews toed the line by ignoring the blatant flaws in the text. See, for a solid counterexample, James Wood, "Jihad and the Novel," *New Republic*, July 3, 2006, http://www.newrepublic.com/article/books-and-arts/jihad-and-the-novel.

56. Dave Eggers, *A Hologram for the King* (New York: Vintage, 2013), 17.

57. Ralph Clare, *Fictions Inc.: The Corporation in Postmodern Fiction, Film, and Popular Culture* (New Brunswick, N.J.: Rutgers University Press, 2014), 6.

58. Sigrun Meinig, "Empathizing with the Experience of Cultural Change: Reflections on Contemporary Fiction on Work," in *Rethinking Empathy through Literature*, ed. Meghan Marie Hammond and Sue J. Kim (New York: Routledge, 2014), 107.

59. McLaughlin, "After the Revolution," 293.

60. Eggers, *A Hologram for the King*, 13.

61. Ibid., 143.

62. Ibid., 151.

63. Meinig, "Empathizing with the Experience of Cultural Change," 110.

64. Liesl Schwabe, "Nothing Is Illuminated: Adam Johnson," *Publisher's Weekly*, November 11, 2011, 26.

65. Adam Johnson, *The Orphan Master's Son* (New York: Random House, 2012), 411.

66. Ibid., 449.

67. Ibid., 452.

CONCLUSION

1. Vendela Vida, *The Diver's Clothes Lie Empty* (New York: HarperCollins, 2015), 27–28.

2. For example, she analyzes the cultural phenomenon of the Sally Field television movie *Not Without My Daughter* in terms of a domestic discourse of female empowerment (see her chapter 5) and also shows how the Pentagon's public relations machine emphasized the ethnic diversity of the U.S. soldiers that fought in the first Iraq War (chapter 6). See McAlister, *Epic Encounters*.

3. Without ever mentioning Bowles, Rolland Murray has mapped an excellent beginning of an answer to this question in his essay analyzing McKnight's *I Get on the Bus*. See Rolland Murray, "Diaspora by Bus: Reginald McKnight, Postmodernism, and Transatlantic Subjectivity," *Contemporary Literature* 46, no. 1 (2005): 46–77. More generally, the strong trend toward a more globalized view of African American letters can be found in the scholarship of Alex Lubin, Vaughn Rasberry, Michelle Stephens, and Cedric Tolliver, which in turn builds on earlier work by Paul Gilroy, Brent Hayes Edwards, and others.

4. In framing this issue, one might compare McAlister's discussion of the emphasis on "multiculturalism" among U.S. troops in the first Iraq War with the following passage from Hardt and Negri's *Empire*: "When one looks closely at U.S. corporate ideology (and to a lesser but still significant extent, at U.S. corporate practice), it is clear that corporations do not operate simply by excluding the gendered and/or racialized Other. In fact, the old modernist forms of racist and sexist theory are the explicit enemies of this new corporate culture. The corporations seek to include difference within their realm and thus aim to maximize creativity, free play, and diversity in the corporate workplace" (153).

5. I have been working with my co-editor, Gayatri Chakravorty Spivak, for almost a decade on two different book series that publish critical theory written outside of Europe and North America. These have demonstrated to me the concrete and institutional obstacles to changing the biases in U.S.-centric intellectual culture. They include the inability to acknowledge the labor of translators and a general absence of global intellectual style available as a vehicle for the rare translators who might be willing to work sans acknowledgment.

Works Cited

Abboushi-Dallal, Jenine. "The Perils of Occidentalism: How Arab Novelists Are Driven to Write for Western Readers." *Times Literary Supplement*, April 24, 1998, 8–9.

Abdel-Malek, Anouar. "Orientalism in Crisis." *Diogenes* 44 (1963): 103–40.

Aboul-Ela, Hosam. *Other South: Faulkner, Coloniality, and the Mariátegui Tradition*. Pittsburgh: University of Pittsburgh Press, 2007.

———. "Review of Sonallah Ibrahim's *Zaat*." *Edebiyat: Journal of Middle Eastern Literatures* 13, no. 2 (2003): 251–68.

Abu-Lughod, Lila. "Do Muslim Women Really Need Saving? Anthropological Reflections on Cultural Relativism and Its Others." *American Anthropologist* 104, no. 3 (2002): 783–90.

Afshari, Reza. "Egalitarian Islam and Misogynist Islamic Tradition: A Critique of the Feminist Reinterpretation of Islamic History and Heritage." *Critique: Journal of Critical Studies of Iran and the Middle East* 3, no. 4 (1994): 13–33.

Agbaw, S. Ekema, and Karson L. Kiesinger. "The Reincarnation of Kurtz in Norman Rush's *Mating*." *Conradiana* 32, no. 1 (2000): 47–58.

Alsultany, Evelyn. *Arabs and Muslims in the Media: Race and Representation after 9/11*. New York: New York University Press, 2012.

———. "Arabs and Muslims in the Media after 9/11: Representational Strategies for a 'Postrace' Era." *American Quarterly* 65, no. 1 (2013): 161–69.

Amin, Samir. *Eurocentrism*. Translated by Russell Moore. New York: Monthly Review Press, 1989.

Ang Cheng Guan. *The Vietnam War from the Other Side: The Vietnamese Communist's Perspective*. New York: RoutledgeCurzon, 2002.

Apter, Emily. *Against World Literature*. New York: Verso, 2013.

Armstrong, Charles. "America's Korea, Korea's Vietnam." *Critical Asian Studies* 33, no. 4 (2001): 527–39.

———. *The Koreas*. 2d ed. New York: Routledge, 2014.

al-'Azm, Sadiq. "Orientalism and Orientalism in Reverse." In Macfie, *Orientalism*, 217–38.

Bassnett, Susan, and Harish Trivedi, eds. *Post-Colonial Translation: Theory and Practice*. New York: Routledge, 1999.

Bayoumi, Moustapha. "The God That Failed: The Neo-Orientalism of Today's Muslim Scholars." In *Islamophobia/Islamophilia: Beyond the Politics of Enemy and Friend*, edited by Andrew Shryock, 79–93. Bloomington: Indiana University Press, 2010.

Bevan, Greg. "Beyond the Father and Son: The Rise of Modern Morocco in Bowles's *The Spider's House*." *Journal of the American Literature Society of Japan* 5 (2007): 21–33.

Biden, Joseph R., and Leslie H. Gelb. "Unity through Autonomy in Iraq." *New York Times*, May 1, 2006. http://www.nytimes.com/2006/05/01/opinion/01biden.html?_r=0.

Blodgett, Harriet. "The Feminist Artistry of *Paradise of the Blind*." *World Literature Today* 75, nos. 3–4 (2001): 31–39.

Boone, Joseph Allen. *The Homoerotics of Orientalism*. New York: Columbia University Press, 2014.

Booth, Marilyn. "'The Muslim Woman' as Celebrity Author and the Politics of Translating Arabic: Girls of Riyadh Go on the Road." *Journal of Middle East Women's Studies* 6, no. 3 (2010): 149–82.

Bowles, Paul. *Collected Stories*. Santa Rosa, Calif.: Black Sparrow, 1997.

———. *In Touch: The Letters of Paul Bowles*. Edited by Jeffrey Miller. New York: Farrar, Strauss & Giroux, 1994.

———. *Let It Come Down*. Santa Barbara, Calif.: Black Sparrow, 1980.

———. *The Sheltering Sky*. New York: HarperCollins, 1999 [1949].

———. *The Spider's House*. Santa Barbara, Calif.: Black Sparrow, 1982.

Brehony, Noel. *Yemen Divided: The Story of a Failed State in South Arabia*. New York: IB Tauris, 2011.

Brenner, Neil. "The Space of the World: Beyond State Centrism?" In Palumbo-Liu, Robbins, and Tanouki, *Immanuel Wallerstein and the Problem of the World*, 101–37.

Brier, Evan. "Constructing the Post-War Art Novel: Paul Bowles, James Laughlin, and the Making of *The Sheltering Sky*." *PMLA* 121, no. 1 (2006): 186–99.

Buell, Lawrence, and Wai-Chee Dimock, eds. *Shades of the Planet: American Literature as World Literature*. Princeton, N.J.: Princeton University Press, 2007.

Casanova, Pascale. *The World Republic of Letters*. Translated by M. B. DeBevoise. Cambridge, Mass.: Harvard University Press, 2007.

Castronovo, Russ, and Susan Gilman, eds. *States of Emergency: The Object of American Studies*. Chapel Hill: University of North Carolina Press, 2009.

Charara, Hayan. "The Prize." *Poetry Magazine*, July/August 2017, https://www.poetryfoundation.org/poetrymagazine/poems/142843/the-prize.

Chaúi, Marilena. *Between Conformity and Resistance: Essays on Politics, Culture, and the State*. Translated by Maite Conde. New York: Palgrave, 2011.

Cheah, Pheng. *What Is a World? On Postcolonial Literature as World Literature*. Durham, N.C.: Duke University Press, 2016.

Choukri, Mohamed. *Bul Bulz wa 'Uzla Tanja*. Tangiers: Altopress, 1996.

———. *For Bread Alone*. Translated by Paul Bowles. London: Telegram Books, 2007.

Clare, Ralph. *Fictions Inc.: The Corporation in Postmodern Fiction, Film, and Popular Culture*. New Brunswick, N.J.: Rutgers University Press, 2014.

Cleary, Joe. *Literature, Partition and the Nation State: Culture and Conflict in Ireland, Israel and Palestine*. New York: Cambridge University Press, 2002.

Coffman, Christopher K., and Daniel Lukes, eds. *William T. Vollmann: A Critical Companion*. Lanham, Md.: Rowman and Littlefield, 2015.

Colla, Elliott. "Revolution on Ice." *Jadaliyya*, January 6, 2014. http://www.jadaliyya.com/pages/index/15874/revolution-on-ice.

Coury, Ralph. "The Twain Met: Paul Bowles's Western and Arab Critics." In *Writing Tangier*, edited by Ralph Coury and Robert Lacey, 129–50. New York: Peter Lang, 2009.

Cumings, Bruce. *The Korean War: A History*. New York: Random House, 2010.

Damrosch, David. *What Is World Literature?* Princeton, N.J.: Princeton University Press, 2003.

Dimock, Wai Chee. *Through Other Continents: American Literature across Deep Time*. Princeton, N.J.: Princeton University Press, 2006.

Djait, Hichem. *Europe and Islam*. Translated by Peter Heinegg. Berkeley: University of California Press, 1985.

Dos Santos, Theotonio. *A teoria da dependência: Balanço e perspectivas* (Rio de Janeiro: Editora Civilização Brasileira, 2000.

Duiker, William J. *The Communist Road to Power in Vietnam*. Boulder, Colo.: Westview, 1996.

Duong Thu Huong. *No Man's Land*. Translated by Nina McPherson and Phan Huy Duong. New York: Hyperion, 2005.

———. *Novel without a Name*. Translated by Nina McPherson and Phan Huy Duong. New York: Penguin, 1995.

Edwards, Brian T. *After the American Century: The Ends of U.S. Culture in the Middle East*. New York: Columbia University Press, 2016.

———. *Morocco Bound*. Durham, N.C.: Duke University Press, 2005.

Eggers, Dave. *A Hologram for the King*. New York: Vintage, 2013.

El-Ariss, Tarek. "Recasting Tradition: Al-Shidyāq and the Orientalists in England and France (1840s–1850s)." In *A Life in Praise of Words: Aḥmad Fāris al-Shidyāq and the Nineteenth Century*, edited by Nadia Al-Bagdadi, Fawwaz Traboulsi, and Barbara Winckler. Wiesbaden, Germany: Reichert, 2016.

Elghandor, Abdelhak. "Atavism and Civilization: An Interview with Paul Bowles." *Ariel: A Review of International English Literature* 25, no. 2 (1994): 7–30.

El Shakry, Omnia. "'History without Documents': The Vexed Archives of Decolonization in the Middle East." *American Historical Review* 120, no. 3 (2015): 920–34.

El-Sherif, Mona. "Reclaiming Tangier: Mohamed Choukri's *Al-Khubz Al-Hafi* and Subaltern Citizenship in Urban Literature." *Research in African Literatures* 44, no. 3 (2013): 101–17.

Ettobi, Mustafa. "Cultural Representation in Literary Translation: Translators as Mediators/Creators." *Journal of Arabic Literature* 37, no. 2 (2006): 206–29.

Fadel, Youssef. *A Rare Blue Bird Flies with Me*. Translated by Jonathan Smolin. New York: American University of Cairo Press, 2016.

Fall, Bernard. *Hell in a Very Small Place: The Siege of Dien Bien Phu*. Cambridge, Mass.: Da Capo, 2002 (1966).

Fieni, David. "French Decadence, Arab Awakenings: Figures of Decay in the Arab *Nahda*." *Boundary 2* 39, no. 2 (2012): 143–60.

Fitzpatrick, Kathleen. *The Anxiety of Obsolescence: The American Novel in the Age of Television*. Nashville: Vanderbilt University Press, 2006.

Flaubert, Gustave. *Flaubert in Egypt: A Sensibility on Tour*. Edited by Frances Steegmuller. New York: Penguin, 1996.

Friedman, Thomas. *The Lexus and the Olive Tree: Understanding Globalization*. New York: Picador, 1999.

Fukuyama, Francis. "The End of History?" *National Interest* 16, no. 16 (1989): 3–18.

———. *The End of History and the Last Man*. New York: Free Press, 2006.

Fulton, Bruce. "The Modern Korean Novel in English Translation." *Journal of Asian Studies* 70, no. 3 (2011): 778–84.

Gibbs, Anna. "After Affect: Sympathy, Synchrony, and Mimetic Communication." In *The Affect Theory Reader*, edited by Melissa Gregg and Gregory Seigworth, 186–205. Durham, N.C.: Duke University Press, 2010.

Gilbert, Marc Jason. "Persuading the Enemy: Vietnamese Appeals to Non-White Forces of Occupation, 1945–1975." In *Vietnam and the West: New Approaches*, edited by Wynn Wilcox, 107–42. Ithaca, N.Y.: Cornell Southeast Asia Program, 2010.

Godden, Richard, and Colin Richmond. "'Blood Meridian,' or the Evening Redness in the East: 'Itinerant Degenerates Bleeding Westwards.'" *Comparative American Studies: An International Journal* 2, no. 4 (2004): 447–60.

Greene, Graham. *The Quiet American*. New York: Penguin, 2004.

Greiff, Louis K. "Soldier, Sailor, Surfer, Chef: Conrad's Ethics and the Margins of *Apocalypse Now*." *Literature/Film Quarterly* 20 (1992): 188–98.

Hafez, Sabry. "Edward Said in Contemporary Arabic Culture." In *Edward Said: A Legacy of Emancipation and Representation*, edited by Adel Iskander and Hakem Rustom, 170–90. Berkeley: University of California Press, 2010.

Halliday, Fred. *Revolution and Foreign Policy: The Case of South Yemen 1967–1987*. New York: Cambridge University Press, 1990.

Hanafi, Hassan. "From Orientalism to Occidentalism." *Hermes* 1, no. 2 (2012): 7–16.

Handley, George. *Postslavery Literatures in the Americas: Family Portraits in Black and White*. Charlottesville: University of Virginia Press, 2000.

Hanssen, Jens, and Max Weiss, eds. *Arabic Thought against the Authoritarian Age: Towards an Intellectual History of the Present*. Cambridge: Cambridge University Press, 2018.

Hardt, Michael, and Antonio Negri. *Empire*. Cambridge, Mass.: Harvard University Press, 2000.

Harrison, Olivia. *Transcolonial Maghreb: Imagining Palestine in the Era of Decolonization*. Stanford, Calif.: Stanford University Press, 2016.

Hartman, Michelle. "Gender, Genre, and the (Missing) Gazelle: Arab Women Writers and the Politics of Translation." *Feminist Studies* 38, no. 1 (2012): 17–49.

Harvey, David. *A Brief History of Neoliberalism*. New York: Oxford University Press, 2007.

Hassan, Wail S. "Translator's Introduction." In Abdelfattah Kilito, *Thou Shalt Not Speak My Language*. Translated by Wail S. Hassan. Syracuse, N.Y.: Syracuse University Press, 2008.

Haykal, Muhammad Hussain. *Hayat Muhammad*. Cairo: Dar al-Ma'arif, 2002 (1935).

———. *Tarajim misriya wa gharbiya*. Cairo: Dar al-Ma'arif, 1985 (1929).

———. *Thawrat al-Adab*. Cairo: Dar al-Ma'arif, 1986 (1933).

Healy, Dana. "From Triumph to Tragedy: Visualizing War in Vietnamese Film and Fiction." *South East Asia Research* 18, no. 2 (2010): 325–27.

Hibbard, Allen. "Expatriation and Narration in Two Works by Paul Bowles." *West Virginia Philological Papers* 32 (1986): 61–71.

———. *Paul Bowles: A Study of the Short Fiction*. Boston: MacMillan, 1993.

Himmich, Ben Salem. *Al-Istishrāq fī ufq insidādihu*. Rabat: Manshūrāt al-Majlis al-Qawmī lil-Thaqāfah, 1991.

Hitchcock, Peter. "The Function of Agon at the Present Time." *Comparatist* 37 (2013): 5–20.

Hoang, Kimberley. *Dealing in Desire: Asian Ascendency, Western Decline, and the Hidden Currencies of Global Sex Work*. Oakland: University of California Press, 2015.

Hoberek, Andrew. *The Twilight of the Middle Class: Post–World War II American Fiction and White Collar Work*. Princeton, N.J.: Princeton University Press, 2005.

Hogue, Lawrence. *Postmodern American Literature and Its Other*. Champaign: University of Illinois Press, 2008.

Hourani, Albert. *Arabic Thought in the Liberal Age, 1789–1939*. New York: Oxford University Press, 1970.

Huntington, Samuel. "The Clash of Civilizations?" *Foreign Affairs* 72, no. 3 (1993): 22–49.

Hwang Sok-yong. *The Guest*. Translated by Kyung-Ja Chun and Maya West. New York: Seven Stories, 2001.

———. "The Pagoda." In *The Voice of the Governor-General and Other Stories of Modern Korea*, 33–61. Translated by Chun Kyung-Ja. Norwalk, Conn.: EastBridge, 2002.

———. *The Shadow of Arms*. Translated by Chun Kyung-Ja. New York: Seven Stories, 2014 (1988).

Ibrahim, Sonallah. *Warda*. Cairo: Dar al-mustaqbal, 2000.

Jābirī, Muḥammad 'Ābid. *Mas'alat al-huwīyah: Al-'Urūbah wa-al-Islām wa-al-Gharb*. Beirut: Markaz Dirāsāt al-Waḥdah al-'Arabīyah, 1995.

Jay, Paul. *Global Matters: The Transnational Turn in Literary Studies*. Ithaca, N.Y.: Cornell University Press, 2010.

Jayawardena, Kumari. *Feminism and Nationalism in the Third World*. London: Zed, 1986.

Johnson, Adam. *The Orphan Master's Son*. New York: Random House, 2012.

Kahf, Mohja. "Packaging 'Huda': Sha'rawi's Memoirs in the United States Reception Environment." In *Going Global: The Transnational Reception of Third World Women Writers*, edited by Amal Amireh and Lisa Suhair Majaj, 148–72. New York: Garland, 2000.

Kaplan, Amy. *The Anarchy of Empire in the Making of U.S. Culture*. Cambridge, Mass.: Harvard University Press, 2002.

Kaplan, Amy, and Donald Pease, eds. *Cultures of United States Imperialism*. Durham, N.C.: Duke University Press, 1993.

Karim, Lamia. "Demystifying Micro-Credit: The Grameen Bank, NGOs, and Neoliberalism in Bangladesh." *Cultural Dynamics* 20, no. 1 (2008): 5–29.

Karnow, Stanley. *Vietnam: A History*. New York: Penguin, 1997.

Keddie, Nikki. *An Islamic Response to Imperialism*. Berkeley: University of California Press, 1968.

———. *Sayyid Jamal ad-Din al-Afghani: A Political Biography*. Berkeley: University of California Press, 1972.

Keegan, Rebecca Winters. "15 Who Had their 15 Minutes of Fame." *Time*, December 25, 2006, http://content.time.com/time/magazine/article/0,9171,1570785,00.html.

Khatib, Ibrahim. *Bul Bulz fi al Maghreb: Aqn'at al Kitaba*. Rabat: Firdaws (Kitab al-Mojat), 1996.

Khatibi, Abdelkebir. *Oeuvres de Abdelkébir Khatibi III: Essais*. Paris: Éditions de la Différence, 2008.

Kim, Hyung-Sook. "Korea's 'Vietnam Question': War Atrocities, National Identity, and Reconciliation in Asia." *Positions: East Asia Cultures Critique* 9, no. 3 (2001): 622–35.

Kinney, Katherine. *Friendly Fire: American Images of the Vietnam War*. New York: Oxford University Press, 2000.

Kinzer, Stephen. *Overthrow: America's Century of Regime Change from Hawaii to Iraq*. New York: Holt, 2006.

Klein, Christine. *Cold War Orientalism: Asia in the Middlebrow Imagination, 1945–1961*. Berkeley: University of California Press, 2003.

Larain, Jorge. *Theories of Development: Capitalism, Colonialism, and Dependency*. Cambridge: Polity, 1989.

Laroui, Abdallah. *Al-'Arab wa al-fikr al-tārīkhī*. Dar al-Beidha: Al-Markaz al-Thaqafi al-'Arabi, 1973.

———. *The Crisis of the Arab Intellectual: Traditionalism or Historicism?* Translated by Diarmid Cammell. Berkeley: University of California Press, 1976.

———. *The History of the Maghreb: An Interpretive Essay*. Translated by Ralph Manheim. Princeton, N.J.: Princeton University Press, 1977.

———. *L'idéologie arabe contemporaine*. Paris: Maspero, (1967) 1982.

———. *Mafhum al-tarikh*. 4th ed. Dar al-Beidha: Al-Markaz al-Thaqafi al-'Arabi, 2005.

Lawrence, Mark Atwood. *The Vietnam War: A Concise International History*. New York: Oxford University Press, 2008.

Lazarus, Neil. *The Postcolonial Unconscious*. Cambridge: Cambridge University Press, 2011.

Lessard, Micheline. "More than Half the Sky: Vietnamese Women and Anti-French Political Activism, 1858–1945." In *Vietnam and the West: New Approaches*, edited by Wynn Wilcox, 91–105. Ithaca, N.Y.: Cornell Southeast Asia Program, 2010.

Levin, Stephen. *The Contemporary Anglophone Travel Novel: The Aesthetics of Self-Fashioning in the Era of Globalization*. New York: Routledge, 2008.

Liparulo, Steven P. "'Incense and Ashes': The Postmodern Work of Refutation in Three Vietnam War Novels." *War, Literature & the Arts: An International Journal of the Humanities* 15, nos. 1–2 (2003): 71–94.

Lockman, Zachary. *Contending Visions of the Middle East: The History and Politics of Orientalism*. New York: Cambridge University Press, 2004.

Lubin, Alex. *Geographies of Liberation: The Making of an Afro-Arab Political Imaginary*. Chapel Hill: University of North Carolina Press, 2014.

Luce, Henry. "The American Century." http://www.informationclearinghouse.info/article6139.htm (accessed July 7, 2016).

Lukes, Daniel. "'Strange Hungers': William T. Vollmann's Literary Performances of Abject Masculinity." In Coffman and Lukes, *William T. Vollmann*, 247–79.

Macfie, Alexander Lyon, ed. *Orientalism: A Reader*. New York: New York University Press, 2000.

Mahmood, Saba. "Feminism, Democracy, and Empire: Islam and the War of Terror." In *Women's Studies on the Edge*, edited by Joan Wallach Scott. Durham, N.C.: Duke University Press, 2008.

Mailer, Norman. *Advertisements for Myself*. Cambridge, Mass.: Harvard University Press, 1992 (1959).

Makdisi, Ussama. "After Said: The Limits and Possibilities of a Critical Scholarship of U.S.-Arab Relations." *Diplomatic History* 38, no. 3 (2014): 657–84.

Mamdani, Mahmoud. *Good Muslim, Bad Muslim: America, the Cold War, and the Roots of Terror*. New York: Pantheon, 2004.

Marr, David G. *Vietnamese Tradition on Trial, 1920–1945*. Berkeley: University of California Press, 1984.

McAlister, Melani. *Epic Encounters: Culture, Media, and U.S. Interests in the Middle East since 1945*. Berkeley: University of California Press, 2005.

McCarthy, Cormac. *Blood Meridian, or That Evening Redness in the West*. New York: Vintage, 1985.

McGurl, Mark. *The Program Era: Postwar Fiction and the Rise of Creative Writing*. Cambridge, Mass.: Harvard University Press, 2011.

McLaughlin, Robert. "After the Revolution: U.S. Postmodernism in the Twenty First Century." *Narrative* 21, no. 3 (2013): 284–95.

Mehrez, Samia. *Egyptian Writers between History and Fiction*. Cairo: American University in Cairo Press, 2005.

Meinig, Sigrun. "Empathizing with the Experience of Cultural Change: Reflections on Contemporary Fiction on Work." In *Rethinking Empathy through*

Literature, edited by Meghan Marie Hammond and Sue J. Kim, 107–18. New York: Routledge, 2014.

Mernissi, Fatima. *Beyond the Veil: Male-Female Dynamics in Modern Muslim Society*. Bloomington: Indiana University Press, 1987 (1975).

———. *Scheherazade Goes West*. New York: Pocket Books, 2001.

———. *The Veil and the Male Elite: A Feminist Interpretation of Rights in Islam*. Translated by Mary Jo Lakeland. New York: Addison-Wesley, 1991.

Mishra, Pankaj. *From the Ruins of Empire: The Revolt against the West and the Making of Asia*. New York: Picador, 2012.

Mitchell, W. J. T. "Representation." In *Critical Terms for Literary Study*, edited by Frank Lentricchia and Thomas McLaughlin, 11–22. Chicago: University of Chicago Press, 1995.

Moore-Gilbert, Bart. *Postcolonial Theory: Contexts, Practices, Politics*. New York: Verso, 1997.

Moretti, Franco. "Conjectures on World Literature." *New Left Review* 1 (2000): 54–68.

Mufti, Aamir. "Comparative Partitions." *Journal of Palestine Studies* 33, no. 1 (2003): 104–5.

———. *Forget English: Orientalisms and World Literature*. Cambridge, Mass.: Harvard University Press, 2016.

Murray, Rolland. "Diaspora by Bus: Reginald McKnight, Postmodernism, and Transatlantic Subjectivity." *Contemporary Literature* 46, no. 1 (2005): 46–77.

Narayanan, S. V. "How Africa Developed Europe." *Frontline*, March 17, 2017, 58–61.

Nguyen, Duy Lap. "Allegories of Developmental Dictatorship in Hwang Sok-Yong's *The Shadow of War*." Paper presented to the Association of Asian American Studies, San Franciso, April 2015.

O'Brien. Tim. *Going After Cacciato*. New York: Broadway Books, 1999 (1978).

———. *If I Die in a Combat Zone*. New York: Broadway Books, 1999 (1975).

O'Nan, Stewart. "First Wave of Major Films." In *The Vietnam Reader*, edited by Stewart O'Nan, 257–77. New York: Anchor, 1998.

Paik Nak-chung. *The Division System in Crisis: Essays on Contemporary Korea*. Translated by Kim Myung-hwan et al. Berkeley: University of California Press, 2011.

———. "Fredric Jameson Interviewed: South Korea as Social Space." In *Global/Local: Cultural Production and the Transnational Imaginary*, edited by Rob Wilson and Wimal Dissanayake, 348–71. Durham, N.C.: Duke University Press, 1996.

Palumbo-Liu, David, Bruce Robbins, and Nirvana Tanoukhi, eds. *Immanuel Wallerstein and the Problem of the World*. Durham, N.C.: Duke University Press, 2011.

Park, Jinim. "The Colonized Colonizers: Korean Experiences of the Vietnam War." *Journal of American–East Asian Relations* 7, nos. 3/4 (1998): 217–40.

Pease, Donald. "U.S. Imperialism: Global Dominance without Colonies." In *A Companion to Postcolonial Studies*, edited by Sangeeta Ray and Henry G. Schwarz, 203–20. Malden, Mass.: Blackwell, 2000.

Phillips, Dana. "History and the Ugly Facts of Cormac McCarthy's *Blood Meridian.*" *American Literature* 68, no. 2 (1996): 433–60.

Prose, Francine. "The Coldest Eye: Acting Badly among the Arabs." *Harper's*, March 2002, 60–65.

Quinn-Judge, Sophie. *Ho Chi Minh: The Missing Years 1919–1941*. Berkeley: University of California Press, 2002.

Renda, Mary. *Taking Haiti: Military Occupation and the Culture of U.S. Imperialism, 1915–1940*. Chapel Hill: University of North Carolina Press, 2001.

Rhouni, Raja. *Secular and Islamic Feminist Critiques in the Works of Fatima Mernissi*. Boston: Brill, 2010.

Robbins, Bruce. "The Worlding of the American Novel." In *The Cambridge History of the American Novel*, edited by Leonard Cassuto, Clare Virginia Eby, and Benjamin Reiss, 1096–1106. New York: Cambridge University Press, 2011.

Rodney, Walter. *Walter Rodney Speaks: The Making of an African Intellectual*. Trenton, N.J.: Africa World Press, 1990.

Rostow, W. W. *The Stages of Economic Growth: A Non-Communist Manifesto*. Cambridge: Cambridge University Press, 1960.

Rountree, Mary Martin. "Paul Bowles: Translations from the Moghrebi." *Twentieth Century Literature* 32, nos. 3–4 (1986): 388–401.

Rush, Norman. *Mating*. New York: Vintage, 1992.

Ryu, Youngju. "Korea's Vietnam: Popular Culture, Patriarchy, Intertextuality." *Review of Korean Studies* 12, no. 3 (2008): 101–23.

———. "Truth or Reconciliation? *The Guest* and the Massacre that Never Ends." *Positions: East Asia Cultures Critique* 23, no. 4 (2015): 633–63.

———. *Writers of the Winter Republic: Literature and Resistance in Park Chung Hee's Korea*. Honolulu: University of Hawai'i Press, 2016.

Said, Edward. *Culture and Imperialism*. New York: Vintage, 1993.

———. *Orientalism*. New York: Vintage: 1994 (1979).

———. "Preface to the Twenty Fifth Anniversary Edition." In *Orientalism*. London: Penguin, 2003.

———. *Reflections on Exile and Other Essays*. Cambridge, Mass.: Harvard University Press, 2002.

Saaf, Abdallah. *Histoire d'Ahn Ma*. Paris: Harmattan, 1996.

———. *Savoir et politique au Maroc*. Rabat: Société Marocaine des Editeurs Réunis, 1991.

Sawyer-Lauçanno, Christopher. *The Invisible Spectator: A Biography of Paul Bowles*. New York: Grove, 1989.

Schaub, Thomas H. *American Fiction in the Cold War*. Madison: University of Wisconsin Press, 1991.

Schwabe, Liesl. "Nothing Is Illuminated: Adam Johnson." *Publisher's Weekly*, November 11, 2011, 26.

Scott, David. "On the Very Idea of a Black Radical Tradition." *Small Axe* 17, no. 1 (2013): 1–6.

Searle, William J. "Dissident Voices: The NVA Experience in Novels by Vietnamese." *War, Literature & the Arts: An International Journal of the Humanities* 10, no. 2 (1998): 224–38.

Shankar, S. *Flesh and Fishblood: Postcolonialism, Translation, and the Vernacular*. Berkeley: University of California Press, 2012.

Sharabi, Hisham. *Neopatriarchy: A Theory of Distorted Change in Arab Society*. New York: Oxford University Press, 1988.

Shehabuddin, Elora. "Gender and the Figure of the 'Moderate Muslim': Feminism in the Twenty-First Century." In *The Question of Gender: Joan W. Scott's Critical Feminism*, edited by Judith Butler and Elizabeth Weed, 102–42. Bloomington: Indiana University Press, 2011.

Shepard, Jim. "The Perfect Man, the Perfect Place, and Yet . . ." *New York Times*, September 22, 1991, http://www.nytimes.com/1991/09/22/books/the-perfect-man-the-perfect-place-and-yet.html?pagewanted=1.

Slotkin, Richard. *Gunfighter Nation: The Myth of the Frontier in Twentieth Century America*. Norman: University of Oklahoma Press, 1992.

Slyomovics, Susan. *The Performance of Human Rights in Morocco*. Philadelphia: University of Pennsylvania Press, 2005.

Smith, Charles. *Islam and the Search for Social Order in Egypt: A Biography of Muhammad Husayn Haykal*. Albany: State University of New York Press, 1983.

Smith, Jon, and Deborah Cohn. *Look Away! The U.S. South in New World Studies*. Durham, N.C.: Duke University Press, 2004.

Smith, Neil. "Contours of a Spatialized Politics." *Social Text* 33 (1992): 54–81.

———. *Uneven Development: Nature, Capital, and the Production of Space*. Athens: University of Georgia Press, 2008.

Smith, Rachel. *Affect and American Literature in the Age of Neoliberalism*. Cambridge: Cambridge University Press, 2015.

Spanos, William V. *American Exceptionalism in the Age of Globalization: The Specter of Vietnam*. Albany: State University of New York Press, 2008.

Spivak, Gayatri Chakravorty. "Can the Subaltern Speak?" In *Marxism and the Interpretation of Culture*, edited by Carey Nelson, 271–315. Urbana: University of Illinois Press, 1988.

———. *Critique of Postcolonial Reason: Toward a History of the Vanishing Present*. Cambridge, Mass.: Harvard University Press, 1999.

———. *Death of a Discipline*. New York: Columbia University Press, 2003.

———. "Globalicities: Terror and Its Consequences." *CR: The New Centennial Review* 4, no. 1 (2004): 73–94.

Suleski, Ronald. "Review: *The Guest*." *Azalea: Journal of Korean Literature and Culture* 1 (2007): 289–93.

Tageldin, Shaden. *Disarming Words: Empire and the Seductions of Translation in Egypt*. Berkeley: University of California Press, 2011.

Takriti, Abdel Razzaq. *Monsoon Revolution: Republicans, Sultans, and Empires in Oman, 1965–1976*. Oxford: Oxford University Press, 2013.

Tanoukhi, Nirvana. "Rewriting Political Commitment for an International Canon: Paul Bowles's *For Bread Alone* as Translation of Mohamed Choukri's *Al-Khubz Al-Hafi*." *Research in African Literatures* 34, no. 2 (2003): 125–44.

———. "The Scale of World Literature." In Palumbo-Liu, Robbins, and Tanoukhi, *Immanuel Wallerstein and the Problem of the World*, 78–99.

Toynbee, Polly. "Behind the Burka." *Guardian*, September 28, 2001, http://www.theguardian.com/world/2001/sep/28/religion.afghanistan

Tu, Mai Thi, and Le Thi Nham Tuyet. *Women in Vietnam*. Hanoi: Foreign Languages Publishing House, 1978.

Tucker, Spencer. *Vietnam*. Lexington: University Press of Kentucky, 1999.

Turner, Karen Gottschang. *Even the Women Must Fight: Memories of War from North Vietnam*. New York: Wiley, 1998.

Turse, Nick. *Kill Anything That Moves: The Real American War in Vietnam*. New York: Picador, 2013.

Updike, John. *Rabbit, Run*. New York: Fawcett, 1996.

Venuti, Lawrence. *The Scandals of Translation: Toward an Ethics of Difference*. New York: Routledge, 1998.

Vida, Vendela. *The Diver's Clothes Lie Empty*. New York: HarperCollins, 2015.

Vollmann, William T. *Butterfly Stories*. New York: Grove, 1993.

Warwick Research Collective. *Combined and Uneven Development: Towards a New Theory of World-Literature*. Liverpool: Liverpool University Press, 2015.

Westad, Odd Arne. *The Global Cold War*. New York: Cambridge University Press, 2007.

Williams, William Appleman. *Empire as a Way of Life: An Essay on the Causes and Character of America's Present Predicament along with a few Thoughts about an Alternative*. Brooklyn: Ig, 2006 (1980).

Wilson, Rob. "Masters of Adaptation: Paul Bowles, the Beats, and 'Fellaheen Orientalism.'" *Cultural Politics* 8, no. 2 (2012): 193–206.

Wood, James. "Jihad and the Novel." *New Republic*, July 3, 2006, http://www.newrepublic.com/article/books-and-arts/jihad-and-the-novel.

Woollacott, Martin. "Europe Losing Faith in American Leadership." *Manchester Guardian Weekly*, June 18, 1995, 10.

Index

Abboushi, Jenine, 144
Abdel-Malek, Anouar, 52, 58–60, 61, 64–65, 66, 68, 110, 206n31
Abdu, Muhammad, 56
Abish, Walter, 44
abstraction: in American discourse, 152, 153–53; in world literature discourse, 169
Adichie, Chimananda, 193
Abu Dib, Kamal, 69
Abulhawa, Susan, 193
Abu-Lughod, Lila, 116, 117–18, 136, 148
Acker, Kathy, 44, 129, 192, 215n41
Afghani, Jamal al-Din al-, 13, 52–58, 59–60, 66, 67, 68, 78, 86, 146, 205n16
Afghanistan War, 117–18, 135
Afshari, Reza, 145, 147
Agbaw, S. Ekema, 138–39
Ahmad Khan, Sayyid, 53
Ahmed, Aijaz, 70
Ahmed, Laila, 147
Alsultany, Evelyn, 160
Alvarez, Julia, 193
American "Third World" novel, 16, 19–20, 23, 25, 43–46, 68, 69, 73, 75, 79, 81, 103, 108, 111, 114, 119, 138–41, 160, 192–93; post-9/11 trajectory of, 182–89, 191–92, 220n55; Vollmann and, 129–31; whiteness of, 193. *See also* Bowles, Paul
Amin, Samir, 11, 70, 154, 167
Anderson, Benedict, 167
Ang Cheng Guan, 108
Apocaylpse Now (Coppola film), 108–9
Apter, Emily, 5, 205n16
Arab intellectual figure, 11, 13, 51, 61–63, 71–73, 144, 146
archivism in fiction, 16, 154, 155, 170–71, 174, 176–77, 179, 182, 219n45, 220n47
Armstrong, Charles, 211n54
'Azm, Sadik Jalal al-, 70

Bacevich, Andrew, 160
Bakhtin, Mikhail, 7
Balfour, Arthur James, 66
Banks, Russell, 44
Bao Ninh, 213n22
Barth, John, 129
Barthes, Roland, 72

Beat writers, 12, 20, 25
Bellow, Saul, 43, 44, 75, 192
Ben Aomar Lahrech, Mohamed (aka Anh Ma), 14, 86–90, 92–94
Bevan, Craig, 38
Biden, Joe, 180
Bin Laden, Osama, 180
Blodgett, Harriet, 214n22
Booth, Marilyn, 144
Bové, Paul, 79
Bowles, Jane, 39–40, 43, 84
Bowles, Paul, 11, 12–13, 20–21, 23–46, 47–50, 64, 68, 74, 75, 102–3, 110, 131–33, 139, 161–62, 182–84, 191–92, 204n4; anti-nationalism of, 25, 34, 44, 82, 132–33; influence of, 16, 26; point of view in, 26–27, 29–36, 38, 42, 82, 84–85, 187; religious views of, 48; scholarship on, 23–24, 26, 36, 38–42, 48–49, 201n13; unwritten Bangkok book, 81–85, 114, 129
  WRITINGS: "A Distant Episode," 38, 84, 184, 202n17; *Let It Come Down*, 27, 32, 33–35, 37, 38, 84, 184–85; *moghrabi* translations, 13, 38–43, 49, 64, 84, 162; "Pages from Cold Point," 26 *The Sheltering Sky*, 20–21, 23–34, 38, 42–43, 45, 82 83, 114, 139–40, 184, 202n17, 203n38; *The Spider's House*, 23, 32–39, 40, 46, 48, 84, 132–33, 184; *Up above the World*, 32, 84; "You Have Left Your Lotus Pods on the Bus," 81, 82–83, 208n5
Brenner, Neil, 16, 169
Burroughs, William, 44, 129, 161
Burton, Richard Francis, 50
Bush, George W., 117, 136, 137, 175
Butler, Robert Olen, 44

Camus, Albert, 34, 36
capitalism, 6, 16, 70, 121, 153, 156, 167–68, 179, 211n54; literature and spread of, 7
Cary, Joyce, 139
Casablanca (Curtiz film), 188, 201n13
Casanova, Pascale, 5, 198n9
Castro, Fidel, 141
Casualties of War (De Palma film), 126–27
Cervantes, Miguel de, 131
Charara, Hayan, 194
Charhadi, Driss Ben Hamed (Larbi Layachi), 40–41, 42
Cheah, Pheng, 198n9, 198n11
Chesler, Phyllis, 119
Choukri, Mohamed, 36, 37, 41–42, 48–49
Chow, Rey, 194
Cleary, Joe, 165–67, 172, 218n18
Clinton, Bill, 3–4, 197n2
Colla, Elliott, 161
colonialism, 12, 53, 152–53, 160, 165; in Bowles, 29, 31, 37–38, 43–44; Orientalism and, 52, 58, 61–62, 65–66, 70–71; U.S. and, 94, 97, 102; women and, 115
comparative literary studies, 5, 7, 168, 198n7
Conrad, Joseph, 33, 36, 43, 109, 138–39, 215n56
contrapuntalism, 63, 107–8, 110, 121, 129, 200n17
Coppola, Francis Ford, 108, 121
core–periphery model, 6–7, 168
counterculture movement, 22, 26, 44
Cromer, Evelyn Baring, Lord, 66
Cumings, Bruce, 170–71

Damrosch, David, 5
Danticat, Edwidge, 193
Darwish, Nonie, 136
decolonization movements, 21, 22, 25, 38, 58–59, 75, 167, 206n31
Deer Hunter, The (Cimino film), 108–9, 212n69
DeLillo, Don, 44, 183
Delta Force, The (Golan film), 189
De Palma, Brian, 108, 126–27
dependency theory, 6–7, 8–9

Derrida, Jacques, 72
Desai, Kirin, 193
development, 6–7, 16, 23, 76, 79, 101, 115–16, 119, 151, 153–55, 157, 160, 168; women and, 15, 116, 135–46, 176
Díaz, Junot, 193
dịch vận strategy, 14, 93, 102
Didion, Joan, 75
Dinesen, Isak, 43
Disraeli, Benjamin, 182
division system concept, 96, 154, 169–70, 175, 210n40
Djaït, Hichem, 71, 110
domestication, 10–11, 15, 21–22, 25, 84, 111, 193, 200n15; in Bowles, 23, 31; post-9/11, 183, 194
Dos Santos, Theotonio, 167
Duong Thu Huong, 122–26, 128, 213n22

Ebershoff, David, 188–89
Edwards, Brian T., 30, 39, 201n13
Eggers, Dave, 11, 16, 45, 130, 183–87, 192
Egyptian fiction, 56–58, 176–78, 217n9
Ehrenreich, Barbara, 119
El-Ariss, Tarek, 204n12
Elghandor, Abdelhak, 47–50, 60, 161, 204n9
Ellison, Ralph, 114
El Shakry, Omnia, 220n47
El-Sherif, Mona, 39, 201n15
Enani, Muhammad al–, 69
Engels, Friedrich, 7
essentialism, 59; in Bowles, 36–37, 49, 50, 203n39
Ettobi, Mustafa, 39, 42
Evans, Oliver, 82–83

Fall, Bernard, 90–92, 94
Fassi, Allal al-, 48
Fitzpatrick, Kathleen, 46
Flaubert, Gustave, 14, 65, 67, 133–34
focalization. *See* perspective
Foer, Jonathan Safran, 183
Forster, E. M., 43
Foucault, Michel, 52, 64, 68, 79
Franzen, Jonathan, 130
Freud, Sigmund, 64, 127
Friedman, Samuel, 156, 159
Fukuyama, Francis, 15, 155–60, 166, 169, 182, 216n2, 217n4, 217n7
Full Metal Jacket (Kubrick film), 126
Fulton, Bruce, 219n39

Gaddis, William, 129
gender issues. *See* women
Giap, Vo Nguyen, 14, 88, 108
Gibb, Hamilton, 57, 68
Gibbs, Anna, 78
Gide, André, 43, 139
Gilbert, Marc Jason, 93, 95
globalism, 21, 26, 116–17, 153, 155, 158–59, 194
Godden, Richard, 164–65, 218n18
Green Berets, The (Wayne film), 109, 126
Greene, Graham, 20, 21, 126, 139
Greiff, Louis K., 109
Gruening, Ernest, 111
Grunebaum, Gustave von, 62–63, 67–68
Gulf War, 32, 152, 158

Hafez, Sabry, 69–70
Haggard, H. Rider, 43
Hakim, Tawfik al-, 178
Halliday, Fred, 220n54
Hardt, Michael, 199n13
Harrison, Olivia, 73, 178
Hartman, Michelle, 144
Hassan, Wail, 72, 207n58
Hassan II, 86, 209n14
Haykal, Muhammad Hussein, 52, 56–58, 60, 65, 66, 68, 178
Hayslip, Le Ly, 127
Hearts and Minds (Davis film), 126
Heaven and Earth (Stone film), 127
Hegel, Georg Wilhelm Friedrich, 156–57
Hemingway, Ernest, 23, 33, 36, 131
Henley, Patricia, 45

Hibbard, Allen, 32–33, 36, 38
Himmich, Bensalem, 75
Hirsi Ali, Ayaan, 136
historical materialism, 154, 155
historicism, 51, 60, 62, 63, 71–72, 74, 155, 207n55
Hitchcock, Peter, 218n31
Hoang, Kimberly, 128–29, 134
Ho Chi Minh, 14, 87–88, 133
Hogue, Lawrence, 46
Hourani, Albert, 54, 56, 73
Huntington, Samuel P., 156, 158, 182
Husayn, Taha, 56
Hwang Sok-yong, 16, 96, 154, 171, 177, 210n43, 211n55
    WORKS: *The Guest*, 171–76, 180, 183, 186, 219n39; "The Pagoda," 97–99, 100; *The Shadow of Arms*, 14, 97, 99–101, 174

Ibrahim, Sonallah, 16, 154, 176–80, 183, 186, 217n9, 219n45, 220n47, 220n49, 220n51
idea. *See* knowledge production
idealism: American, 15–16, 34, 154, 157, 160, 162; Cartesian, 104
identitarianism, 9, 117, 118
Iraq War, 17–18, 107, 135
Islam: al-Afghani and, 53–55; al-'Azm and, 70; al-Jabiri and, 76; feminism and, 118, 145–46; Fukuyama and, 158–59, 217n7; Haykal and, 56–57; Huntington and, 158–59; Islamophobia, 146, 158; Said and, 69

Jabiri, Mohamed Abed al-, 73–74, 75–76, 78, 85, 87, 110, 146
James, C. L. R., 61
Jameson, Fredric, 199n14
Jarrar, Randa, 193
Jayawardena, Kumari, 121
Jim Crow laws, 22, 30, 32
Johnson, Adam, 16, 45, 183, 186–89
Johnson, Dennis, 45
Johnson, Lyndon, 81, 94, 110
Joudah, Fady, 193

Kafka, Franz, 34
Kahf, Mohja, 116, 136, 144
Kaplan, Amy, 160, 199n15
Karim, Lamia, 136–37
Karnow, Stanley, 94, 108, 113–14, 128
Keddie, Nikki, 54–55, 56, 205n16
Kerouac, Jack, 192, 201n13
Kesey, Ken, 114
Khatib, Ibrahim, 48–49
Khatibi, Abdelkebir, 71–73, 74, 78, 86, 146, 207n58
khususiya, al, 73–74, 85
Kiesinger, Karson L., 138–39
Kilito, Abdelfattah, 72, 207n58
Kim Hyun-Sook, 101, 209nn34–35
Kingsolver, Barbara, 44–45
Kinney, Katherine, 127
Kipling, Rudyard, 43, 44
Kissinger, Henry, 110, 121
Klein, Christine, 21–22, 25, 46, 160
knowledge production, 8, 13, 67, 68–69, 73, 112, 117; Arabs and, 49–50, 54–64, 93, 148, 160, 181, 200n19; Fukuyama on, 157, 181; women and, 115
Kojève, Alexandre, 156
Korean War, 10, 13, 94–96, 170–71, 175; novels about, 95–96, 170–75

Lane, Edward, 50, 140
Laroui, Abdallah, 11, 13, 52, 60–64, 66, 67–68, 71–75, 77, 78, 86, 92, 110, 140, 146, 168, 209n22; Bowles and, 50, 204n9; on "no-idea-producing" slur, 50–51, 148, 181, 200n19
Lawrence, Mark Atwood, 107
Lee, Chang Rae, 193
Lessard, Micheline, 121
Liang Qichao, 53
liberalism, 153, 156–60
Liparulo, Steven P., 213n22

Luce, Henry, 21
Lukes, Daniel, 214n37

Mahmood, Saba, 116, 118–19, 136
Mailer, Norman, 26, 202n17
Makdisi, Ussama, 206n38
Mamdani, Mahmood, 32
Manji, Irshad, 136, 137
Mariátegui tradition, 60, 206n32
Marr, David, 213n13
Marx, Karl, 7, 52, 60, 64, 70, 79, 156
*M*A*S*H* (novel, film, TV series), 210n38
Massignon, Louis, 65, 67, 68, 77
Mattawa, Khaled, 193
McAlister, Melani, 32, 160, 192, 221n2, 222n4
McCarthy, Cormac, 44, 161–65, 177, 192, 217n13, 218n18
McCarthyism, 22, 25, 91, 202n15
McGurl, Mark, 46, 84, 85, 187
McKnight, Reginald, 44, 193
McNamara, Robert, 110
Meinig, Sigrun, 186
Melville, Herman, 131
Mernissi, Fatema, 11, 145–48, 220n49
microcredit system, 136–37
Miller, Ken, 130
Mishra, Pankaj, 53, 56
Mitchell, W. J. T., 78
Moore-Gilbert, Bart, 52
Moretti, Franco, 5, 6, 168–69, 198n9
Morocco, 13–14, 19, 48–49, 56, 64, 73, 86–87, 191–92, 201n15. *See also* Bowles, Paul
Mosteghanemi, Ahlam, 177–78
Mrabet, Mohammed, 39, 41
Mufti, Aamir, 218n21
multiculturalism, 32, 193, 222n4
Murray, Rolland, 222n3

Nahdah movement, 56, 73
Nasreen, Taslima, 147
Negri, Antonio, 199n13
Nguyen, Duy Lap, 211n54
Nguyen, Viet Thanh, 193
Nixon, Richard, 110–11

O'Brien, Tim, 11, 14, 44, 95, 103–8, 109, 110, 111, 121, 123, 127, 133, 142, 192, 211n64, 214n31
O'Grady, Scott, 3–4
Olympus Has Fallen (Fuqua film), 189
O'Nan, Stewart, 212n69
Orientalism, 8, 9, 13, 47, 99, 133–34; Arab critiques of, 50–79, 205n30; Western European vs. Eastern European, 60. *See also* Said, Edward: *Orientalism*
Other, the, 13, 14, 29, 32, 42–43, 76, 93, 131, 133–34, 135, 137, 159–60, 187, 189

Paik Nak-chung, 11, 16, 96–97, 100, 101, 154, 169, 175, 180–81, 210n40
Palestine, 73, 166
Palumbo-Liu, David, 6
Park, Jinim, 97
partitioning, 15, 94, 96–97, 154–55, 165–67, 172, 180–81
Pascone, Paul 86
Patchett, Ann, 45
Pease, Donald, 160
Peckinpah, Sam, 162
perspective (point of view), 13–14, 85–86, 91, 98, 100, 127; McGurl on, 84, 85, 187. *See also* Bowles, Paul: point of view in
Phillips, Dana, 217n13
Pol Pot, 133
Porter, Katherine Anne, 44
postcolonial studies, 9, 12, 23, 47, 49; U.S. imperialism and, 102, 166, 211n58
post-postmodernism, 130, 131, 133
Powers, Richard, 130
primitivism, 13, 25, 42, 47, 77, 90, 161–62
Prose, Francine, 38
Pynchon, Thomas, 43, 44, 131, 161

Quiet American, The (Mankiewicz film), 20, 126

Reagan, Ronald, 197n2
Renan, Ernest, 50, 53–54, 55, 63, 68, 205n16, 206n44, 217n7
representation, 51–52, 70–71, 75, 77–79, 107
Rhouni, Raja, 145–46, 147
Richmond, Colin, 164–65, 218n18
Robbins, Bruce, 6
Rodinson, Maxime, 70
Rodney, Walter, 61, 167, 168
Rostow, W. W., 217n4
Rountree, Mary Martin, 39, 40–41
Rush, Norman, 11, 15, 44, 137–43, 192, 215n56
Ryu, Youngju, 171, 174, 210n43, 211n55

Saaf, Abdallah, 11, 13, 86–90, 91–94; point of view in, 89–90
Saddam Hussein, 152, 158–59, 182
Said, Edward, 50, 58, 194; on Flaubert, 14, 65, 67, 133; on Gide, 139; *Orientalism*, 8, 13, 14, 51–52, 59, 60, 61, 63, 64–79, 102, 110, 133–34, 205n30, 206n38
Salinger, J. D., 114
Sartre, Jean-Paul, 24, 36
scale, 16, 167–70, 172, 174, 181–82, 183, 218n31
Schaub, Thomas Hill, 31
Senghor, Léopold Sédar, 58
September 11 attacks, 135, 159, 175, 181, 183
sex workers. *See* women's issues
Shacochis, Bob, 44
Shankar, S., 5
Sharabi, Hisham, 72
Sha'rawi, Huda, 144
Shehabuddin, Elora, 116, 119, 136, 147
Sheltering Sky, The (Bertolucci film), 47
Simpson, Mona, 44
Slotkin, Richard, 162, 164–65
Smith, Charles, 56–57
Smith, Neil, 16, 167–69
Smith, Rachel, 46
Smith, Wilfrid C., 53
Soueif, Ahdaf, 147
Spanos, William V., 107, 211n64
Spivak, Gayatri Chakravorty, 5, 14, 40, 79, 115–17, 119, 120, 194, 203n39, 222n5
Stein, Gertrude, 23
Stone, Robert, 44
Styron, William, 95
Sultan, Wafa, 136

Tageldin, Shaden, 5
Tagore, Rabindrinath, 53
Takriti, Abdel Razzaq, 219n45
Tanoukhi, Nirvana, 6, 16, 39, 42, 168–69, 218n27, 218n31
Theroux, Paul, 44
Third World Marxist liberationist thought, 60
1001 Arabian Nights, 147–48
Tibawi, Abdul Latif, 52
Toynbee, Polly, 117, 119
translation, 5–6, 17, 41, 144, 195, 203n42
"tricontinental" designation, 50, 60, 206n31
Tru'ng sisters, 120–21
Tu, Mai Thi, 121
Tucker, Spencer, 107
Turner, Karen Gottschang, 121–22
Turse, Nick, 111
Tuyet, Le Thi Nham, 121

United States: camouflaging efforts of, 10, 43, 46, 111, 153, 160, 165, 167, 170; exceptionalism and, 9–10, 160, 195; imperialism of, 9–11, 13, 17, 25, 84, 102–3, 111, 115–18, 144, 148, 153, 162, 165–68, 170, 193, 201n2; nationalism of, 85, 137, 129–30, 160; racism and, 111, 147; superpower status

of, 19, 21–22, 151–52. *See also* Vietnam: U.S. war in
Updike, John, 44, 95, 114, 183, 221n55

Vida, Vendela, 45, 191
Vietnam: French rule of, 86–94, 121; movies about, 108–10, 126–27; U.S. war in, 10, 13, 81, 94, 96–111, 113–15, 121–29, 209nn34–35, 211nn54–55; women in, 113, 120–29, 212n2, 213n13
Vollmann, William T., 15, 44, 129–35, 137–38, 141, 142, 192, 215n41

Walker, Alice, 44, 193
Wallace, David Foster, 130
Wallerstein, Immanuel, 6–7, 8, 16, 154, 169–70
War on Terror, 14, 16, 38, 114–16, 135, 148, 182–83
Warwick Research Collective, 197n8, 199n14
Washington Consensus, 6, 115, 116, 141, 154
Westad, Odd Arne, 200n1
WID (women in development), 15, 116, 136–37, 176
Williams, William Appleman, 189
women 14–15, 113–49; captive stereotype, 119, 135–36, 143, 177; sex workers, 113–14, 119, 120, 126, 128–35, 148, 208n12, 212n2; thinker figure, 119, 143–48; woman warrior figure, 119–26, 148, 176–77, 178
Woollacott, Martin, 3–4
world literature discourse, 5, 169–70, 194, 197n5, 198n9, 198n11, 199n12, 218n27, 218n31
world systems theory, 6–7, 8, 154, 169–70, 175, 210n40
Wright, Stephen, 44

Yacoubi, Ahmad, 39
Yates, Richard, 114
Yemen, 176, 180–81, 219n45
Young, Robert J. C., 206n31
Yunus, Muhammad, 136

Zidane, Zineddine, 200n16

FLASHPOINTS

1. *On Pain of Speech: Fantasies of the First Order and the Literary Rant,* Dina Al-Kassim
2. *Moses and Multiculturalism,* Barbara Johnson, with a foreword by Barbara Rietveld
3. *The Cosmic Time of Empire: Modern Britain and World Literature,* Adam Barrows
4. *Poetry in Pieces: César Vallejo and Lyric Modernity,* Michelle Clayton
5. *Disarming Words: Empire and the Seductions of Translation in Egypt,* Shaden M. Tageldin
6. *Wings for Our Courage: Gender, Erudition, and Republican Thought,* Stephanie H. Jed
7. *The Cultural Return,* Susan Hegeman
8. *English Heart, Hindi Heartland: The Political Life of Literature in India,* Rashmi Sadana
9. *The Cylinder: Kinematics of the Nineteenth Century,* Helmut Müller-Sievers
10. *Polymorphous Domesticities: Pets, Bodies, and Desire in Four Modern Writers,* Juliana Schiesari
11. *Flesh and Fish Blood: Postcolonialism, Translation, and the Vernacular,* S. Shankar
12. *The Fear of French Negroes: Transcolonial Collaboration in the Revolutionary Americas,* Sara E. Johnson
13. *Figurative Inquisitions: Conversion, Torture, and Truth in the Luso-Hispanic Atlantic,* Erin Graff Zivin
14. *Cosmopolitan Desires: Global Modernity and World Literature in Latin America,* Mariano Siskind
15. *Fiction Beyond Secularism,* Justin Neuman
16. *Periodizing Jameson: Dialectics, the University, and the Desire for Narrative,* Phillip E. Wegner
17. *The Practical Past,* Hayden White
18. *The Powers of the False: Reading, Writing, Thinking Beyond Truth and Fiction,* Doro Wiese
19. *The Object of the Atlantic: Concrete Aesthetics in Cuba, Brazil, and Spain, 1868–1968,* Rachel Price
20. *Epic and Exile: Novels of the German Popular Front 1933–1945,* Hunter Bivens
21. *An Innocent Abroad: Lectures in China,* J. Hillis Miller
22. *Form and Instability: East Europe, Literature, Postimperial Difference,* Anita Starosta
23. *Bombay Modern: Arun Kolatkar and Bilingual Literary Culture,* Anjali Nerlekar
24. *Intimate Relations: Social Reform and the Late Nineteenth-Century South Asian Novel,* Krupa Shandilya
25. *Media Laboratories: Late Modernist Authorship in South America,* Sarah Ann Wells
26. *Acoustic Properties: Radio, Narrative, and the New Neighborhood of the Americas,* Tom McEnaney

27. *The New Woman: Literary Modernism, Queer Theory, and the Trans Feminine Allegory*, Emma Heaney
28. *Civilizing War: Imperial Politics and the Poetics of National Rupture*, Nasser Mufti
29. *Late Colonial Sublime: Neo-Epics and the End of Romanticism*, G. S. Sahota
30. *Globalizing Race: Anti-Semitism, Empire, and the Politics of Scale in Modern French and European Culture*, Dorian Bell
31. *Domestications: American Empire, Literary Culture, and the Postcolonial Lens*, Hosam Aboul-Ela